Gerold Schneider

Hybrid Long-Distance Functional Dependency Parsing

Gerold Schneider

Hybrid Long-Distance Functional Dependency Parsing

A hybrid, deep-syntactic Dependency Grammar parser for English, combining statistical performance and formal grammar-based competence approaches

Südwestdeutscher Verlag für Hochschulschriften

Impressum/Imprint (nur für Deutschland/ only for Germany)
Bibliografische Information der Deutschen Nationalbibliothek: Die Deutsche Nationalbibliothek verzeichnet diese Publikation in der Deutschen Nationalbibliografie; detaillierte bibliografische Daten sind im Internet über http://dnb.d-nb.de abrufbar.
Alle in diesem Buch genannten Marken und Produktnamen unterliegen warenzeichen-, marken- oder patentrechtlichem Schutz bzw. sind Warenzeichen oder eingetragene Warenzeichen der jeweiligen Inhaber. Die Wiedergabe von Marken, Produktnamen, Gebrauchsnamen, Handelsnamen, Warenbezeichnungen u.s.w. in diesem Werk berechtigt auch ohne besondere Kennzeichnung nicht zu der Annahme, dass solche Namen im Sinne der Warenzeichen- und Markenschutzgesetzgebung als frei zu betrachten wären und daher von jedermann benutzt werden dürften.

Verlag: Südwestdeutscher Verlag für Hochschulschriften Aktiengesellschaft & Co. KG
Dudweiler Landstr. 99, 66123 Saarbrücken, Deutschland
Telefon +49 681 37 20 271-1, Telefax +49 681 37 20 271-0, Email: info@svh-verlag.de
Zugl.: Zurich, University, Diss., 2008

Herstellung in Deutschland:
Schaltungsdienst Lange o.H.G., Berlin
Books on Demand GmbH, Norderstedt
Reha GmbH, Saarbrücken
Amazon Distribution GmbH, Leipzig
ISBN: 978-3-8381-0723-3

Imprint (only for USA, GB)
Bibliographic information published by the Deutsche Nationalbibliothek: The Deutsche Nationalbibliothek lists this publication in the Deutsche Nationalbibliografie; detailed bibliographic data are available in the Internet at http://dnb.d-nb.de.
Any brand names and product names mentioned in this book are subject to trademark, brand or patent protection and are trademarks or registered trademarks of their respective holders. The use of brand names, product names, common names, trade names, product descriptions etc. even without a particular marking in this works is in no way to be construed to mean that such names may be regarded as unrestricted in respect of trademark and brand protection legislation and could thus be used by anyone.

Publisher:
Südwestdeutscher Verlag für Hochschulschriften Aktiengesellschaft & Co. KG
Dudweiler Landstr. 99, 66123 Saarbrücken, Germany
Phone +49 681 37 20 271-1, Fax +49 681 37 20 271-0, Email: info@svh-verlag.de

Copyright © 2009 by the author and Südwestdeutscher Verlag für Hochschulschriften
Aktiengesellschaft & Co. KG and licensors
All rights reserved. Saarbrücken 2009

Printed in the U.S.A.
Printed in the U.K. by (see last page)
ISBN: 978-3-8381-0723-3

Abstract

This thesis proposes a robust, hybrid, deep-syntatic dependency-based parsing architecture and presents its implementation and evaluation. The architecture and the implementation are carefully designed to keep search-spaces small without compromising much on the linguistic performance or adequacy. The resulting parser is deep-syntactic like a formal grammar-based parser but at the same time mostly context-free and fast enough for large-scale application to unrestricted texts. It combines a number of successful current approaches into a hybrid, comparatively simple, modular and open model.

This thesis reports three results:

> We suggest, implement, and evaluate a parsing architecture that is fast, robust and efficient enough to allow users to do broad-coverage parsing of unrestricted texts from varied domains.

> We present a probability model and a combination between a rule-based *competence* grammar and a statistical lexicalized *performance* disambiguation model.

> We show that inherently complex linguistic problems can be broken down and approximated sufficiently well by less complex methods. In particular (1) on the level of long-distance dependencies, the majority of them can be approximated by using a labelled DG, context-free finite-state based patterns, and post-processing, (2) on the level of long-distance dependencies, a slightly extended DG allows us to use mildly context-sensitive operations known from Tree-Adjoining Grammar (TAG), (3) on the base phrase level, parsing can successfully be approximated by the more shallow approaches of chunking and tagging. We conclude that labelled DG is sufficiently expressive for linguistically adequate parsing.

We argue that our parser covers the middle ground between statistical parsing and formal grammar-based parsing. The parser has competitive performance and has been applied widely.

Contents

1	**Introduction**			**2**
	1.1	Ambiguity		4
	1.2	Approaches to Parsing		6
		1.2.1	Full or Shallow Parsing	6
		1.2.2	Formal Grammar Based Parsing Approaches	8
		1.2.3	Probabilistic Parsers	8
		1.2.4	Mixed Models	9
	1.3	Task-Specific Division of Labour		10
	1.4	Relations and Differences to Current Approaches		11
	1.5	Overview of this Thesis		14
2	**Overview of the Parser and the Architecture**			**18**
	2.1	The Modular Architecture		18
	2.2	Integrating Linguistic Knowledge into the System		32
		2.2.1	The Boundedness of Long-Distance Dependencies	32
		2.2.2	Constraints on Grammar Rules	33
		2.2.3	Mapping Grammatical Relations for the Probability Estimation	33
3	**Dependency Grammar**			**36**
	3.1	Conceptions of DG		36

	3.1.1	Extended Valency Grammar	37
	3.1.2	Government Grammar	39
	3.1.3	Terminal Node Context-Free Grammar	40
	3.1.4	A Version of X-bar Theory	49
3.2	Characteristics of functional DG		52
	3.2.1	Definition of Head	52
	3.2.2	Projectivity	58
	3.2.3	Functionalism	59
3.3	The Relationship of DG to HPSG and LFG		61
	3.3.1	HPSG	61
	3.3.2	LFG	64
3.4	Conclusions		64

4 State of the Art — 66

4.1	Introduction		66
4.2	PP attachment disambiguation		67
	4.2.1	The question	67
	4.2.2	Hindle and Rooth	69
	4.2.3	Collins and Brooks	70
4.3	Treebank-Based Statistical Parsers		71
	4.3.1	Collins 1996	71
	4.3.2	Model 1, 1997	78
	4.3.3	Model 2	79
	4.3.4	Model 3	80
	4.3.5	Recovering empty nodes and functional tags with Treebank-Based Statistical Parsers	81
4.4	Dependency-oriented Statistical Parsers		82
	4.4.1	Link Grammar	82
	4.4.2	Eisner	82

	4.4.3	MacDonald et al.	83
	4.4.4	Nivre et al.	83
	4.4.5	Yamada and Matsumoto	85
4.5	Data-Oriented Parsing (DOP)		86
4.6	Statistical Formal Grammar Parsers		87
	4.6.1	Lexical-Functional Grammar (LFG)	87
	4.6.2	Head-Driven Phrase Structure Grammar (HPSG)	91
	4.6.3	Combinatory Categorial Grammar (CCG)	93
	4.6.4	Tree-Adjoining Grammar (TAG)	94
4.7	Shallow Parsing, Finite-state Cascading		94
	4.7.1	Tag-Based Chunking and Partial Parsing Grammars	95
	4.7.2	Grefenstette, Brants	97
4.8	Memory-Based Grammatical Relation Finding		97
	4.8.1	Daelemans et al. 1999	98
	4.8.2	Buchholz 2002	99
4.9	Conclusions		100

5 Grammar Engineering   102

5.1	Introduction		102
	5.1.1	The Penn Treebank	103
	5.1.2	The Difficulty of Writing Grammars	104
	5.1.3	Benefits of a Hand-Written Grammar	107
5.2	Subcategorisation and Lexicalisation		109
5.3	The Rules in Detail		110
	5.3.1	Major Types of Grammar Rules	111
	5.3.2	Minor Types	121
	5.3.3	Unconventional Types	123
5.4	Conclusion		124

6 Extended Locality: Treatment of Long-Distance Dependencies in Functional Dependency Grammar — 126

- 6.1 Introduction — 126
- 6.2 The Boundedness of Long-Distance Dependencies — 128
  - 6.2.1 Local Relations — 129
  - 6.2.2 Nonlocal Relations — 131
- 6.3 A Quantitative Analysis of Types of Empty Nodes — 137
  - 6.3.1 Overview — 137
  - 6.3.2 NP Traces — 139
  - 6.3.3 NP PRO — 139
  - 6.3.4 WH Traces — 140
- 6.4 A Qualitative Analysis of Types of Empty Nodes — 147
  - 6.4.1 Tree-Adjoining Grammar — 151
  - 6.4.2 TAG Adjoining and mild context-sensitivity — 152
  - 6.4.3 The Nature of Elementary and Auxiliary Trees — 155
  - 6.4.4 Sketching TAG Adjoining in DG — 156
  - 6.4.5 An Implementation at the Functional Level — 160
  - 6.4.6 Ambiguous WH-attachment — 161
  - 6.4.7 Subjacency and Barriers — 170
  - 6.4.8 Minimality and Relativized Minimality — 171
- 6.5 TAG Adjoining and LFG — 172
  - 6.5.1 Functional Uncertainty — 172
  - 6.5.2 A chunks and F-structure version of LFG — 173
- 6.6 Conclusions — 173

7 Evaluation and Discussion — 176

- 7.1 Introduction — 176
  - 7.1.1 Traditional Syntactic Evaluation: Labelled Bracketing — 176
  - 7.1.2 Dependency-Based Evaluation: Lin 1995 — 177

	7.1.3	Desiderata	178
	7.1.4	An Annotation Scheme for Evaluation: Carroll et al. 1999, 2003	179
7.2	GREVAL: A standard 500 sentence test corpus	180
	7.2.1	Bidirectional Mapping of Pro3Gres to GREVAL	181
	7.2.2	Unidirectional Mapping of Pro3Gres to GREVAL	184
	7.2.3	Long-Distance Dependencies	192
	7.2.4	Comparison to Lin's MINIPAR	195
	7.2.5	Comparison to Carroll and Briscoe's RASP	195
	7.2.6	Comparison to Buchholz, Charniak, and Collins, according to Preiss	199
	7.2.7	Comparison to Collins's Model 1	200
7.3	Tentative Comparison to Nivre's MaltParse	203
	7.3.1	Comparison Across Different Corpora	203
	7.3.2	Comparing with the same Corpus: Participation in CoNLL-XI Shared Task	207
7.4	Evaluation on Biomedical Term-Annotated Corpora	209
	7.4.1	Evaluation on 100 Random Sentences from the GENIA Corpus	210
	7.4.2	Evaluation with the Stanford Dependency Scheme on 900 BioInfer sentences	212
	7.4.3	Task-Oriented, Practical Evaluation of Pro3Gres relation extraction	213
7.5	Exploring Precision and Recall Trade-Offs	216
	7.5.1	High Recall Parsing	219
	7.5.2	High Precision Parsing	219
7.6	Baseline, Distance Measure, Lexicalisation	232
	7.6.1	The Baseline System	232
	7.6.2	The Distance Measure	234
	7.6.3	Lexicalisation	236

7.7	Disambiguation from the Parsing Context	240
	7.7.1 Parsing Speed, Pruning, and Local Maxima	240
	7.7.2 Local Readings Constrain Each Other	242
7.8	Linguistic constraints	244
7.9	Conclusions	245

8 Conclusions   **246**

8.1	The Cornerstones of Pro3Gres	246
8.2	A Hybrid Architecture	248
8.3	Applications	250

A tgrep Queries for Grammatical Relations   **270**

B Gradience and Mapping: A Small Selection of Problematic Cases   **277**

List of Figures

2.1 Pro3Gres flowchart 19
2.2 Parser output of the sample sentence *What could rescue the bill would be some quick progress on a bill amending the National Defense Education Act of 1958* in the classical arrow notation 20
2.3 Parser output of the sample sentence *What could rescue the bill would be some quick progress on a bill amending the National Defense Education Act of 1958* in stemma notation 21
2.4 Complete CYK chart for an example sentence with 6 terminals . . 24
2.5 Parser output 32

3.1 Dependency tree example 42
3.2 Constituency tree example 43
3.3 Pro3Gres analysis of the sentence: Mutations affecting the 5' guanine residues of the kappa B site were unable to compete for these NF-kappa B-related proteins. 48
3.4 Pro3Gres analysis of the sentence: The transcription of the human immunodeficiency virus type 1 (HIV-1) is under the control of cellular proteins that bind to the viral long terminal repeat (LTR). . . 48
3.5 The partial CFG tree corresponding to the local DG passive subject relation. 49

6.1 Prototypical subject configuration 129
6.2 Explicit Penn-II subject relation 130
6.3 Extraction pattern for active subject-verb relations 130

6.4	Extraction pattern for passive subjects	132
6.5	First experiment pattern for passive subjects: Coreference is not enforced	132
6.6	Second experiment pattern for passive subjects: Forcing *no* trace in the object position	132
6.7	Extraction pattern for passive *dub* verb subjects	134
6.8	Extraction pattern for subject control (left) and object control (right)	134
6.9	The extaction pattern for the *modpart* relation. The NP is explicitly a non-subject NP	140
6.10	Actual parser output for example sentence *William got a present to which Peter believes I will contribute*	143
6.11	Actual parser output for example sentence *William got a present Peter believes I will contribute to*	144
6.12	Actual parser output for example sentence *William got a present I believe which suits Peter*	145
6.13	Actual parser output for example sentence *William got a present I believe that Peter likes*	146
6.14	An example of the Substitution operation. The rewritten node is boxed.	152
6.15	An example of the Adjoining operation. The foot node is boxed. .	152
6.16	An example of the Adjoining operation. The foot node is boxed. .	153
6.17	Adjoining for WH-questions. The deep recursion of the auxiliary trees introduces mild context-sensitivity. The foot node is boxed. .	154
6.18	An unlabelled DG representation and its X-bar equivalents	157
6.19	An unlabelled DG representation and its TAG equivalents. The foot node is boxed.	158
6.20	Actual parser output for example sentence *What do you think that Peter believes I will contribute to*	166
6.21	Actual parser output for example sentence *What do you eat that Peter believes I will contribute to*	167
6.22	Actual parser output for example sentence *Why do you think that Peter believes*	168

LIST OF FIGURES   xii

6.23 Actual parser output for example sentence *Why do you think Peter believes* 169

7.1 The hierarchy of grammatical relations suggested in GREVAL .. 179
7.2 Bidirectional Mapping the Pro3Gres output to the GREVAL format. GREVAL relations bear a c-subscript 182
7.3 Mapping the Pro3Gres output to the GREVAL format for precision, and the reverse mapping for recall 187
7.4 Mapping for the preterminal $clausal_c$ relation 196
7.5 Semantic and syntactic dependency annotation of *New York Stock Exchange* 206
7.6 A sample sentence illustrating the complexity of noun-modifying PPs, with its top-ranked grammatical relation annotation 211
7.7 Graph of percentage results of recall among first N-ranked analyses on the GREVAL corpus 217
7.8 Graph of percentage results of recall among first N-ranked analyses on GENIA 218
7.9 Graph of Precision of Experiment 4 on GREVAL 221
7.10 Graph of Recall of Experiment 4 on GREVAL 222
7.11 Graph of Precision of Experiment 4 on GENIA 223
7.12 Graph of Recall of Experiment 4 on GENIA 224
7.13 Graph of Precision of Experiment 5 on GREVAL 226
7.14 Graph of Recall of Experiment 5 on GREVAL 227
7.15 Graph of Precision of Experiment 5 on GENIA 228
7.16 Graph of Recall of Experiment 5 on GENIA 229
7.17 Graph of Precision of Experiment 6 on GREVAL 231
7.18 Comparison between Baseline, Distance Measure Only, Full Model without Distance Measure, and Full Model 233
7.19 F-Score Comparison between Baseline, Distance Measure Only, Full Model without Distance Measure, and Full Model 235
7.20 Comparison of Levin or Wordnet verb classes for backing off ... 239

LIST OF FIGURES

B.1   Aberrant but intentional analysis 278

List of Tables

3.1	Zwicky's definition of heads	54
3.2	Hudson's definition of heads	54
4.1	Alpino 2001 in comparison to Pro3Gres	92
5.1	The Penn Treebank Tagset	105
5.2	Penn Treebank Functional Labels	106
5.3	The major Pro3Gres dependency types	112
6.1	Important Pro3Gres Dependency types	129
6.2	The distribution of the 10 most frequent types of empty nodes and their antecedents in the Penn Treebank (adapted from Johnson 2002). Row numbers in parentheses indicate cases that are inherently local in our functional DG	138
6.3	Coverage of the patterns for the most frequent NP traces [row 1]	138
6.4	Coverage of the patterns for the most frequent NP PRO [row 2]	139
7.1	Examples of grammatical relations in the GREVAL scheme	180
7.2	Currently best results on evaluating Pro3Gres on GREVAL test corpus on subject, object and PP-attachment relations	184
7.3	Error Classification of Subject Precision errors of all GREVAL corpus sentences	185
7.4	Evaluating Pro3Gres on the GREVAL corpus on PP-attachment relations	188

7.5	Detailed Analysis of the PP-attachment errors in the first 100 GREVAL sentences	190
7.6	Manual categorisation of the first 10 $iobj_c$ recall errors on GREVAL	191
7.7	Evaluation of Long-Distance Dependencies	193
7.8	The distribution of the 10 most frequent types of empty nodes and their antecedents in the Penn Treebank (adapted from Johnson 2002). Row numbers in parentheses indicate cases that are inherently local in our functional DG	194
7.9	Comparison of Pro3Gres to Lin's MINIPAR	195
7.10	RASP evaluation results compared to Pro3Gres	196
7.11	Percentage and absolute values for chunk-internal relations	198
7.12	Percentage and absolute values for the PP-attachment argument/adjunct distinction	199
7.13	Preiss's precision (P) and recall (R) evaluation results of Buchholz, Charniak, and Collins, compared to Pro3Gres	200
7.14	Comparison of parsing performance between Collins Model 1 and Pro3Gres	202
7.15	Nivre (2006) Dependency Types	203
7.16	Nivre (2006) Evaluation Results	205
7.17	Prec.&recall of DEPREL	208
7.18	Prec.&recall of DEPREL+ATTACHMENT	209
7.19	Evaluation comparing LTChunk chunking ("dirty") and near-perfect multi-word knowledge ("clean") on GENIA corpus	212
7.20	Some example sentences of the task-oriented evaluation on biomedical texts	215
7.21	Distribution of GENIA parsing errors in the application-oriented evaluation	216
7.22	Percentage results of Experiment 1: keeping only sentences with identical tags from two taggers, on the GREVAL corpus on subject, object and PP-attachment relations	220
7.23	Percentage results of Experiment2: keeping only agreeing relations arising from parsing with two taggers, on the GREVAL corpus on subject, object and PP-attachment relations	220

LIST OF TABLES

7.24 Percentage results of Experiment 3: discarding the most ambiguous relation in each sentence, for subject, object, PP-attachment and subordinate sentence relations 225

7.25 PP-attachment backoff level legend 230

7.26 Evaluation of the currently best parser output on the GREVAL corpus on subject, object and PP-attachment relations, discarding backoff levels 5 and 6 for non-*by*-PP-attachment 230

7.27 Percentage results of Experiments 3, 4 and 5 combined at threshold 0.4 and distances 1 to 5 232

7.28 Backoff decision points for the Fully Lexicalized, Backed-Off System on the GREVAL corpus 238

7.29 Beam size effects on parsing speed and performance 241

7.30 Disambiguation from the Context. Maximal span size effects on parsing speed and performance 243

7.31 Currently best system on the GREVAL corpus with the standard grammar and the grammar without restrictions compared 244

LIST OF TABLES

Acknowledgements

I would like to thank my supervisors, Prof. Michael Hess and Dr. Paola Merlo, for the continued support they have given me during the writing of this thesis. I am grateful to the Swiss National Science Foundation grant 21-59416.99 to Paola Merlo at the University of Geneva, for partly supporting me during this research. I am also grateful to the European Network of Excellence project REWERSE (reference number 506779) grant to Dr. Norbert E. Fuchs at the University of Zurich, and to the Department of English of the University of Zurich, for partly supporting me during the finishing phase of the thesis.

I would also like to thank the following people for inspiring linguistic discussions, comments on earlier versions of the thesis, for their co-operation in research projects, and for their wonderful support (the list is in alphabetical order): Samuel Bayer, Matthias Buch-Kromann, John Carroll, Ralph Debusmann, James Dowdall, Norbert Fuchs, Josef van Genabith, James Henderson, Timo Järvinen, Eric Joanis, Frank Keller, Kaarel Kaljurand, Sandra Kübler, Hans Martin Lehmann, Diego Mollá Aliod, Joakim Nivre, Sampo Pyysalo, Fabio Rinaldi, Patricia Ronan, Rolf Schwitter, and Martin Volk.

INTRODUCTION

Chapter 1

Introduction

This thesis proposes a robust, deep-syntactic dependency grammar parsing architecture and presents its implementation and evaluation. The architecture and the implementation are carefully designed to keep search-spaces small without compromising much on the linguistic performance or adequacy. The resulting parser is deep-syntactic like a formal grammar parser but fast enough for large-scale application to unrestricted texts. It combines a number of successful current approaches into a comparatively simple, extendable and adaptable model. It is hybrid since we use a hand-written part-of-speech grammar combined with lexicalised probabilistic disambiguation.

Parsing has always been a fundamental task in Natural Language Processing. Most natural language applications, such as information extraction, machine translation, question answering, or speech recognition, can almost certainly profit from high-accuracy syntactic parsing. The aim of parsing is to map a sentence input onto a syntactic and possibly shallow semantic analysis, which usually consists of a hierarchy of substrings, a syntax tree. The syntactic analysis also expresses the grammatical functions (GF, or GR for grammatical roles) of the substrings, either implicitly based on their position in so-called *configurational* approaches, or explicitly by labeling the functions in so-called *functional* approaches. The approach presented here follows the latter paradigm, which is often used in a class of grammars called Dependency Grammars (DG). There is a growing interest in dependency-based representations for the purpose of many Natural Language Processing tasks, such as text mining or information extraction (de Marneffe, MacCartney, and Manning, 2006; Rinaldi et al., 2007), semantic space construction (Henderson et al., 2002; Weeds et al., 2005; Padó and Lapata, 2007), question answering (Aliod et al., 2000), etc. One of the advantages of dependency based syntactic representations is that they can be mapped easily into a semantic representation, or and they allow easy identification of the arguments of complex relations.

We propose to combine a rule-based approach with a statistical approach. We rely on a hand-written and editable syntactic *competence* grammar over part-of-speech tags, and use statistical lexical information to estimate the probabilities of the application of these rules for *performance*-based disambiguation. Linguists are often very efficient at writing grammar rules, particularly when using a framework that is close to traditional school grammar assumptions, such as DG (Tesnière, 1959). But the scope of application and the amount of ambiguity a rule creates is easily beyond imagination and better handled by a statistical system. The statistical model that we suggest is not probabilistic in the sense that it captures the probability of *generating* a sentence (Collins, 1999), but models the decision process of parsing. The probabilities of possible decisions at an ambiguous point in the derivation are assumed to add up to 1. Its probability estimation is thus a *discriminative* model (Charniak, 1996; Johnson, 2001).

Although we use a context-free CYK parsing algorithm (Younger, 1967), we are able to treat the majority of English long-distance dependencies, by (1) using and modelling dedicated patterns across several levels of constituency subtrees partly leading to dedicated but fully local dependency syntactic relations, by (2) lexicalized post-processing rules, and by (3) modelling mildly context-sensitive phenomena in DG. We also show that some non-local dependencies are simply artifacts of the grammatical representation.

This thesis reports three results:

> We suggest and implement a parsing architecture that is fast, robust and accurate enough to allow users to do broad-coverage parsing of unrestricted texts from unrestricted domains. We have parsed the 100 million word British National Corpus and similarly large amounts of medical scientific literature.
>
> We present a probability model and a combination between a rule-based *competence* grammar and a statistical lexicalized *performance* disambiguation model.
>
> We show that inherently complex problems can be approximated and broken down sufficiently well by less complex methods. In particular (1) on the level of long-distance dependencies, the majority of them can be approximated by using a labeled DG, context-free finite-state based patterns, and post-processing, (2) on the level of long-distance dependencies, a slightly

extended DG allows us to use mildly context-sensitive operations known from Tree-Adjoining Grammar, (3) on the base phrase level, parsing can successfully be approximated by the more shallow approaches of chunking and tagging. We conclude that a representationally minimalist theory such as labeled DG is sufficiently expressive for linguistically adequate parsing.

One of the main challenges of parsing natural language is ambiguity, as we illustrate in section 1.1. In section 1.2 we give a a brief introduction to the major approaches of parsing natural language texts. Since full parsing is very resource-intense, we argue in section 1.3 that it is beneficial to employ different techniques for the various different tasks required to attain full parses. In section 1.4 we give a high-level comparison between our parser and a number of related parsers. To conclude the introduction chapter, we give an overview of the contents of each chapter of the thesis in section 1.5.

1.1 Ambiguity

Parsing of natural language, unlike the parsing of formal language, is difficult due to the inherent ambiguity of natural language at all levels. Ambiguity is a primary motivation for using statistical methods. We now give some examples of syntactic ambiguity for illustration. Except for the first example, they are all examples of structural ambiguity. All of the ambiguity types discussed here occur frequently in real-world texts.

Part-of-speech (POS) ambiguity *run* is a verb in *I like to run* but a noun in *He liked the run*. Even for the seemingly clear-cut and very frequent POS classes verb and noun, there are areas of gradience. The two semantically nearly identical sentences *I like him running* and *I like his running* suggest a verb reading for the former and a noun reading for the latter case. With the female pronoun *her* a distinction can no longer be made.

PP-attachment *I saw the man with glasses* has at least 2 possible analyses: one in which I use the glasses as an instrument for seeing, and one where the man happens to carry glasses.

Coordination *The director ran and left the factory* can mean that the director first ran the factory, but has left his position in the meantime, or that he physically accelerated before he stepped outside the factory.

Complex NP or 2 NPs *She sold BP shares* can either mean that she sold unspecified shares to BP or that she sold shares of BP to somebody unspecified.

Object or adjunct *I hate Mondays; but by Tuesday afternoon I usually stop hating* has a hidden reading of which most readers only become aware in the second part of the sentence.

Adjunct or sentential complement *The news reported last Friday was bad* can either mean that last Friday was bad or that the reporting of the news happened last Friday. Readers can be unsure where the unrealized, or zero, relative marker should occur. Lexical statistics used in *lexicalized* statistical models such as the one introduced in this thesis are a natural way to express readers' expectations.

Superordinate Clause or Zero-Relative *Something the reporter said is unconvincing* is ambiguous if punctuation is absent. Either the reporter has discovered an unconvincing item or listeners find that one of the reporter's utterances fails to convince.

Functional role *Stolen Painting Found by Tree*. Only a semantic role analysis expresses the ambiguity between a geographical adjunct or a passive agent adjunct.

The vast majority of ambiguities that arise during the parsing process remain local, because the parsing context does not allow them to lead to a full parse, but they still tremendously slow down the parsing process. Sentences with dozens of global readings and thousands of local partial readings are rather the rule than the exception. Several mutually compatible analyses lead to an exponential increase in the number of sentences. Church and Patil (1982) note on PP attachment that a sequence <verb-NP-PP*> with n PPs has C_{n+1} analyses, where C_{n+1} is the $(n+1)$'th Catalan number. The Catalan number Cn is defined as $\frac{1}{n+1}\binom{2n}{n}$. Other types of ambiguity show a similar exponential behaviour. Average sentence length in the Wall Street Journal (WSJ) is around 23 words, 7 % being above 40 words. Large-coverage grammars have very many rules, so that the combination of a large grammar, long sentences and exponential ambiguity factors lead to enormous search spaces, which make parsing a very complex and error-prone challenge.

While ambiguity often leads to an enormous number of potential readings for a sentence, the *types* of ambiguity are restricted and relatively few. We will discuss in section 1.4 that we model less than 10 types of ambiguity.

1.2 Approaches to Parsing

1.2.1 Full or Shallow Parsing

Many natural language applications have in fact dismissed full parsing as too complex and too error-prone and suggested to use shallow parsing as a viable alternative. Shallow parsing is a popular alternative to full parsing, which is fast, because it is based on finite-state techniques, and robust, because only partial unconnected strings instead of full sentences are analysed. Recursion is absent or strictly limited. Typically, the text to be analyzed is run through a sequence of finite-states machines, which build up a partial structure in a bottom-up fashion (Appelt et al., 1995; Abney, 1996). Each finite-state machine corresponds to a level of syntactic processing: tagging for POS disambiguation, chunking for Base-Phrase recognition (in some systems followed by a PP-chunker for PPs), a verbal (and sometimes nominal) attacher for the phrase level. Super-phrasal attachment is rarely done, long-distance dependencies are usually neglected, ambiguous PPs remain unattached, non-canonical word-order also leads to unattached constituents, or to wrong analyses. Because of the sequential processing, each finite-state transducer taking as input the output of the previous transducer, these shallow parsers are often called cascaded finite-state transducers. While this approach is highly promising and reliable for the low-level cascades – tagging and base phrase chunking – the performance for high-level chunking drops off. Nerbonne et al. (2001) confirm that a variety of chunking methods applied to parsing tasks do not reach the levels of probabilistic parsers like Collins (1999) or Charniak (2000).

Briscoe and Carroll (2002) summarise the current view on shallow parsing in the computational linguistics community. They state that shallow parsing output is neither as complete nor as accurate as state-of-the-art statistical parsers, and that it is unlikely that they will achieve the same level. A major problem for the development of accurate shallow parsers is that heuristics like longest match interact in complex ways with the large number of manually coded rules required in a wide-coverage system. This makes effective development of further rules increasingly difficult, and it requires increasingly painstaking manual specification of the contexts of legitimate application for each rule. A second problem is the pipeline approach, which requires that the output from each phase of processing is deterministic, thus many decisions need to be taken too early in the processing chain, favouring local maxima. A third problem is that many such systems achieve much of their domain independence by basing rules as much as possible on part-of-speech (PoS) tags, rather than specific lexical items, in order to limit the number of rules required.

In the IE community, the opinion that there is not yet a viable alternative to shallow parsing is still predominant. Shatkay and Feldman (2003) summarise the current view on shallow parsing as follows:

> *Efficient and accurate parsing of unrestricted text is not within the reach of current techniques. Standard algorithms are too expensive to use on very large corpora, and are not robust enough. A practical alternative is shallow parsing. ... Shallow parsing has the benefit of both speed and robustness of processing, which comes at the cost of compromising the depth and the fine-granularity of the analysis*
>
> (Shatkay and Feldman, 2003)

They dismiss full parsing as too slow and too error-prone. Since the approaches of the authors they quote in their work, large-scale parsing has made tremendous progress, both in terms of speed and accuracy. We thus argue that their verdict merits re-assessment.

Full and fast parsing of unrestricted texts is within the reach of current techniques, as described in this thesis. On the one hand full parsing is already widely applied in Computational Linguistics with a surface-syntax approach, namely probabilistic context-free parsing (Collins, 1999; Charniak, 2000; Henderson, 2003), and on the other hand, deep-syntactic approaches are currently becoming more robust, scalable and faster, so that the first systems allowing full, deep-syntactic parsing of unrestricted amounts of texts from unrestricted domains are becoming available (Riezler et al., 2002; Clark and Curran, 2004; Miyao, Ninomiya, and Tsujii, 2005).

We describe a system in this thesis that uses finite-state techniques for the low-level tasks of lemmatising, part-of-speech tagging and base-phrase chunking, but uses full parsing for finding the syntactic relations between base phrases and clauses, thus profiting from the speed, robustness and small search-spaces of finite-state techniques, and employing resource-intense parsing approaches only where they are beneficial.

1.2.2 Formal Grammar Based Parsing Approaches

A variety of parsers that are based on a formal linguistic theory have existed for a number of years. To name only a few, they are: The Alvey tools (Briscoe et al., 1987) have been developed for Generalized Phrase Structure Grammar (GPSG). Lingo (Copestake and Flickinger, 2000) and Babel (Müller, 1996) has been developed for Head-Driven Phrase Structure Grammar (HPSG). FIPS (Wehrli, 1997) and PAPPI (Fong, 1991) parse using Government & Binding (GB) grammars. MINIPAR (Lin, 1998) and FDG (Tapanainen and Järvinen, 1997) use Dependency Grammar (DG). Parsers for Combinatory Categorial Grammar (CCG) include e.g. Steedman (2000). XTAG (Group, 2001) has been developed for Tree-Adjoining Grammar (TAG). The Xerox Grammar Writer's Workbench (Kaplan and Maxwell, 1996) has been developed for Lexical-Functional Grammar (LFG).

Formal grammars have been developed to formalise all phenomena that natural language exhibit. In their original form, formal grammar based parsers rely on *competence* data only. They are also referred to as grammar-based parsers. Parsers that are based on them are linguistically satisfactory, but their accuracy varies, and processing times are often considered too long for large-scale application. Also, developing and maintaining hand-written grammars and disambiguation scoring systems in complex formalisms can be labour-intensive. As an alternative, probabilistic parsers have been developed.

At the same time, some deep linguistic grammars have also achieved the coverage and robustness needed to parse large corpora, for two reasons. First, linguistic performance is increasingly included into these parsers, leading to the mixed approaches which we discuss below. A second important reason for the increasing speed and robustness of deep-linguistic grammars are recent developments in the context-free and mildly context-sensitive parsing of of long-distance dependencies (LDD), which will be discussed in chapter 6.

1.2.3 Probabilistic Parsers

Broad-coverage syntactic parsers that learn from syntactically annotated corpora have become available. Classical probabilistic parsers (Eisner, 1996; Collins, 1999; Charniak, 2000; Henderson, 2003) use context-free history-based grammar representations (Black et al., 1993).

Implementations of probabilistic parsers can be very efficient. The CYK parsing algorithm has parsing complexity $O(n^3)$ (see e.g. (Eisner, 2000; Nivre, 2003)), which means that large-scale parsing of real-world texts becomes possible. Lexical information, but also entire grammars, can be learnt from annotated data.

Probabilistic parsers analyse sentences by means of imitation following annotated linguistic *performance* data. Grammars are either learnt automatically or exist implicitly in the form of statistical data. These parser are also referred to as data-driven parsers. They generally have good performance, both in terms of speed, accuracy, and robustness. Until recently, they were linguistically not convincing, since they produced pure CFG trees as output, i.e. trees that do not include the deep-syntactic information known from formal grammars, i.e. neither annotation for grammatical function nor the empty nodes and long-distance annotation which are actually provided in Treebanks such as the Penn Treebank (Marcus, Santorini, and Marcinkiewicz, 1993b; Bies et al., 1995) on which they are usually trained. Collins (1999) uses head-driven and dependency-based models, which are discussed in detail and compared to our approach in chapter 4.

Recently, both the discovery of deep-syntactic information (Johnson, 2002; Dienes and Dubey, 2003; Jijkoun and de Rijke, 2004; Campbell, 2004; Musillo and Merlo, 2005) and probabilistic parsing that includes deep-syntactic information (Gabbard, Kulick, and Marcus, 2006) have made great progress.

The problem of grammar size is not necessarily solved in probabilistic systems, but can be aggravated by a naive probabilistic parser implementation, in which e.g. all CFG rules permitted in the Penn Treebank are extracted. From his 300,000 words training part of the Treebank (Charniak, 1996) obtains more than 10,000 CFG rules, of which only about 3,000 occur more than once. It is therefore necessary to either discard infrequent rules, do manual editing, use a different rule format such as individual dependencies (Collins, 1996), compress the representation (Henderson, 2003), or use a hand-written grammar as we and other mixed models do.

1.2.4 Mixed Models

Recently, parsers that mix grammar-based and probabilistic data-driven approaches have been particularly successful. They include the first LFG system that has managed to parse the entire Treebank (Riezler et al., 2002), the first HPSG parser to attain similar robustness (Miyao, Ninomiya, and Tsujii, 2005), and recent parsers in the CCG framework (Curran and Clark, 2004; Clark and Curran, 2004). Kaplan et al. (2004a) compare speed and accuracy of a successful probabilistic context-free parser (Collins, 1999) to a robust LFG system based on (Riezler et al., 2002). They show that their mixed model clearly outperforms Collins (1999). The system we present in this thesis is also a mixed model, relying on the one hand on a hand-written competence grammar, while using probabilistic performance data obtained from the Penn Treebank for disambiguation and pruning.

1.3 Task-Specific Division of Labour

Not all NLP tasks are equally hard or resource-intense, and there is no single approach that is suitable for all levels of processing. Parsing proper is very resource-intense, using parsing algorithms for all levels of analysis can be seen as an overkill if simpler algorithms deliver the same level of performance. Morphological analysis (morphology can be parsed with CFG rewrite rules), part-of-speech annotation (disambiguation can be done according to the highest ranked parse) or base phrase detection can be efficiently handled by linear, finite-state algorithms (Abney, 1991). While finite-state algorithms are less resource-intense, and while they typically do not reach the accuracy of parsing approaches at the complex phrase and clause level (Briscoe and Carroll, 2002), the debate whether finite-state algorithms or parsing delivers better accuracy is still open. We summarise the results of Prins (2005) below. Dienes and Dubey (2003) have shown that a task that seems inherently hard, finding the landing sites for long-distance dependencies, can be handled quite successfully by a finite-state tagging approach.

Kaplan et al. (2004b) discuss the integration of finite-state technology into a formal grammar based parser using Lexical-Functional Grammar (LFG). The use of finite-state morphology greatly decreases the lexicon development task. The integration of finite-state morphology and part-of-speech tagging is described as an essential step for the development of truly broad-coverage grammar, such as Riezler et al. (2002).

Approaches integrating part-of-speech taggers as filters for the parser typically show a considerable increase in parsing speed and robustness, and a slight increase in accuracy. For example, Prins (2005, 72-74) reports detailed results on applying such a filtering system to parsing. He shows that tagging preprocessing systems are up to 10 times faster, and that the accuracy increases slightly if reasonable filtering parameters are used. Also, very long sentences typically cause parser to run out of memory if no filter is used. Approaches integrating base phrase chunking, such as Prins (2005), typically report the same level of accuracy at moderately reduced parsing time. We employ a hand-written grammar. The fact that the grammar writer is freed from the task of writing base NP rules provided an additional practical motivation for integrating chunking into our parser.

1.4 Relations and Differences to Current Approaches

A number of different approaches have been used in parsing. We give a high-level overview of approaches that are related to ours. Collins (1999) uses head-driven and dependency-based models in his work, which is discussed in detail and compared to our approach in chapter 4.

We have mentioned that some deep linguistic grammar based parsers have also achieved the coverage and robustness needed to parse large corpora, by means of adding performance data. Riezler et al. (2002) show how a hand-crafted LFG grammar scales to the Penn Treebank with Maximum Entropy probability models. Hockenmaier and Steedman (2002) acquires a wide-coverage CCG grammar from the Penn Treebank automatically, Burke et al. (2004) an LFG grammar. Sarkar and Joshi (2003) apply TAG to statistical parsing. These approaches are discussed in chapters 4. An important reason for the increasing speed and robustness of deep-linguistic grammars are recent developments in the context-free and mildly context-sensitive parsing of long-distance dependencies (LDD), which will be discussed in chapter 6.

The system we propose and implement in this thesis, Pro3Gres, is a hybrid system on many levels, which combines successful parsing and finite-state approaches[1].

It occupies a middle ground between using a formal grammar and a probabilistic parser. Recently, progress has been made at closing the gap between deep-linguistic formal grammar-based parsing and probabilistic parsing. We have introduced these approaches as mixed models above. An important example is Kaplan et al. (2004a). Our work is in the same spirit. Like Kaplan et al. (2004a) our system explores the middle ground between systems like Collins (1999) and Riezler et al. (2002). Pro3Gres largely uses simple context-free parsing, but it delivers deep-syntactic analyses comprising most long-distance dependencies. It integrates efficient finite-state techniques like taggers and chunkers. Pro3Gres can be used as an alternative to formal grammars that integrate finite-state LDD approximations, discussed in chapter 4 (Riezler et al., 2002; Burke et al., 2004; Hockenmaier and Steedman, 2002; Miyao, Ninomiya, and Tsujii, 2003).

It can be seen as a statistical extension of Tapanainen and Järvinen (1997). Tapanainen and Järvinen (1997) is a popular dependency parser which relies on constraint grammar (Karlsson et al., 1995), heuristics and a manually written gram-

---

[1] The abbreviation Pro3Gres signifies PRObabilistic, PROlog-implemented, Parser-based RObust Grammatical Relations Extraction System

1.4. Relations and Differences to Current Approaches

mar, but it does not have a statistical disambiguation component. Mollá and Hutchinson (2003) have conducted an evaluation of Tapanainen and Järvinen (1997) on a 500 sentence test corpus (Carroll, Minnen, and Briscoe, 1999). Comparing the results of their evaluation to our results in chapter 7 indicate that we perform better.

It can be seen an extension of deterministic dependency parsing (Nivre, 2003; Nivre, 2004; Nivre, 2006b) to non-deterministic but still low-complexity parsing by using a beam search instead of an oracle based on a short look-ahead.

It is an extension from PP-attachment as in Collins and Brooks (1995) to all dependency relations, including the majority of long-distance dependencies (Schneider, 2003) as we discuss in chapter 4. It also extends Collins (1999) from ad-hoc dependencies to functional dependencies, including the majority of long-distance dependencies.

It can be seen as version of the chunking & dependency model proposed by Abney (1995) that includes the treatment of long-distance dependencies. Pro3Gres integrates shallow parsing methods in order to reduce the parsing cost (Schneider, 2004). We also present Pro3Gres as a statistical, broad-scale extension of Frank (2003)'s LFG chunk and F-structure model. We show that fully-fledged C-structures can be obviated in a functional dependency and chunks model that employs mild context-sensitivity (Schneider, 2005).

Our pattern-based finite-state recognition of long-distance dependencies can be seen as an extension to the patterns in Johnson (2002) and a parsing application to Jijkoun and de Rijke (2004).

Instead of simple and error-prone mapping schemes as in Collins (1999) or Nivre (2006b) to map the Treebank to dependency representations, we use a functionally oriented, relatively involved mapping scheme, which is explained in chapters 3 and 6 and which is detailed in the appendix. We believe that the merit of attaining a linguistically highly motivated dependency representation outweighs the disadvantage of using a non-trivial, relatively complex mapping.

Unlike many other probabilistic parsers, Pro3Gres models a closed and clearly defined set of ambiguities. They are the following ambiguities.

1. **PP-attachment:** PPs can be attached to a verb or to an noun. In *I ate the steak with fries* the PP attaches to the noun, in *I ate the steak with a fork* the PP attaches to the noun.

2. **Words tagged _IN as preposition or complementizer:** The Penn Treebank tagset uses the tag _IN for both prepositions and complementizers. In *I work*

for I like it the word *for* is a complementizer; in *I work for the money* the word *for* is a preposition.

3. **Subject or reduced relative clause:** A noun preceding a verb can be this verb's subject or it may be modified by a reduced relative clause headed by this verb. In *The newspaper published the article* the noun *newspaper* is the subject of the verb *published*; in *The article published last month* the noun *article* is modified by a reduced relative clause headed by the verb *published*. The reduced relative clause reading is only possible for verb participles. Since the performance of taggers in distinguishing simple past and participle forms is relatively poor, also simple past forms need to be treated as ambiguous.

4. **Object or adjunct noun:** A noun following a verb may be an object or an adjunct. In *Jane ate the excellent fish* the NP headed by *fish* is an object; in *Jane ate only last Friday* the NP headed by *Friday* is an adjunct.

5. **Participles as verbs or as adjectives:** Participles may serve as adjectives or as full verbs. In *Computer aided design* the participle *aided* is an adjective; in the headline *Computer aided to design spacecrafts* it is a full verb.

6. **Subordinate clause attachment:** Subordinate clauses attach to a verb or a noun. In *John wanted his girlfriend to leave* the subordinate clause headed by *leave* attaches to the matrix verb *wanted*; in *John wanted a reason to leave* the subordinate clause headed by *leave* attaches to the matrix object *reason*.

7. **Matrix verb dependent or subordinate clause subject:** Nouns between the matrix verb and the subordinate verb may depend on either of them if a complementizer is absent. In The news reported the earthquake was bad the noun *earthquake* depends on the subordinate verb; in The news reported yesterday was bad the noun *yesterday* depends on the matrix verb. This example hinges on a subject vs. reduced relative clause ambiguity. Independent examples are possible, but less obvious, as they are not acceptable in all English dialects: In John realized the apple was bad the noun *apple* depends on the subordinate verb; in John ate the apple was bad the noun *apple* depends on the matrix verb and is modified by a zero-relative clause.

8. **Object or subject:** A closed class of verbs, typically introducing direct speech, may use subject-verb inversion if the matrix clause occurs in sentence-final position. In *"Yes", said the student* the subject and verb are inverted, *student* is then the subject; in The student said something there is no inversion, *something* is the object.

In addition to these 8 types of ambiguities, some ambiguities are addressed by post-processing, for example the distinction between a PP acting as a complement or as an adjunct. Long-distance dependency ambiguities are partly treated as post-processing and partly during parsing, as chapter 6 explains.

1.5 Overview of this Thesis

The further layout of this thesis is as follows.

Overview of the Parser and the Architecture Chapter 2 gives an overview of the parser by discussing an example sentence. Each module is introduced and briefly discussed. An introduction to the probabilistic model of the parser is given. Detailed discussions are postponed to the later chapters.

Dependency Grammar Chapter 3 introduces and defines the grammar formalism that we use: Dependency Grammar. We discuss the common core of all Dependency Grammar approaches, and the characteristics of our version of Dependency Grammar. Our version of Dependency Grammar is labelled with grammatical roles, partly underspecifies word order, is mildly context-sensitive, mostly allows content words only to be heads, and integrates tagging and chunking. This chapter also paves the way for our treatment of long-distance dependencies in chapter 6.

Related Approaches In chapter 4, a summary of related approaches is given. They are compared to our approach. We review research on PP-attachment as an especially ambiguous relation, then we discuss probabilistic approaches (Collins, 1999; Charniak, 2000). They are relatively fast and robust, but quite shallow, since they typically do not express long-distance dependencies. Some formal grammar based parsers have now become robust enough for wide-coverage parsing. We discuss that the complexity class occupied by Tree-Adjoining Grammar (TAG) is a good candidate for expressing the amount of context-sensitivity found in natural language. A non-parsing approach aiming at the expression of grammatical roles is also discussed.

Grammar Engineering In chapter 5, we discuss our hand-written grammar in detail. Advantages and disadvantages of hand-written grammars are discussed. It is discussed that one advantage is that sentence types that are rare in the training domain but important for the application domain, such as questions, which are rare in the Penn Treebank but important for question answering (QA), can be manually tuned or extended. A hand-written grammar is also perspicuous and maximally flexible. Since dependency rules are binary and the Penn Treebank tagset quite limited the expense needed for writing a large-scale grammar is manageable. Grammars are re-usable since they are not very domain-dependent. The hand-written grammar does explicitly not model rare and marked phenomena, and places strong, linguistically well-founded constraints, which leads to a considerable search space reduction. As rare phenomena have very low probabilities, precision and recall values are hardly affected.

Extended Locality: Modelling Long-Distance Dependencies in a Context-Free Fashion Context-free grammars are appealing as they allow a parser to use very fast parsing algorithms, for example the $O(n^3)$ CYK algorithm. But context-free grammars cannot express non-local information (long-distance dependencies, LDDs) at least not in the traditional way involving empty nodes and structure-sharing, co-indexation or movements. We will explore in chapter 6 how the majority of LDDs can be expressed in a context-free way.

In particular, we will show that the vast majority of non-local dependencies except for few WH-traces can be treated as local dependencies by (1) using and modelling dedicated patterns across several levels of constituency subtrees partly leading to dedicated but fully local dependency syntactic relations, by (2) lexicalized post-processing rules, by (3) modelling mildly context-sensitive phenomena in DG. We also show that (4) some non-local dependencies are simply artefacts of the grammatical representation.

We will first explore how unbounded LDDs really are, then we will give a quantitative analysis of our findings for the ten most frequent types of empty nodes in the Penn Treebank 6.2, which cover more than 60,000 of the approximately 64,000 empty nodes of sections 2-21 of the Penn Treebank. Then we will describe the importance of the particular grammar formalism we are using, Functional DG, to achieve the goal of expressing most LDDs locally. We will also explain how we deal with the LDDs that that we found to be really unbounded, namely indexed gerunds and WH-non-subject questions. The former remain underspecified, the latter are treated either with a simple pre-parsing approach, or with a slightly extended DG that allows us to express mildly context-sensitive constructions known from Tree-Adjoining Grammar (TAG) in DG. The relation to TAG (Frank, 2002; Frank, 2004) and LFG (Bresnan, 2001) is discussed.

Evaluation In chapter 7, an extensive evaluation is given, from an unlexicalized baseline to the lexicalized versions of the parser. The evaluation is based on GREVAL (Carroll, Minnen, and Briscoe, 1999) and on a selection of the GENIA corpus. We also evaluate relations involving long-distance dependencies, as far as this is possible. It is shown that the parser's performance is comparable to a selection of statistical parsers and to a classical robust full parser. The roles of pruning, backing-off, distances, lexicalisation and linguistic constraints are investigated.

Chapter 2

Overview of the Parser and the Architecture

In this chapter we first give an overview of the parser with an example. Each module is introduced and briefly discussed. More detailed discussions are postponed to the appropriate chapters. In the second part we give three examples of how we integrate linguistic knowledge into our system.

2.1 The Modular Architecture

Pro3Gres is a modular system. Each problem is broken down into sub-problems, and a simplified solution is used. As much of the processing and disambiguating as reasonably possible is done before and after the costly parsing stage. The parsing itself is also least resource-intense thanks to reasonably reducing search spaces and restricting to mostly CFG parsing. Fig. 2.1, a flowchart, gives an overview of the parsing architecture.

We will now illustrate the information flow by sketching the on-line processing of the following example sentence, respectively the off-line processing of Treebank training sentences.

(1) What could rescue the bill would be some quick progress on a bill amending the National Defense Education Act of 1958

Its top-ranked parser output can be seen in figures 2.2 and 2.3. Figure 2.2 uses the classical arrow notation, in which labelled dependencies are drawn as

2.1. The Modular Architecture

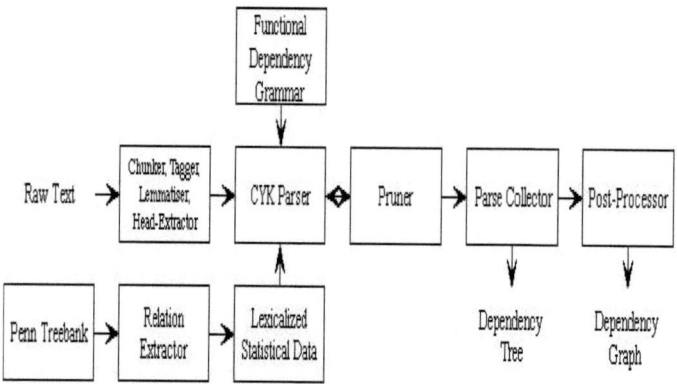

Figure 2.1: Pro3Gres flowchart

arrows from the governor to the dependent. Figure 2.3 uses the classical stemma notation, in which governors appear higher than dependents, the dependency labels appear directly below the head. The stemma notation was introduced by (Tesnière, 1959) and illustrates the similarity of dependency of constituency, which we will discuss in chapter 3. Both representations are completely equivalent, only a few parameters in the tree display routine differ, the graphical interface offers both as display options.

Tagging The raw text is part-of-speech tagged using a state-of-the-art tagger. We have used LTPos (Mikheev, 1997) and, alternatively, Ratnaparkhi's Maximum Entropy tagger (Ratnaparkhi, 1996).

Almost all current taggers reach accuracy of 95-97% for tagging the Penn Treebank with the Penn Treebank tagset.Only an evaluation on unknown words is reported inMikheev (1997), but LTPos is a popular tagger because it supports XML and integrates a chunker, which made it particularly easy to integrate into our processingpipeline. Ratnaparkhi (1996) report an accuracy of 96.6%. The tagged text of our example sentence is shown in (2).

(2) What_WP could_MD rescue_VB the_DT bill_NN would_MD be_VB some_DT quick_JJ progress_NN on_IN a_DT bill_NN amending_VBG the_DT National_NNP Defense_NNP Education_NNP Act_NNP of_IN 1958_CD

2.1. The Modular Architecture

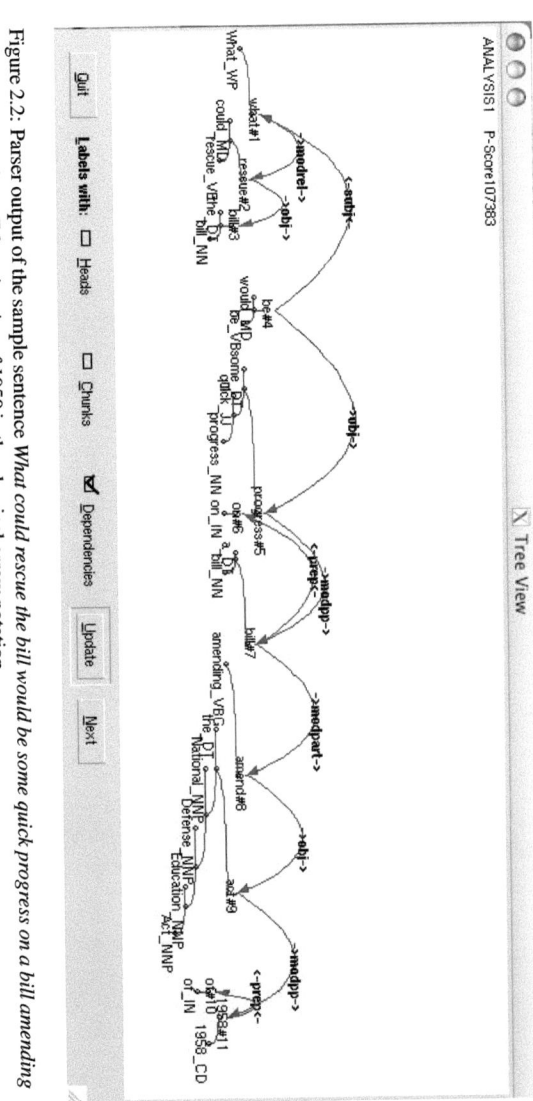

Figure 2.2: Parser output of the sample sentence *What could rescue the bill would be some quick progress on a bill amending the National Defense Education Act of 1958* in the classical arrow notation

2.1. The Modular Architecture

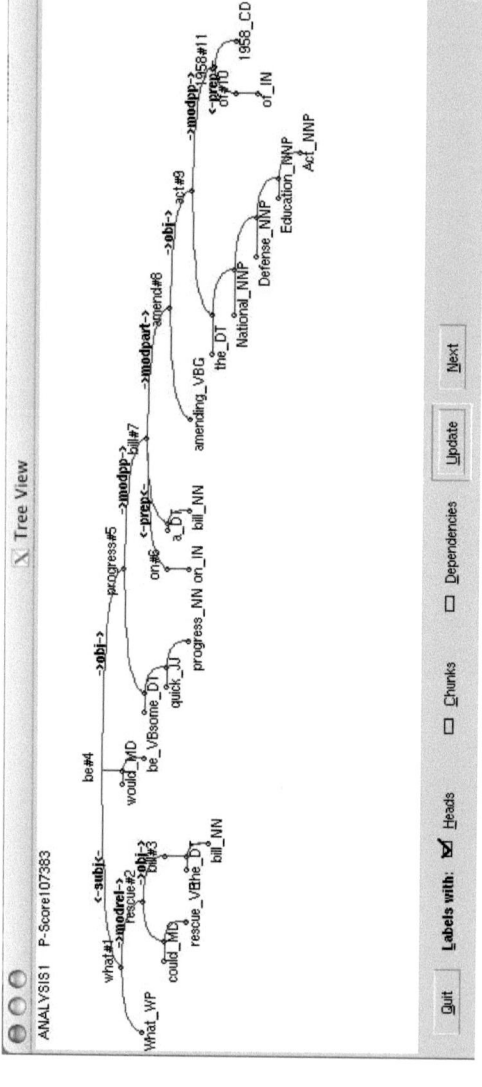

Figure 2.3: Parser output of the sample sentence *What could rescue the bill would be some quick progress on a bill amending the National Defense Education Act of 1958* in stemma notation

2.1. The Modular Architecture

Chunking The tagged text is chunked for verb groups, indicated by parentheses and base NPs indicated by square brackets with LTChunk (Mikheev, 1997). Because LTChunk was not robust enough for chunking the whole British National Corpus, we have used Carafe, a conditional random field chunker for that task[1]. The resulting text is shown in (3).

(3) What_WP (could_MD rescue_VB) [the_DT bill_NN]
    (would_MD be_VB) [some_DT quick_JJ progress_NN] on_IN
    [a_DT bill_NN] amending_VBG [the_DT National_NNP
    Defense_NNP Education_NNP Act_NNP] of_IN 1958_CD

Head Extraction The linguistic heads are extracted using our own implementation of Magerman rules (Magerman, 1995). The original chunk and the tag are associated to the head. The linguistic head is the semantic and syntactic core of the chunk. It has frequently been suggested (see e.g. (Abney, 1995; Collins, 1996)) that it is sufficient to parse between heads of chunks. The sentence reduced to (head,tag) pairs is shown in (4).

(4) What_WP rescue_VB bill_NN be_VB progress_NN on_IN
    bill_NN amending_VBG Act_NNP of_IN 1958_CD

Lemmatizing The extracted heads are lemmatised. We use Morpha (Minnen, Carroll, and Pearce, 2000).

Functional Dependency Grammar The hand-written grammar is based on part-of-speech tags and on few closed-classed words. For example, the leftmost parsing step, combining what and rescue with a *relative modification* dependency is licensed by a rule involving closed class words, because it is restricted to only a subset of all WH-pronouns. First, only a subset of WH-pronouns can generally serve as relative pronoun, secondly, the relative dependency here is special since *what* is both the modified noun and the relative pronoun, short for that which. This rule is restricted to the what WH-pronoun only. The second left parsing step which leads to the analysis in fig. 2.2, the rule that licenses the *object* dependency, is very general and applies to any verb tag followed by any noun tag.

Parsing A CYK parser (Younger, 1967) is used. CYK is a generalised, all path version of chart-based shift-reduce parsing for CNF grammars. CYK is a bottom-

---

[1]Carafe is a programming project available at http://sourceforge.net/projects/carafe/

up algorithm, the structure is built up in a breadth-first fashion from the lexical item, level by level.

The algorithm in pseudo-code is as follows (N is the number of chunks in the sentence):

```
for j = 2 to N           # length of span
  for i = 1 to N-j+1     # beginning of span
    for k = i+1 to i+j-1 # separator position
      if Z → XY and X in chart[i to k], Y in chart[k+1 to j]
        and Z not in chart[i to j]
      then insert Z into chart[i to j]
```

At the first level, where the span length j is 2, all combinations between adjacent words are built, as far as they are licensed by the grammar. The combination of A and B, the span from A to B, can either have A as head, (which can be noted as $A(B)$) or B as head (which can be noted as $B(A)$). The following graph illustrates the build-up at level 2 for the first 6 words in the sentence.

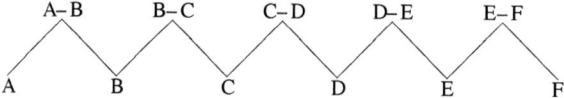

In our example, $A - B$ is $What - rescue$ which can be licensed by a *subject* relation, in which B is the head, $B(A)$ or by a *modification by relative clause* relation, in which A is the head, $A(B)$.

$B - C$ is $rescue - bill$ which can be be licensed by an *object* or an *adjunct* or a *subject* relation, in all cases *rescue* being the head. The *object* relation rule succeeds and creates a chart entry. Since the inverted *subject* relation rule is restricted to a closed class of verbs, it fails. The adjunct relation rule is restricted to a closed class of dependents, namely temporal expressions, and thus fails.

$C - D$ is $bill - is$ which licenses a *subject* relation. This relation will not lead to a globally connected parse due to the parsing context, but it is possible locally, the rule succeeds and a chart entry is created.

Analogously, structures of span length 2 are constructed for the rest of the sentence.

At the next level, j is 3, structures with span length 3 are constructed. $A - C$

2.1. The Modular Architecture

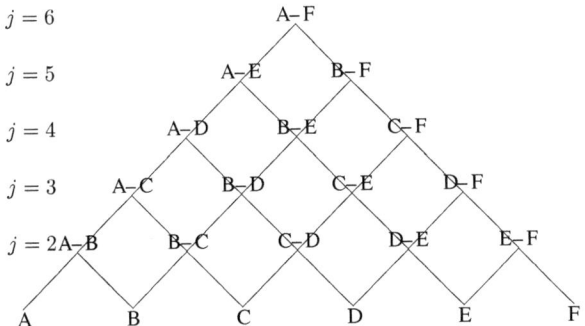

Figure 2.4: Complete CYK chart for an example sentence with 6 terminals

is $What(rescue(bill))$ with a *modification by relative clause* relation, or $rescue(what)(bill) = rescue(what, bill)$ with a *subject* relation. Analogously, the whole structure is built up, in exactly N levels, where N is the number of words per longest parse span. All the theoretically possible chart entries for the cell $A-C$ are listed in the following illustration.

$$A + (B(C)) = A(B(C)) \, or \, B(A, C)$$
$$A + (C(B)) = A(C(B)) \, or \, C(A, B)$$
$$C + (A(B)) = C(A(B)) \, or \, A(B, C)$$
$$C + (B(A)) = C(B(A)) \, or \, B(A, C)$$

The algorithm continues analogously until one or several spans covering the entire sentence are found. In our example, that is at $j = 6$, because this example has 6 terminals. Figure 2.4 shows the complete chart for this example.

In order to alleviate the overhead of keeping loop variables or executing loops

2.1. The Modular Architecture

that do not find results, a data-driven, fully declarative version of the CYK algorithm has been implemented. For every chart entry X (where start i and end j are provided by chart entry X), if there is a chart entry Y (starting at $j + 1$, and whose end k is provided by the chart entry Y), if there is a grammar rule $Z \rightarrow X, Y$, then a new chart entry Z (starting at i and ending at k) is inserted into the chart. Its pseudo-code is as follows. We use lambda notation in order to indicate unbound variables.

1. Add all terminals (heads of chunks) to chart

2. Loop: `foreach chart entry` $X\lambda i.\lambda k.[i$ `to` $k]$
    `foreach chart entry` $Y\lambda j.[k$+1 `to` $j]$ # adjacent
        `if ¬ tried`(X, Y)
            `foreach` $Z \rightarrow X, Y$ `assert` $Z[i$ `to` $j]$ `to chart`
            `assert tried`(X, Y)

3. If any rule was successful, prune and then Loop again, else terminate.

Relation Extraction Each chart entry is weighted by a lexicalized probability. The frequency counts for the lexicalized statistics are obtained from the Gold Standard, which is the Penn Treebank (Marcus, Santorini, and Marcinkiewicz, 1993b; Bies et al., 1995), at an off-line stage, before the parsing starts. Structural patterns expressing grammatical relations are applied to the Gold Standard. For local relations the patterns are relatively simple, for long-distance dependencies they can be quite complex (see chapter 6), spanning a large number of tree generations. Since the lexical heads need to be extracted, all patterns comprise more than one generation.

Let us consider a simple example of a *subject relation*. The first sentence in the Penn Treebank is annotated as follows.

(5)

```
( (S
    (NP-SBJ (NNP Mr.) (NNP Vinken) )
    (VP (VBZ is)
      (NP-PRD
        (NP (NN chairman) )
        (PP (IN of)
          (NP
            (NP (NNP Elsevier) (NNP N.V.) )
            (, ,)
            (NP (DT the) (NNP Dutch) (VBG publishing) (NN group) )))))
    (. .) ))
```

A subject relation holds between an NP with a functional label *SBJ* and its VP sister. In order to extract the lexical head, the extraction pattern needs to comprise the possible subtrees of the NP and the VP. They can both be arbitrarily nested, in our simple example that is not the case, both NP and VP immediately dominate their heads. The subject NP immediately dominates two nouns, however. The structural pattern selects the rightmost noun as the head. It thus reports a count for the (*noun,verb*) pair (*Vinken_NNP, is_VBZ*). The counts are lemmatized after the extraction, and back-off counts with semantic classes, tags, and only a subset of the heads specified are also calculated.

Lexicalized Statistical Data from the Treebank During the build-up of the parse, three sources contribute to the disambiguation: first, the parsing context only allows a small subset of local structures to be combined into a full parse. Second, the analyses are ranked by the product of the probabilities of the parsing decisions. Third, analyses whose products of probabilities fall below a certain threshold are abandoned.

A Maximum Likelihood Estimation (MLE) probability model is used for the second and third source. We use the hash symbol (#) to symbolise frequency. The general Pro3Gres MLE estimation is as follows. We estimate the probability of dependency relation R at distance (in chunks) $dist$, given the lexical head a of the governor and the lexical head b of the dependent. By application of the chain rule we get:

$$P(R, dist|a, b) = P(R|a, b) \cdot P(dist|R, a, b) \cong \frac{\#(R, a, b)}{\#(a, b)} \cdot \frac{\#(R, dist, a, b)}{\#R, a, b} \quad (2.1)$$

We then take the assumption that the distance depends only on the relation type, but not on the lexical items. We have observed that some relations, for example the subordinating clause relation *sentobj* or the PP-attachment relations *modpp* and *pobj* can span many chunks, while for example in the object relation *obj* the object noun is almost always immediately adjacent to its governing verb chunk. We have also observed that there is only little variation based on lexical differences, so that including them would considerably increase the sparseness of the data at probably very little benefit.

$$P(R, dist|a, b) \cong P(R|a, b) \cdot P(dist|R) \cong \frac{\#(R, a, b)}{\#(a, b)} \cdot \frac{\#(R, dist)}{\#R} \quad (2.2)$$

Some relations use variations of this general estimation rule. Let us look at the ending of our example sentence, ... *a bill amending the National Defence Education Act of 1958*. The final PP, which is introduced by *of*, can syntactically be attached to 5 positions: *be, progress, bill, amend,* or *act*. For PP-attachment, a variation on the above MLE estimation, following Collins and Brooks (1995), is used. It includes the PP-internal noun (we will refer to it as description noun). a is the head (a verb or a subject), b the preposition and c the description noun, R is labelled *modpp* for noun-attachment and *pobj* for verb-attachment.

$$P(R, dist|a, b) \cong P(R|a, b) \cdot P(dist|R) \cong \frac{\#(R, a, b, c)}{\#(a, b, c)} \cdot \frac{\#(R, dist)}{\#R} \quad (2.3)$$

The co-occurrence count in the denominator expresses the sum of attachment cases and attachment candidates (i.e. syntactically licensed, potential attachments). Because potential attachment interacts with the rest of the parsing progress in complex ways it needs to be approximated. Following (Collins and Brooks, 1995) we model PP-attachment as 2-way ambiguous between noun- and verb-attachment[2]. As regards our above example, where attachment is 5-way ambiguous, that means that all 5 attachment possibilities are never compared directly. The denominator generally expresses the sum of competing relations. The MLE estimations for *pobj* and *modpp* are thus the distance factor times all attachment cases divided by all attachment cases plus all cases where the attachment went to any competing relation.

$$P(pobj, dist|verb, prep, desc.noun) \cong$$
$$\frac{\#(pobj, verb, prep, desc.noun)}{\#(verb, prep, desc.noun)} \cdot \frac{\#(pobj, dist)}{\#pobj}$$

$$P(modpp, dist|noun, prep, desc.noun) \cong$$
$$\frac{\#(modpp, noun, prep, desc.noun)}{\#(noun, prep, desc.noun)} \cdot \frac{\#(modpp, dist)}{\#modpp}$$

---

[2]There are other approximations, e.g. (Collins, 1996) uses the entire sentence as a window. Merlo, Crocker, and Berthouzoz (1997) model 3-way ambiguous situations

2.1. The Modular Architecture

Since we model PP-attachment as ambiguous between verbal and nominal attachment (as discussed in section 1.4), we make the approximation that the competing relations are only *pobj* and *modpp*, hence that the denominator is the sum of all nominal plus all verbal attachments given the lexical items. This approximation is appropriate, because PPs can usually only attach to nouns (*modpp*), to verbs (*pobj*) or to predicative adjectives (which is subsumed under the *pobj* relation). If we based our counts on all 2-way ambiguous verb-noun-pp sequences (Collins and Brooks, 1995) we could get the following probabilities.

$$P(pobj, dist|verb, noun, prep, desc.noun) \cong$$
$$\frac{\#(pobj, verb, noun, prep, desc.noun)}{\#(pobj, verb, noun, prep, desc.noun) + \#(modpp, verb, noun, prep, desc.noun)}$$
$$\cdot \frac{\#(pobj, dist)}{\#pobj}$$

$$P(modpp, dist|verb, noun, prep, desc.noun) \cong$$
$$\frac{\#(modpp, verb, noun, prep, desc.noun)}{\#(modpp, verb, noun, prep, desc.noun) + \#(pobj, verb, noun, prep, desc.noun)}$$
$$\cdot \frac{\#(modpp, dist)}{\#modpp}$$

We need a slightly different model for three reasons. First, this model only counts occurrences where a PP appears in an ambiguous position in the text. We would like to profit from the many cases in which informative PP-attachments in the Gold Standard do not appear in ambiguous positions, for example a sentence initial noun attaching an immediately following PP, or a verb attaching the immediately following PP. The latter case includes intransitive verbs, which are only in an ambiguous position if they are followed by an adjunct noun. Second, the parser needs attachment probabilities, for 2-way ambiguous, unambiguous, or multi-way ambiguous attachments alike. Third, when an attachment probability during parsing needs to be assigned, the analysis we have of the sentence is very incomplete and does not know which other attachment possibilities there will be. Let us look at the parsing situation where *act* and *of 1958* are about to be combined, when the probability of the noun attachment with *act* as governor and *of 1958* as dependent needs to be assigned. At this stage, there is no certain way of knowing that *act* will in fact be in competition with *amend*, *bill* and *progress* over attaching *of 1958*, nor that it will not be in competition with *what* and the first occurrence of the word *bill* in the sentence. An object dependency from *rescue* to the first occurrence of *bill* rendering it inaccessible as potential governor for *of 1958* will exist in the chart at this stage, but we cannot know if it will feature in the highest ranked analysis. These intricate interdependencies arising from the parsing context are very hard to estimate.

We have therefore decided to model PP-attachment as generally ambiguous between noun attachment and verb attachment (the latter including adjective attachment), that is to use the putative parsing context of Collins and Brooks (1995) as an approximation, where every verb is in competition with one noun, and every noun is in competition with one verb. The actual competitions during parse time are never in direct comparison, but indirectly via the comparison of the putative parsing context.

Generally, an MLE probability is the result of the positive counts divided by the candidate counts. For our PP-attachment model, positive counts are cases that do attach in the Gold Standard, and candidate counts are cases that do attach in the Gold Standard *plus* cases that could attach but that do not, according to the putative parsing context. For verb attachment, then, candidate cases are all cases where attachment as *pobj* occurs, *plus* all cases where in the ambiguous context of a verb-noun-PP sequence the PP attaches to the noun (the label will be *modpp*).

$$P(pobj, dist | verb, prep, desc.noun) \cong$$
$$\frac{\#(pobj, verb, prep, desc.noun)}{\#(pobj, verb, prep, desc.noun) + \#(modpp, verb, \sum(noun), prep, desc.noun)}$$
$$\cdot \frac{\#(pobj, dist)}{\#pobj} \qquad (2.4)$$

$$P(modpp, dist | noun, prep, desc.noun) \cong$$
$$\frac{\#(modpp, noun, prep, desc.noun)}{\#(modpp, noun, prep, desc.noun) + \#(pobj, \sum(verb), noun, prep, desc.noun)}$$
$$\cdot \frac{\#(modpp, dist)}{\#modpp} \qquad (2.5)$$

The counts are backed off across several levels, following Merlo and Esteve Ferrer (2006) by including semantic classes, the WordNet lexicographer file ID for nouns and the Levin top class for verbs. The probabilities used for the attachment of the PP *of 1958* in the example sentence are as follows.

2.1. The Modular Architecture

Probability of attachment of the PP *of 1958* to the noun *bill*

$$P(modpp, dist|noun, prep, desc.noun) \cong$$
$$\frac{\#(modpp, bill, of, Class18) = 8}{\#(modpp, bill, of, Class18) + \#(pobj, \sum(verb), bill, of, Class18) = 8}$$
$$\cdot \frac{\#(modpp, dist) = 677}{\#modpp = 53591} = 0.0126$$

Probability of attachment of the PP *of 1958* to the verb *amend*

$$P(pobj, dist|verb, prep, desc.noun) \cong$$
$$\frac{\#(pobj, \sum(verb), of, \sum(noun)) = 420}{\#(pobj, \sum(verb), of, \sum(noun)) + \#(modpp, verb, \sum(noun), of, desc.noun) = 5586}$$
$$\cdot \frac{\#(pobj, dist) = 25650}{\#pobj = 46124} = 0.0418$$

Probability of attachment of the PP *of 1958* to the noun *act*

$$P(modpp|noun, prep, desc.noun) \cong$$
$$\frac{\#(modpp, act, of, Class18) = 14}{\#(modpp, act, of, Class18) + \#(pobj, \sum(verb), act, of, Class18) = 14}$$
$$\cdot \frac{\#(modpp, dist) = 11918}{\#modpp = 53591} = 0.2224$$

As we have mentioned, there is no direct competition between different possible noun-PP attachments in this model. For example *bill* and *act* are not in direct competition in this model, their probabilities differ due to the distance and their relative probabilities when in competition to verb attachment.

We have now explained the probability for a single parsing decision, equalling a single attachment. The probability of a tree for a given sentence is the product of all the single decisions that build up the tree. As can be seen in the triangular chart that is built up by the CYK algorithm (see figure 2.4), the number of chart entries m is related to the number of terminals n as follows.

$$m = \frac{(n-1)^2 + (n-1)}{2} \tag{2.6}$$

The probability of a tree T given a sentence S with n terminals is therefore:

$$P(T|S) = \prod_{i=1}^{m} P(R_i, dist_i | a_i, b_i) \qquad (2.7)$$

We estimate the probability of a tree given a sentence. We thus use a discriminative, not a generative model (Johnson, 2001).

MLE is not the statistical method leading to the best possible results. However, Bikel (2004, 109 ff) points out that using advanced statistical methods does often not improve performance considerably. He only reports a 1 % increase in parsing performance on a Collins (1999) parser when replacing the MLE model by a Maximum Entropy model. We have therefore decided to investigate into a sophisticated back-off model rather than into alternative statistical methods.

Pruner In complex real-world sentences, constructing all possible chart entries can become very time-consuming. It has been shown (see e.g. Brants and Crocker (2000)) that discarding locally very improbable partial analyses hardly affects a parser's performance, because the chance that locally very improbable analyses become parts of the most probable analysis later is very small. Pruning happens during parsing, as indicated by the double arrow in figure 2.1. Pruning is a standard procedure, used in all beam parsers (Ratnaparkhi, 1997; Henderson, 2003).

We use the following three pruning methods: hard local cut, fixed beam pruning, and large chart panic mode. The hard local cut method rules out local attachments that are very improbable. As a default, all attachments that have a probability below 1 % are immediately cut. The fixed beam pruning method restrict the number of chart entries for each span. As a default value for robust, large-scale parsing we use 5. The large chart panic mode is used to cope with very complex real-world sentences. It only has an effect in a small minority of real-world sentences. When the total number of chart entries exceeds a certain threshold (we use 1000 as a default) the value used for the hard local cut is increased according to a heuristic function which takes the span length of the chart entries and the total number of chart entries into account. The large beam panic mode entails that in very complex sentences some permissible spans are never found, but it allows the parser to deliver a set of long partial analyses for every sentence. The largest sentence we have encountered in the British National Corpus consists of over 200 chunks.

Parse Collection In case no complete span for an input sentence can be found, the parser needs to resorts to collecting partial parses. Starting from the most probable longest span, recursively the most probable longest span to left and right is

2.2. Integrating Linguistic Knowledge into the System 32

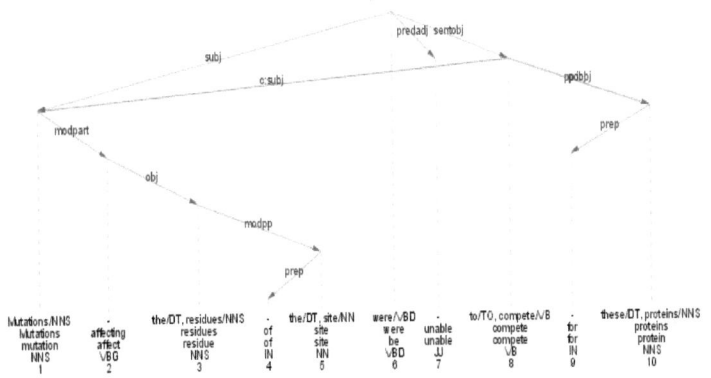

Figure 2.5: Parser output

collected. There are two reasons why no complete span can be found in some sentences. Either it contains a (rare, highly marked or potentially unacceptable) construction that is not covered by our grammar, or the pruner prevents a possible complete structure from being created.

Post-Processing After parsing, a post-processing module converts the dependency tree into a graph structure which contains additional, deep-syntactic relations, so-called long-distance dependencies. An example of a sentence involving a long-distance dependency is shown in figure 3.3, a so-called control structure, where *mutations* becomes the subject of the subordinate verb *compete* due to the semantic of the control adjective *unable*. We give a short overview of long-distance dependencies in the following, and discuss them in detail in chapter 6.

2.2 Integrating Linguistic Knowledge into the System

2.2.1 The Boundedness of Long-Distance Dependencies

Long-distance dependencies are traditionally grouped into two classes (see e.g. Pollard and Sag (1994)). In the first class, there is an overt constituent in a nonargument position that represents the absent constituent (the trace) in the argument position. In this class we find topicalisations, WH-questions, WH-relative clauses and pseudo-cleft constructions. In the second class there is a constituent in an argument position that also represents an argument of a different predicate. In this class we find control and raising, relative clause, passive, and it-cleft constructions.

We show in chapter 6 that all cases of the first class type except for complex WH-movements can be treated locally in Dependency Grammar. For the second class type, context-free parsing is sufficient, because the coreference of the argument position can be resolved at the post-processing stage by means of a statistical method. Let us look at an example of a control structure.

(6) John wanted to leave.

Every subordinate clause which is subjectless and infinitival, such as *to leave* here, triggers the post-processing module to take a decision based on the lexical probability of the matrix verb (*want*) which introduces subject control, object control, or neither. In this case, the outcome of the decision constructs a coreference to the subject of the matrix verb, indicating that on the deep-syntactic level *John* is also the subject of *leave*. Complex WH-movements needs a different treatment. A simple mildly context-sensitive approach is discussed and implemented in chapter 6.

2.2.2 Constraints on Grammar Rules

Linguistic knowledge allows us to place strong restrictions on the co-occurrence of different relation types. Verbs that have attached adjuncts cannot attach complements, since this would violate X-bar constraints. Verbs that have no object cannot attach secondary objects. The application of dependency rules can often be lexically restricted: for example, only temporal expressions occur as NP adjuncts. We have noticed during the development of the grammar that these restrictions play a crucial role for the improvement of the parser's performance. We describe the grammar in detail in chapter 5, we assess the impact on speed and performance of these constraints in section 7.8.

2.2.3 Mapping Grammatical Relations for the Probability Estimation

We integrate a wide selection of knowledge sources in our system, and a variety of techniques. Integrating grammatical knowledge does not only have an impact on the grammar rules. We now give an example of how grammatical knowledge can be used for the probability estimation.

2.2. Integrating Linguistic Knowledge into the System

We have discussed the MLE estimation in general in section 2.1, and the case of PP-attachment relations. Some relations have models that slightly differ from the general estimation. For example, the noun-participle relation integrates linguistic knowledge about similar grammatical relations.

The noun-participle relation is also known as reduced relative clause. Examples are *the report written* or *the soldiers returned home were greeted*. Reduced relative clauses are frequent enough to warrant a probabilistic treatment, but considerably sparser than verb-subject or verb-object relations. They are in direct competition with the subject-verb relation (as discussed in section 1.4), because both are licensed by a NP followed by a VP. We have a subject-verb relation in *the report announced the deal* and a noun-participle relation in *the report announced yesterday*. The majority of modification by participle relations, if the participle is a past participle, functionally correspond to passive constructions (*the report written* ≅ *the report which has been written*). In order to reduce data sparseness, we have added the verb–passive-subject counts ($psubj$) to the noun–participle counts. Some past participles also express adjunct readings (*the week ended Friday*); therefore the converse, i.e. adding noun–participle counts to verb–passive-subject counts, cannot be recommended.

The probability estimation for the $modpart$ relations across all backoff levels is as follows (we map the noun a to its Wordnet-class $\mathring{a}$ and the verb b to its Levin-class $\mathring{b}$).

$$P(modpart, dist | a, b) = \qquad (2.8)$$

$$\begin{cases} \frac{\#(modpart,right,a,b)+\#(psubj,left,a,b)}{\#(modpart,right,a,b)+\#(psubj,left,a,b)+\#(asubj,left,a,b)} & if>0, else \\ \frac{\#(modpart,right,\mathring{a},b)+\#(psubj,left,\mathring{a},b)}{\#(modpart,right,\mathring{a},b)+\#(psubj,left,\mathring{a},b)+\#(asubj,left,\mathring{a},b)} & if>0, else \\ \frac{\#(modpart,right,b)+\#(psubj,left,b)}{\#(modpart,right,b)+\#(psubj,left,b)+\#(asubj,left,b)} & if>0, else \\ \frac{\#(modpart,right,a)+\#(psubj,left,a)}{\#(modpart,right,a)+\#(psubj,left,a)+\#(asubj,left,a)} & \end{cases} \cdot \frac{\#(modpart,dist)}{\#modpart}$$

As the last backoff, a low non-zero probability is assigned for most relations. Again, based on grammatical knowledge, there are exceptions to this: the verb–adjunct relation can only occur with a closed class of nouns, mostly with adverbial expressions of time. In order reduce parsing complexity, only the backoff levels that include the adjunct noun or its class are used. The backoff hierarchy is also changed. Before using a semantic class on the dependent and keeping the lexical head of the governor, the adjunct relation keeps the head of the dependent and uses the semantic class of the verb. While predicates place selectional restrictions on their arguments, adjuncts are themselves a restricted class, a class that can, however, be selected by almost any predicate (Merlo and Esteve Ferrer, 2006).

Chapter 3

Dependency Grammar

In this chapter we give a detailed introduction to Dependency Grammar (DG). We need to discuss DG in detail for a number of reasons. First, it motivates out mapping of the constituency representation of the Penn Treebank to a dependency representation. Second, we need to clarify what we mean by *functional* in functional dependency grammar. Third, the discussion of headedness and projectivity is an important preparatory step for our treatment of long-distance dependencies, which hinges on the fact that functional DG naturally extends locality to the clause level. We discuss long-distance dependencies in chapter 6. Fourth, we elucidate the close relationship of DG to Head-Driven Phrase Structure Grammar (HPSG), and to Lexical-Functional Grammar (LFG).

There exist a number of different versions of DG. In section 3.1 we present four important conceptions of the common core of all DG versions. In section 3.2 we then discuss some characteristics of the version of DG that we use, which is best described by the term *functional DG*.

3.1 Conceptions of DG

In the following we will present four conceptions of what DG is. First we give a historical, informal definition of the intuition of DG as an extended valency grammar. Second we discuss that the government relation is the fundamental DG primitive. Third we give a more formal definition and discuss in which ways DG has been presented as equivalent to constituency, and in which ways it is not. Finally, we discuss that DG can be mapped to X-bar under certain conditions.

3.1.1 Extended Valency Grammar

Intuitively, DG is a valency grammar. The term *valency* or *valence* is borrowed from the definition of valency in chemistry. Different verbs take a specific number and type of complement. A monovalent verb like *sleep* typically takes a subject (*she sleeps*) but cannot take an object **she sleeps it*. A bivalent verb like *eat* typically takes a subject and an object (*she eats it*), although the object may also be absent. A trivalent verb like *give* typically takes a subject, a direct object and an indirect object (*she gives him flowers* or *she gives flowers to him*). The type of complement, typically nouns, prepositional phrases or subordinate clauses, is often restricted. While for example epistemic verbs may take subordinate clauses (*he thinks that she sleeps*), the majority of verbs cannot (**he eats that she sleeps*). Also the type of argument can be restricted. For example, the type of complementizer introducing a subordinate clause depends on the matrix verb.

(7) I think that you will come.

(8) *I wonder that you will come.

(9) *I think whether you will come.

(10) I wonder whether you will come.

Valency is closely related to transitivity, intransitive verbs being monovalent, transitive verbs being bivalent, and ditransitive verbs being trivalent. Transitivity typically does not refer to restrictions on the type of arguments and does not include the subject valency.

Valency is not restricted to verbs only. Relational nouns and some predicative adjectives also open valencies. Predicative adjectives have in common with verbs that different subclasses of them take different complements, usually certain PPs and complementizers. For example, *afraid* requires a PP introduced by *of*, *ready* needs a PP introduced by *for*:

(11) I am afraid of action.

(12) *I am afraid for action.

(13) *I am ready of action.

(14) I am ready for action.

Nouns that are derived from verbs or adjectives partly keep the valencies. Valencies for PPs are usually kept, the subject of object valency often corresponds to a PP introduced by *of*.

(15) The offer of a present to the guest

(16) ?The house of a present to the guest

Valencies have been extended from verbs to many other word classes, and from syntax into semantics (Helbig, 1992, 108). Valency theory was also influenced by (Fillmore, 1968)'s Case Grammar and by collocation analysis.

Especially from the viewpoint of the German DG tradition (see e.g. Tapanainen and Järvinen (1997, 3)), DG is based on valency. Weber (1997, 34) stresses the influence of the seminal valency work by Tesnière (1959) on an entire generation of German lexicographers. The word opening a valency is defined as *governor* or equivalently *head* in DG, the word filling the valency is called *dependent*. Unlike constituency grammar, DG leaves the distinction between mother node, governor and head underspecified. The traditional stemma notation places the governor above the dependent and draws a line between them. In example 17 we see a stemma DG notation (a.), a redundant stemma DG notation (b.) in which the head as a daughter of the governor is explicitly added, and a constituency representation (c.), in which the governor is a phrasal category. We will discuss the relation between DG and constituency in more detail in section 3.1.3.

(17) eats pizza

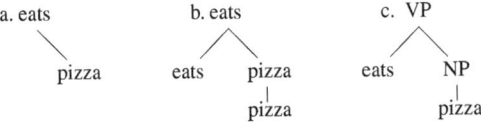

In DG, valency was also extended from argument to adjuncts and even to function words in order to be able to build up complete dependency structures. Some dependencies are not valencies or grammatical functions in a strict sense. For example, the dependence of a subordinate verb on the complementizer that introduces the subordinate sentence is difficult to explain on valency grounds. But where possible, Tesnière's conception of *nucleus* was kept to alleviate the need to create an unlimited number of dependencies for which valency cannot account. A nucleus is a content word plus its attributed function words[1]. Only nuclei have dependency relations among each other. For a verb, typical function words are auxiliaries. For a noun, typical function words are determiners. Content words typically form open classes, function words closed classes. Valency focuses on events between content words, usually underspecifiying definiteness, polarity, modality, aspect and tense. This valency background of DG is a major reason why the definition of heads in DG is often diametrically opposed to the definition of heads in GB (where function word categories often dominate content words) or in Montague grammar (where determiners dominate nouns). We will discuss head definitions in section 3.2.1.

There is a substantial overlap between the practical notion of verb and noun *chunk* and the theoretical concept of *nucleus*, but there are also differences. For example, a predicative adjective can be seen to form a nucleus with a copula. For practical parsers, they can be considered similar enough, so that chunking plus parsing between chunk heads as suggested by Abney (1995) follows the philosophy of valency grammar and gives it a thorough theoretical linguistic motivation.

3.1.2 Government Grammar

DG leaves the distinction between governor and head underspecified. DG is a grammar in which the government relation is a fundamental primitive. Government, a relatively complex constituent relation in GB, which is needed for example to assign Case, is available in dependency as a primitive. Covington (1992, 4) concludes that since only lexical items can govern in DG, dependency and government coincide. Covington (1992, 4) equates government to immediate dependency, the most local form of dependency. The restriction to immediate dependency is a DG version of the Minimality condition (Chomsky, 1986; Rizzi, 1995).

As a first approximation, lexical government can be defined as c-command in GB. c-command is defined as follows. α c-commands β iff:

1. the first branching node dominating α also dominates β
2. α does not dominate β.

This definition is not sufficient to assign case to subjects. Subject case is assumed to be assigned by I. I does not c-command the subject NP due to the intervening I' node.

---
[1] Nuclei are also known as bonetsus from the Japanese grammar tradition.

3.1. Conceptions of DG

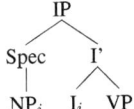

In order to allow I to govern the subject NP the notion of m-command was introduced and the definition of government was adapted. Typical definitions of government also constrain the governor to be a terminal category and require that Minimality be respected.

α c-commands β iff:

1. the first maximal projection dominating α also dominates β
2. α does not dominate β and β does not dominate α.

α lexically governs β iff:

1. α is an X^0 category
2. α m-commands β
3. Minimality is respected.

As DG leaves the distinction between words and maximal projections (phrases) underspecified, it can be assumed that the version of government expressed by DG dependency corresponds to m-command. Since DG only knows lexical categories (words), the restriction to X^0 is redundant in DG. We will return to Minimality in chapter 6.

3.1.3 Terminal Node Context-Free Grammar

We will now compare DG and constituency in detail. We give formal definitions of a version of context-free DG and context-free constituency. They are proven to be equivalent, but they miss out on important characteristics of DG.

We have seen in section 3.1.1 that DG leaves the distinction between mother node and lexical head underspecified. DG is a context-free constituent grammar (CFG) that only knows terminal nodes. We repeat the example: in 18 we see a stemma DG notation (a.), a redundant stemma DG notation (b.) in which the head as a daughter of the governor is explicitly added[2], and a constituency representation (c.), in which the governor is a phrasal category.

(18) eats pizza

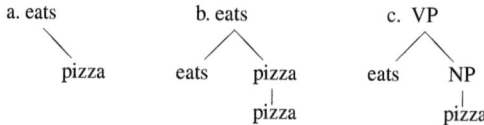

This is a classical conception of DG. It has been used by Gaifman (1965) for his proof that DG is a proper subset of CFG. It turned out that this proof is an oversimplification. It has come under criticism for several reasons. First, Abney (1994) shows that the essential DG property of headedness has been supressed by Gaifman (1965). Second, Baumgärtner (1970) was the first to discuss that the definition used by Gaifman (1965) fails to reflect an important property of Tesnière's conception of DG: DG expresses immediate dominance[3] but may leave linear precedence[4] underspecified. Third, Baumgärtner (1970), Tapanainen and Järvinen (1997) and Nivre (2006a) discuss that Gaifman (1965) assumes a projective version of DG, while at least Tesnière's original DG conception is non-projective[5] (see section 3.1.3). Fourth, DG often uses dependency labels, typically containing grammatical relation information (such as *subject* or *object*, see section 3.1.1). Covington (1994) discusses how they can be used to map DG to and from X-bar. We illustrate these points in more detail in the following.

Headedness

We follow Abney (1994) for his definition of Gaifman's DG and CFG. A DG is a quadruple $G = (\Sigma, P, S, L)$, in which Σ is a set of word categories, P is a set of productions, $S \subset \Sigma$ is the set of start symbols, and L is the lexicon of words. Productions P licence trees. Abney (1994) defines their form as $X(\alpha; \beta)$, X is a

---

[2]This explicitly expresses the essential DG characteristic that one daughter and the head are identical. In (a.) this is not expressed, as it is redundant information
[3]dominance is defined as appearing higher in a tree representation. Immediate dominance is defined as a direct mother-daughter relation in a tree representation
[4]Precedence is an order relation. Precedence of A over B is defined as A appearing before B. Linear precedence is defined as order relation in the unannotated, hence non-hierarchical, linear text.
[5]Projectivity of a tree is defined as follows: If for every node in the tree, for every n, the rightmost daughter of its nth daughter appears before the leftmost daughter of its $n + 1$th daughter, then the tree is projective.

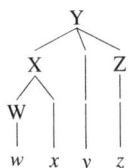

Figure 3.1: Dependency tree example

category, α and β are sequences of categories: α is the sequence of dependents to the left of X, in the listed order, β is the sequence of dependents to the right of X, in the listed order

A DG lexicon L relates words to categories. In a word-only DG, words and categories are equated, but in most practical DG's, categories are pre-terminals such as part-of-speech tags.

For example, the following DG licences the dependency tree in figure 3.1.

Categories Σ	Productions P	Lexicon L	Start Node S
W	$X(W;\epsilon)$	$w \in W$	$S = Y$
X	$Y(X;Z)$	$x \in X$	
Y		$y \in Y$	
Z		$z \in Z$	
		$\epsilon \in \epsilon$	

A CFG is a quintuple $G = (V, \Sigma, P, S, L)$, in which V is a set of nonterminal categories, and, like in DG, in which Σ is a set of word categories, P is a set of productions, S is the set of start symbols, and L is the lexicon of words. Unlike in DG, $S \in V$, and productions P are of the form $X \to \alpha$, where $X \in V$ and $\alpha \in (V \cup \Sigma \cup L)$. Productions P licence trees. The production $X \to Y_1, ...Y_n$ licences a node iff the node has category X and its children have categories $Y_1, ...Y_n$, in the given order.

For example, the following CFG licences the phrase structure tree in figure 3.2.

Categories Σ and V	Productions P	Lexicon L	Start Node S
W	$X \to W *X$	$w \in W$	$S = Y$
X	$Y \to X *YZ$	$x \in *X$	
Y		$y \in *Y$	
Z		$z \in Z$	

Except for the extra non-terminal nodes introduced in CFG, the DG and CFG

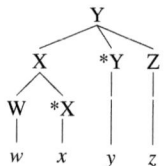

Figure 3.2: Constituency tree example

representations seem identical. Tree 3.2 can be induced from tree 3.1, $*X$ and $*Y$ are non-terminal categories representing the heads of X and Y. While this seems like a small change, it contains a crucial difference: the newly introduced categories $*X$ and $*Y$ are only related to X and Y because the production rules of this example happen to enforce it; but it is no inherent characteristic of CFG (Abney, 1994, 3).

The essential characteristic of DG that one daughter is the head is not a part of the CFG formalism. Gaifman (1965)'s proof thus loses much of its interest as it is based on wrong assumptions, as Abney (1994, 4) concludes.

Abney (1994) thus suggests to compare DG to Headed Context-Free Grammar (HCFG), a CFG in which a unique child of each node is distinguished as a head. Formally, productions are defined as pairs (r, i), in which r is a CFG production, and i is the index of the head, with $1 \leq i \leq |r|$.

A HCFG can be related to a unique DG, which Abney (1994) calls *projection dependency grammars*. A DG can be related to several HCFGs, however. In order to understand this point, it is important to clarify the distinction between productions P and DG rules. Productions are not DG rules, but they licence DG trees that arise from the application of DG rules. DG rules are binary by definition, they relate a governor to a dependent. In the example tree 3.1, the application of two DG rules, both with Y as governor, with X as dependent to the left in one DG rule, and with Z as dependent to the right in a second DG rule leads to the one production $Y(X; Z)$. The order of application of these two rules is left underspecified.

If we define *projection category* as a sequence of projections in a headed tree, we can define dependencies between projections. For example, in the headed tree of example 19, the projection category (B, D, S) has one left dependent, (A), and one right dependent, (C).

(19)

3.1. Conceptions of DG

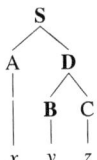

One can map a headed tree to a unique dependency tree. Each projection p in the headed tree maps to a node π in the *projection dependency tree*. The category of π is the projection category of p. Projections $q1, ..., q_n$ that are dependents of p in the headed tree map to the dependents of π in the projection tree. The projection dependency tree of (19) is (20):

(20)

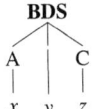

The projection dependency tree of a headed tree is unique, but several headed trees may have the same projection dependency tree. The projection dependency tree (20) corresponds to the two headed trees in (21). Projection-dependency trees thus abstract away from the order in which dependents are combined with their governor (Abney, 1994, 6).

(21)

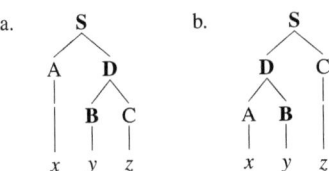

The fact that DG underspecifies the attachment order has also led to the observation that DG is an X-bar Grammar without intermediate nodes (Covington, 1992; Miller, 2000), and the suggestion that the labels in labelled DGs may be used to recover the X-bar intermediate nodes (Covington, 1994). We discuss this in section 3.1.4.

Linearity

Another reason why Gaifman (1965)'s proof has been criticised is that it does not respect the property of Tesnière's original DG that dependencies express immediate dominance (ID) but not linear precedence (LP). There is a family of formal grammars distinguishing between ID and LP, so-called ID/LP grammars (Shieber, 1983). CFG incorporates dominance and precedence into a single rule, while ID/LP grammars maintain separate rule sets. The ID/LP approach is used in head-driven phrase structure grammar (HPSG) and lexical-functional grammar (LFG).

In some versions of DG, linear precedence is left underspecified in the representation. This entails that these versions are unable to reconstruct the linear order from the representation. They are thus unsuitable for language generation purposes.

Baumgärtner (1970) was the first to note that Gaifman (1965)'s proof suppresses the ID/LP distinction. Gaifman (1965) uses the following general form for his proof.

w are dependents to the left, in the order from m to 1, x is the head, y are dependents to the right, in the order from 1 to n.

$$w(m)...w(1) \quad x \quad y(1)...y(n) \tag{3.1}$$

Baumgärtner (1970, 57) explains that this formula allows easy comparison between constituency and dependency, because it can be transformed into the following rewrite rule (where [#] is at the position of the governing symbol)

$$x \rightarrow w(m)...w(1) \ [\#] \ y(1)...y(n) \tag{3.2}$$

Such a DG is equivalent to CFG (except for headedness, see the paragraph *headedness* above) but supresses the underspecification of linearity, an important characteristic of many DG versions. Baumgärtner (1970, 60-61) points out that the linear ordering is not expressed in DG, but that this proof forces the linear ordering onto DG, thus making incorrect assumptions. At the same time he admits that linearity may play a secondary role.

An advantage of a grammar that focuses on ID is that for free word-order phenomena an inversion of the "canonical" dependency direction under well-defined conditions can be allowed in the grammar, without the need to resort to long-distance dependencies. Such phenomena are the English subject-verb inversion in non-support questions (22) or sentence-final verbs of utterance (23), or clause order inversions with sentence-final verbs of utterance (24).

(22) *Is Peter* tall?

(23) Peter is tall, *says he*.

(24) Peter *is* tall, he *says*.

A disadvantage of such a grammar is that parsing complexity increases. Barton (1985) proves that ID/LP parsing is actually NP-complete. In practical terms, the fact that linearity may play a secondary role, constraining the direction of dependencies wherever possible, alleviates this theoretical problem. Barton (1985, 77) elaborates on the practical implications of the increase in parsing complexity for ID/LP grammars. First, he observes that parsing time only explodes in practice if the amount of ambiguity is high, if linearity remains largely unconstrained. Second, he observes that although parsing time may exponentially increase, expanding an ID/LP grammar into all possible CFG rewrite rules, a so-called object grammar, leads to much worse time behaviour, since the object grammar very easily explodes.

> *[T]he use of Earley's algorithm on the expanded object grammar constitutes a parsing method for the fixed-grammar ID/LP parsing problem that is indeed no worse than cubic in sentence length. However, the most important aspect of this possibility is that it is devoid of practical significance. The object grammar could contain trillions of rules in practical cases (Shieber, 1983, 4).*
>
> (Barton, 1985, 80)

In practice, linearity can indeed be constrained in the majority of cases. In the above examples, in (22) only questions allow an inversion of the verb and the subject; in example (23) only the closed class of epistemic verbs allow an inversion of the verb and the subject; the subordinate clause relation $sentobj$ of example 24 is indeed a dependency relation that can always go in either direction, but most relations are considerably or fully constrained in English.

Projectivity

Tesnière's original DG is not context-free. It does not rule out crossing dependencies. Levy (2005) proves that non-projecitivity and crossing constituency are identical. The few DG implementations that aim to follow Tesnière are thus often context-sensitive, notably Tapanainen and Järvinen (1997) and Nivre (2006a). Surprisingly, there are few context-sensitive DG parsers. Nivre (2006a, 74) states that although extensions to context-free grammar have been studied quite extensively, few corresponding dependency-based systems exist.

Let us look at an example sentence containing non-projective dependencies. Figure 3.3 shows the Pro3Gres analysis of the sentence *Mutations affecting the 5' guanine residues of the kappa B site were unable to compete for these NF-kappa B-related proteins*. Only the heads of domain terms are represented in the tree. *mutations* is the surface-syntactic, projective subject of the main verb *unable*, but on a deep-syntactic level, *mutations* is also the subject of *compete*. This dependency is non-projective, since it crosses other dependencies. Non-projective dependencies appear in a number of phenomena, their frequency may depend on how deep-linguistic the analysis is. Figure 3.4 shows an example of relative pronoun resolution and the optionally available feature of expanding appositions by means of non-projective dependencies.

Neuhaus and Bröker (1997) have proven that unconstrained context-sensitivity leads to an NP-complete recognition problem for dependency parsing. Context-sensitivity thus needs to be restricted to a minimum. We will suggest in chapter 6 that most English long-distance dependencies can be expressed in context-free fashion, and discuss that for the few remaining long-distance dependencies, mild context-sensitivity is sufficient.

Some characteristics of DG entail that it needs fewer long-distance dependencies than classical CFGs. We have seen in the *linearity* paragraph that free word order can be modelled in an ID grammar without the need for long-distance dependencies. We have seen in the *headedness* paragraph that DG underspecifies the order of attachment and projection levels. This entails that different verbal projections such as VP and S are not distinguished, no distinction between internal and external argument is maintained. Accordingly, fronted positions are available locally to the verb in DG as illustrated in example (25). Generally, constituents that appear semantically closer need not appear linearly closer in the text. The dislocated verbal particle *up* in example (26) can be attached locally to the verb, even though in a typical parsing process it will be attached later than the object *her*.

(25) *In God* we trust

3.1. Conceptions of DG   48

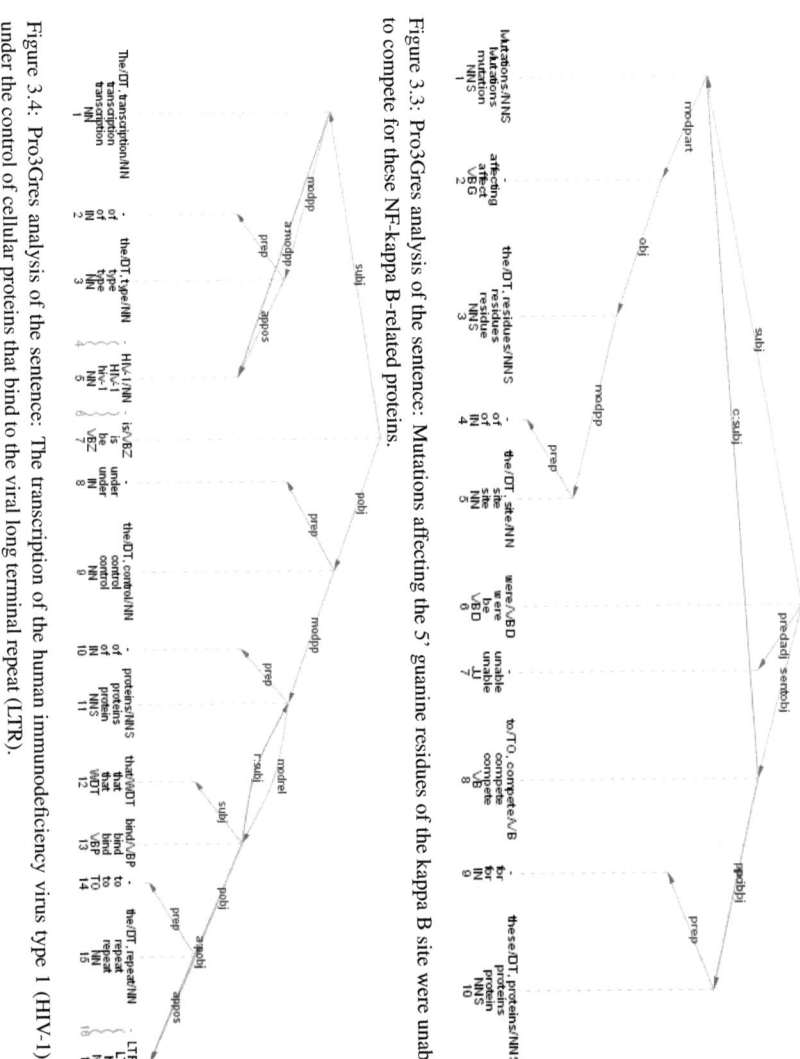

Figure 3.3: Pro3Gres analysis of the sentence: Mutations affecting the 5' guanine residues of the kappa B site were unable to compete for these NF-kappa B-related proteins.

Figure 3.4: Pro3Gres analysis of the sentence: The transcription of the human immunodeficiency virus type 1 (HIV-1) is under the control of cellular proteins that bind to the viral long terminal repeat (LTR).

3.1. Conceptions of DG

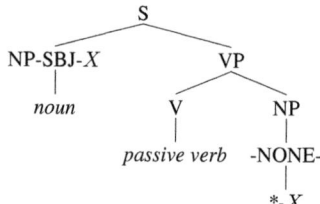

Figure 3.5: The partial CFG tree corresponding to the local DG passive subject relation.

(26) He called *her up*

Dependency Labels

Many DG versions use relation labels, which typically express grammatical relations. Such labels are unknown in CFG. Labels can be used to map non-local partial trees onto a local labeled DG relation. For example, partial trees from the Penn Treebank expressing the passive subject relation are of the form shown in figure 3.5 (where X is the co-indexation). The same information can be expressed by using a dedicated DG label, a label that expresses the passive subject only.

In section 3.1.4 we will see that relation labels can also be used to map DG representations to X-bar representations.

3.1.4 A Version of X-bar Theory

We have seen above in subsection 3.1.3 in the paragraph *headedness* that DG can be compared to a headed CFG (HCFG). A subset of HCFG which has become widely used is the linguistic theory of X-bar (Chomsky, 1970; Jackendoff, 1977). It was recognised early that natural language does not need the full set of rules that can be expressed by CFG rewrite rules. Rewrite rules in which lexical categories project to phrases of the same category (the category of the phrase is endocentric) are sufficient. It was also observed that these categories share the same build-up, and that the rewrite rules for these phrases can be unified into a universal scheme in which the category type X can be instantiated by any lexical category. This universal set of patterns is called X-bar scheme. Its intermediate level of projection, X-bar, is recursive, attaching an adjunct at each recursion. A pattern with no recursion of X-bar and a pattern with one recursion of X-bar can look as follows.

3.1. Conceptions of DG

(27)

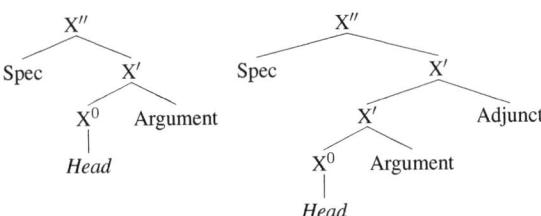

The recursion at the projection level of X' ensures that an arbitrary number of adjuncts can be attached, while the number of arguments is fixed, determined by the subcategorisation of the head. Stowell (1981) summarises the characteristics of X' as five conditions.

1. Every phrase is endocentric.

2. Specifiers appear at the X"-level; subcategorised complements appear within X'.

3. The head always appears adjacent to one boundary of X'.

4. The head is one bar level lower than the immediately dominating phrasal node.

5. Only maximal projections may appear as non-head terms within a phrase.

While a HCFG can be mapped to a unique DG representation, a DG representation may correspond to several headed trees, due to the DG characteristics that the attachment order is underspecified. The projection dependency tree of (20) can be mapped to both headed trees (21), repeated here as (28) and (29).

(28)

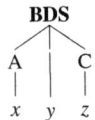

(29)

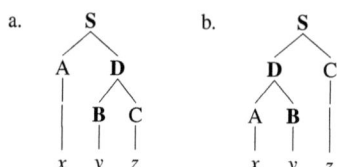

    The projection category (B, D, S) corresponds to the projections of a lexical category X in X-bar theory. D corresponds to the intermediate category X'. When mapping from the projection dependency tree (28) to a headed tree (29), S always dominates all categories, B always dominates the head only, but it is unclear whether the intermediate category D dominates B and C as in tree 29a. or A and B as in tree 29b. We can thus conclude that while X-bar expresses the distinction between the different levels of projections, the bar levels, DG is not able to do so. Covington (1992, 2) defines DG in terms of X-bar with only one non-terminal bar-level. The distinction between terminals and projections is possible because terminals have no dependents. But a distinction between maximal projections (X'') or intermediate projections (X') is not possible.

    X-bar theory uses three types of dependencies: *specifier*, the non-head dependent of X''; *adjunct*, a non-head dependent of X' with X' as sister; and *argument*, a non-head dependent of X' with X^0 as sister. If one uses a labelled DG that knows these three types or can map to them unambiguously, then DG and X-bar are equivalent (Covington, 1994).

> *[I]nstead of being considered equivalent to flat X-bar trees, dependency structures can be mapped onto X-bar trees that introduce stacking in a principled way. Here is a sketch of such a reinterpretation, consistent with current X-bar theory. Given a head (X) and its dependents, attach the dependents to the head by forming stacked X nodes as follows:*
>
> *1. Attach subcategorized complements first, all under the same X node. If there are none, create the X node anyway.*
>
> *2. Then attach modifiers, one at a time, by working outward from the one nearest to the head noun, and adding a stacked X node for each.*

> 3. *Finally, create an X node at the top of the stack, and attach the specifier (determiner), if any.*

(Covington, 1994, 7)

We can conclude that a labelled DG using labels that can be mapped to specifier, argument, and adjunct functions is a notational variant of X-bar.

3.2 Characteristics of functional DG

The informal definitions in section 3.1 have allowed us to introduce some characteristics of DG. We would now like to introduce the characteristics of our version of DG, which is best represented by the term *functional DG*, in which functional is closely related to the sense of LFG f-structure (Bresnan, 1982; Kaplan and Maxwell, 1996; Bresnan, 2001). We will discuss the close relation between LFG and our DG in section 6.5.

An LFG f-structure conception presumes the use of a labelled DG, in which the labels express grammatical relations. The distinction between configurational and functional structure is not always straightforward, however. Let us consider three examples. First, LFG uses the relations COMP for subordinated clauses, and XCOMP for subordinated clauses in which argument is shared by means of syntactic control). One may argue that the clausal or phrasal status of an argument is coincidential – we therefore use the label sentential object ($sentobj$) for COMP and XCOMP. Second, LFG has a clause level relation TOPIC, which houses fronted constituents that are consequently shared to their deep-syntactic subject, object, or adjunct functions. One may argue that TOPIC is a configurational concept. We attach fronted constituents directly to their deep-syntactic functions. Third, some relations that do not have a clearly functional character need to be admitted to the label set for practical parsing purposes, both in LFG and DG. In our robust parser, they include *compl* for attaching complementizers to a verb, *prep* for connecting the preposition and the noun in a PP, or *nchunk* to correct underchunking (the rules are presented in detail in chapter 5). We discuss our notion of functionalism in section 3.2.3.

3.2.1 Definition of Head

We have seen in section 3.1.3 that headedness is an essential property of DG. As in other theories where headedness is essential (e.g. X-bar, LFG, HPSG), a detailed linguistic discussion of what a head is has to arise. If two items A and B are combined, the mother node has to be either A or B. Interestingly, X-bar (as part of GB) and HPSG have often taken opposite views, partly based on valency considerations discussed in section 3.1.1. In practical terms, the differences between the definitions of what a head is are as important as the small formal grammar differences discussed in 3.1.

Engel (1994, 28), although firmly rooted in the German valency tradition, takes the extreme view that ultimately all head definitions are arbitrary.

Other linguists have disagreed about the definition of heads. The importance of the issue is, for instance, mirrored by the fact that a third of Jung (1995), a general book on DG, is devoted to the question of head-definition.

There are different uses and definitions of the notion of head in different types of grammars. They may be semantic, as in the case of Categorial Grammar, where the functor is the head, and the argument is the dependent. In X-Bar theory, on the other hand, heads are defined by syntactic means. On a morphological basis, one may also come to different conclusions about what is the head. For instance, in a simple Subject+Verb Construction, the subject may be seen as selecting person and number of the Verb.

Zwicky (1985, 4-14) suggests the following arguments for determining the head of a combination of two constituents:

a. The semantic argument: in a combination X+Y, crudely put, X is the "semantic head" if X+Z describes a kind of the thing being described by X.

b. The subcategorisand: the constituent which is subcategorized with respect to its sisters. For example, in a PP, the preposition is subcategorised by the verb, unlike its sister NP. The preposition is therefore a head candidate.

c. The morphosyntactic locus: the (actual) inflectional locus within a construction is a candidate for the head of the construct. For example, for a VP, the auxiliary verb carries the inflection and is a head candidate.

d. The governor: the constituent which determines the morphosyntactic form of some sister. For example, in a VP, the verb is head candidate, because it determines the case of an object.

e. The determinant of concord: the constituent with which some or other constituent must agree. For example, in a sentence, the subject N is head candidate because the main verb must agree with it.

f. The distributional equivalent: the constituent that belongs to a category with

3.2. Characteristics of functional DG

	V+NP	P+NP	NP+VP	DET+N	AUX+VP	COMP+S
(a) Semantic Argument	NP	NP	NP	N	VP	S
(b) Subcategorisand	V	.	.	DET	.	COMP
(c) Morphosyntactic locus	V	P	VP	N	AUX	S
(d) Governor	V	P	VP	.	AUX	.
(e) Determinant of Concord	NP	.	NP	N	.	.
(f) Distributional Equivalent	V	.	.	N	VP	S
(g) Obligatory Constituent	V	P	VP	N	VP	S

Table 3.1: Zwicky's definition of heads

	V+NP	P+NP	NP+VP	DET+N	AUX+VP	COMP+S
(a) Semantic Argument	V	P	VP	DET	AUX	COMP
(b) Subcategorisand	V	P	.	DET	.	COMP
(c) Morphosyntactic locus	V	P	VP	DET	AUX	COMP
(d) Governor	V	P	VP	.	AUX	.
(f) Distributional Equivalent	V	.	.	DET	AUX	COMP
(g) Obligatory Constituent	V	P	VP	DET	AUX	COMP

Table 3.2: Hudson's definition of heads

roughly the same distribution as the construct as a whole. For example, in a NP, adjective + noun and noun only are both NPs. This results in the noun being a head candidate.

g. The obligatory constituent: the constituent which has to be present if the mother is to be categorized as it is. For example, in an ADJP, an adjective is obligatory and therefore head candidate, while adverbs are not.

h. The rulers in dependency grammar: the ruler is the word on which other words depend. Since the head discussion here should support a head definition for dependency, using this argument here would lead to circularity. We will ignore it.

Zwicky discusses these arguments by use of the following English constructions: DET + N, as in *those penguins*; V + NP, as in *control those penguins*; AUX + VP, as in *must control those penguins*; P + NP, as in *toward those penguins*; NP + VP, as in *we control those penguins*; COMP+S, as in *that we control those penguins*. Zwicky's findings are summarized in table 3.1. Undeciable cases are marked with a dot. Hudson (1987) re-analysed Zwicky (1985), using the same arguments except for (e.) determinand of concord, and came up with the completely different results presented in table 3.2. Hudson (1987)'s head definition has influenced and foreshadowed the headedness definition in GB, including the DP hypothesis, which views NPs as a complement of DPs (see e.g. Cook and Newson (1996)) and which facilitates the semantic analysis of quantifier scopes.

Functional Heads or Markers

We would like to show now that alternative head definitions are also possible, based on the lexical rather than the functional heads.

It can be observed that functional words in X-bar syntax are usually required to project to a maximal projection. The stacking of functional projections is a noticeable feature of GB analyses. Determiners were an exception to this in the pre-DP-hypothesis view. Now they are likewise assigned a maximal projection. While functional projections are uncontested, especially HPSG raised the question whether it would not be possible to use a representation in which content words are heads. The four most contested constructions in tables 3.1 and 3.2 involve a functional category (P+NP, DET+N AUX+VP and COMP+S). Before discussing each construction in detail, we would like to point out that different levels of analysis have different heads.

Research on the definition of heads reveals that morphological, surface syntactic, deep syntactic and semantic levels of analysis often come to different conclusions. On the morphological level, Mel'čuk (1988, 109) discusses that morphological dependencies themselves pose opposing head definitions: In Russian *dve volny* (= two waves), the numeral *dve* is morphologically dependent on the noun *volny* according to gender (feminine), but *volny* is dependent on *dve* according to number (sg.) and case (genitive). On the surface syntactic level, GB, TAG, versions of LFG, and other formal syntactic theories including the dependency-based Word Grammar (Hudson, 1984; Hudson, 1990), use functional projections. On the semantic level, there is no doubt that quantifiers dominate NPs in a first-order predicate logic representation and that modal verbs dominate VPs in a modal logic representation. But for the deep-syntactic level, HPSG proposes that functional words are non-heads and fall outside the dependency types available in X-bar, (specifier, argument, adjunct), as we discuss in the following paragraph. The purpose of the deep-syntactic level is to offer direct access to the grammatical relations (also called functions) between content words, largely normalised for alternations, quantification and surface phenomena. From a practical viewpoint, a representation that assumes content words to be heads facilitates the implementation of lexicalisation since it gives local access to content word heads. For tasks such as information retrieval and text mining such representations are particularly useful as they represent the semantic structure more directly (see e.g. de Marneffe, MacCartney, and

Manning (2006),Rinaldi et al. (2007)).

The majority of formal grammars distinguish between several levels of analysis by using a multi-stratal approach. GB maps between surface syntax and deep syntax by means of transformations, LFG relies on functional annotations to map from the surface-oriented c-structure to the deep-syntactic functional f-structure, HPSG uses an advanced system of co-indexation, although often leaving the level unspecified, thus profiting from constraint-based approaches such as the commutative unification operation. In contrast, many versions of DG are monostratal. For a multistratal version of DG, see (Debusmann et al., 2004). This does not entail that monostratal DGs fail to recognise that there are several levels of analysis, but it contains the (usually implicit) claim that it is possible to underspecify the levels that remain unexpressed without affecting the linguistic expressiveness or parsing performance. Chapter 6 of this thesis is largely devoted to showing that a functional level of representation can deliver accurate deep-syntactic descriptions even if we underspecify the surface syntactic level.

Constructions with Functional Heads

We now discuss the four contested constructions involving a functional head (P+NP, DET+N, AUX+VP, COMP+S) in more detail.

Prepositions Prepositions can have semantic content, directly expressing local, temporal, or benefactive relations. But in the following constructions, the preposition has no semantic character. It is grammatical in nature and often and language-specific. It is often associated to a case marker.

(30) Peter depends *on* Susan.

(31) Peter is afraid *of* spiders.

In a functionally oriented representation, alternations such as the dative shift should receive identical or closely related analyses.

(32) Mary gives the book to John.

(33) Mary gives John the book.

This is only possible if NPs and PPs are treated on a par. Dependency theory, partly under the influence of languages like Finnish, French, German, or English, where case assignment and prepositions largely overlap, has always been sceptical of the status of prepositions. (Tarvainen, 1981, 10) states that prepositions have no syntactic valency, they have at best a grammatical valency that corresponds to case endings.

LFG assigns head character to both the noun and the prepositions, thus leaving the head definition underspecified. In practice, we follow the same approach: although the noun appears as the head of the PP in the dependency representation, PP-attachment is lexicalized both on the preposition and the noun (if available). Since prepositions are less sparse and more discriminant, the preposition plays a larger role in the attachment task. LFG has also suggested to distinguish between semantic and non-semantic prepositions, where semantic prepositions are governors and non-semantic prepositions are dependents of their noun. A practical problem of such a forced distinction is its high gradience leading to low inter-annotator agreement.

Complementizers In GB, LFG and TAG, complementizers are functional heads with a sentential complement. One potential practical problem with such an analysis is that empty heads need to be assumed in the case of zero-complementizers. When parsing, it is difficult to decide where to insert empty categories.

(34) Sandy thinks (that) Kim is foolish.

(Pollard and Sag, 1994) use examples like the following to argue that complementizers are non-heads:

(35) I demand that he leave/*leaves immediately.

If *demand* determines the form of the verb in the complement clause then this may suggest that the verb is the head of the complement, else we need a non-local dependency or a distinction between different types of complement clauses. Complementizers are a prime example for the introduction of *markers* in HPSG. Pollard and Sag (1994, 44-45) define markers as functional or grammatical words whose semantic content is logical.

We have decided to use markers, as a class of dependents with dedicated relation labels, in our DG. The reasons for this decisions are rather practical than theoretical in nature.

Determiners In GB, TAG and versions of LFG, determiners are functional heads with a noun complement. Analogously to complementizers, it is difficult to decide where to insert empty categories when parsing.

(36) Sandy saw (the) pictures of Kim.

In our DG approach, we only parse between heads of chunks – the distinction between DP or NP analysis remains underspecified. The DP hypothesis is not used. Although the noun chunk typically includes the determiner and is thus equivalent to a DP, the notion of *head extraction* always refers to the head noun.

Auxiliary Verbs Chunkers delivering verb groups underspecifiy the distinction between auxiliary and main verb. HPSG does not treat auxiliaries as markers, but uses so-called argument composition, which uses co-indexation to the effect that auxiliaries and the main verb share all complements.

For practical reasons of consistency, we also treat auxiliaries as dependents of the main verb. This leads to representations in which all types of dependency (specifier, arguments, adjuncts), plus all markers, are available locally to the main verb. In other words, locality naturally extends to the clause level. We discuss in chapter 6 that this leads to a DG which has the same locality as TAG extended locality.

3.2.2 Projectivity

Levy (2005) proves that non-projectivity and crossing constituency are identical. We will use the term non-projectivity.

The question of whether non-projectivity is needed for parsing has been debated for a long time. Approaches assuming the equivalence of CFG and DG are projective. For example, early robust DG parsers, Eisner (1996) and Collins (1996) are fully projective. Some of the first researchers to point out that Tesnière's DG conception is non-projective included the creators of the first broad-coverage DG parser that is explicitly non-projective (Tapanainen and Järvinen, 1997). Tapanainen and Järvinen (1997, 3) note that for a long time linguists took Gaifman (1965)'s proof for granted.

Truly non-projective DG parsers are still very rare, due to the large processing overhead. Theoretically, fully non-projective DG parsing is NP-complete, and also in practice, the overhead is very substantial (Nivre, 2006a). Accordingly, research, both in DG and other robust parsing approaches, rather focuses on the question of how to maximally constrain non-projectivity, how much non-projectivity is needed, and up to which point post-processing and CFG and finite-state approximations can replace non-projectivity. Nivre (2006a) sums this up concisely:

> *Most of this work has so far focused either on post-processing to recover non-local dependencies from context-free parse trees (Johnson, 2002; Jijkoun and De Rijke, 2004; Levy and Manning, 2004; Campbell, 2004), or on incorporating nonlocal dependency information in nonterminal categories in constituency representations (Dienes and Dubey, 2003; Hockenmaier, 2003; Cahill et al., 2004) or in the categories used to label arcs in dependency representations (Nivre and Nilsson, 2005). By contrast, there is very little work on parsing methods that allow discontinuous constructions to be represented directly in the syntactic structure, whether by discontinuous constituent structures or by non-projective dependency structures. Notable exceptions are Plaehn (2000), where discontinuous phrase structure grammar parsing is explored, and McDonald et al. (2005b), where nonprojective dependency structures are derived using spanning tree algorithms from graph theory.*

(Nivre, 2006a, 73)

As there is very little research on non-projective extensions in DG frameworks (Nivre, 2006a, 74), it is highly advisable to adopt research from other grammar formalisms: In chapter 6 we therefore investigate in detail how Tree-Adjoining Grammar (TAG) and Lexical-Functional Grammar (LFG) deal with non-projective phenomena in natural language. We also show how the choice of grammar representation largely influences the amount of non-projectivity needed. Research showing to which surprising amount the grammar representation influences the amount of non-projectivity is only just starting. While it was classically assumed, for example, that German is a language exhibiting a particularly high amount of non-projectivity, Kübler (2006) shows that this assumption largely rests on the representation of grammar: while trees in NEGRA format (Brants et al., 1997) have a high amount of non-projectivity, trees in the TüBa format (Telljohann, Hinrichs, and Kübler, 2004) have only very little, although they do not contain less information. We show in chapter 6 that our DG representation keeps non-projectivity to a minimum. Only nested WH-questions are truly non-projective.

3.2.3 Functionalism

Tapanainen and Järvinen (1997) call their DG approach Functional Dependency Grammar. Functionalism is an important notion for a deep-syntactic DG, for several reasons, as we outline in the following. The term functionalism has a number

3.2. Characteristics of functional DG

of meanings. Each of the following points represents a possible meaning of functional.

Grammatical Function

Our labelled DG is perhaps most obviously functional in the sense that labels express grammatical functions such as subject or object as far as possible. This is also a main reading of *functional* in Lexical-Functional Grammar. In order to obtain full parses, some configurational, surface-syntactic labels are also needed, as mentioned in 3.1.1. The set of functional and configurational labels are strictly disjoint.

Predicate-Argument Relations

Due to its valency tradition, DG representations are easily mappable to predicate-argument relations. DG representations are functions in the mathematical sense, a grammatical function or relation from a head to a dependent[6], a grammatical function or relation from a dependent to a head[7]. This aspect of functionalism is largely owed to the choice of lexical heads and chunks as an approximation to nuclei or bonetsus (see 3.1.3).

Abstracting away from surface configurations

The use of an ID/LP grammar allows us to abstract away from form, i.e. surface word order, to function. The use of our headedness definition allows us to map alternations and verb configurations. Importantly, the fact that non-projectivity could be reduced to a minimum allows us to use a monostratal approach that can leave other representation levels underspecified.

A Functional Conception of Word Classes

Tesnière's DG uses a functional conception of word classes. We could only partly model this functional aspect. Subordinate clauses are seen as clause-level objects,

---

[6] In most cases they are a function. If a long-distance chain has more than one element, they are a relation. In the case of adjuncts, there may equally be several dependents on the same head with the same function (adjunct), they are thus a relation

[7] In most cases they are a function. There is a post-processing module that expands conjunctions and appositions, which can lead to a dependent having several heads. Then they are a relation

hence their label *sentobj*. Gerunds are ambivalent between verbal and nominal status. In the sentence

(37) John likes eating bananas.

eat takes an object like a verb, but functions as nominal object to *like*. We allow gerunds to attach as objects. Tesnière refers to change of word class as *translation* and uses it extensively. In our DG, we use it more restrictively, e.g. in order to allow adjectives (e.g. *the poor*) or numbers to function as nominal objects in the absence of a noun, thus obviating the need for empty categories. Our choice of the noun as the head of a PP also follows this philosophy: the functions of PPs and cases in alternations (Levin, 1993) such as the dative shift or the alternation mapping the saxon genitive to an of-PP are representationally more similar.

There are a number of closed class words which (before becoming grammaticalised) can function as words of different word classes. Examples that are modelled in our grammar comprise the gerunds *including* or *using* which can function as prepositions.

3.3 The Relationship of DG to HPSG and LFG

The formal grammar theories Head-Driven Phrase Structure Grammar (HPSG) and Lexical-Functional Grammar (LFG) are closely related to DG. HPSG (Pollard and Sag, 1994) is largely based on DG, the f-structure layer of LFG (Bresnan, 2001) expresses labelled dependency information.

3.3.1 HPSG

HPSG shares crucial characteristics with DG. The DG endocentricity constraint is a fundamental HPSG grammar principle, and HPSG rule schemata are largely based on X-bar theory, which is equivalent to DG. A closer investigation reveals additional similarities such as HPSG's valency-based lexicalist character, the use of graph theory by means of structure-sharing, and the monostratal orientation.

HPSG insists on using typed feature structures. While versions of DG using such structures are conceivable, no such restrictions on implementational issues are made. There is one major linguistic difference, however: HPSG typically aims to integrate semantics to a higher degree than DG.

Any well-formed constituent in HPSG needs to conform to the 3 main components of HPSG: grammar principles, grammar rules, and lexical entries.

3.3. The Relationship of DG to HPSG and LFG

Grammar Principles The major HPSG grammar principles are the head feature principle and the subcategorisation principle. The head feature principle, a grammar universal, is formulated as follows.

$$[\text{DTRS}\ _{headed\ structure}[]] \Rightarrow \begin{bmatrix} \text{SYNSEM} \mid \text{LOC} \mid \text{CAT} \mid \text{HEAD}\ \boxed{1} \\ \text{DTRS} \mid \text{HEAD-DTR} \mid \text{SYNSEM} \mid \text{LOC} \mid \text{CAT} \mid \text{HEAD}\ \boxed{1} \end{bmatrix}$$

In words, each feature structure containing the feature *daughters (DTRS)* with a feature structure of type *headed structure* needs to abide to the head feature principle, which expresses that, by means of structure sharing, the HEAD feature of the mother node and the HEAD feature of the head daughter are identical, just as the DG endocentricity constraint enforces.

The subcategorisation or valency principle makes sure that valencies are saturated. The SUBCAT feature contains a list of all required, but still missing valencies of a constituent. A feature structure whose SUBCAT list is empty has all valencies filled. The subject is also part of the SUBCAT list, and all complements. The elements are ordered according to the obliqueness hierarchy. The least oblique element, i.e. the subject, comes first. The subcategorisation principle ensures that the SUBCAT list is emptied, i.e. its requirements are met.

$$[\text{DTRS}\ _{headed\ structure}[]] \Rightarrow \begin{bmatrix} \text{SYNSEM} \mid \text{LOC} \mid \text{CAT} \mid \text{SUBCAT}\ \boxed{2} \\ \text{DTRS}\ \begin{bmatrix} \text{HEAD-DTR} \mid \text{SYNSEM} \mid \text{LOC} \mid \text{CAT} \mid \text{SUBCAT append}(\boxed{1},\boxed{2}) \\ \text{COMP-DTRS}\ \boxed{1} \end{bmatrix} \end{bmatrix}$$

In words, the subcategorisation requirements of a phrase are identical to those of the head daughter, minus those satisfied by the complements (COMP-DTRS) attached at the same level. The subcategorisation principle is also a grammar universal. In later versions (Pollard and Sag, 1994, chapter 9), specifiers get their own subcat list, but the general principle remains unaltered. For the discussion of grammar rules, we use the version where specifiers have their own SUBCAT list – the specifier subcat list is called SPR, and the complement subcat list is called COMPS – but any other method identifying specifier dependencies would have the same effect.

In DG, the endocentricity constraint has the side effect that the filling of valencies is not automatically enforced. On the one hand, this has the robustness advantage that unfilled valencies never cause a parse to fail. On the other hand, a mechanism preferring satured valencies is needed. The preference for longer partial structures (if possible structures spanning the whole input string) ensures just that. Any element of a sentence will get attached somewhere whenever possible, as a consequence valencies will be filled unless there is no way according to the grammar to fill them. Internally we also use probability scores (Probability * 2) instead of probabilities, which has the effect that an element with a likely attachment is more likely than the element without the attachment. We have not investigated up to which point this may render our preference for longer partial structures redundant, or if it may lead to better results, leading to better partial structure breaks when no span covering the entire input string is found.

Grammar Rules In X-bar theory, PSG grammar rules are only rule schemata, constrained by bar levels and endocentricity. The same applies to HPSG grammar rules, where most rule schemata are strictly derived from X-bar theory. HPSG rule schemata comprise the head-specifier rule, the head-complement rule, the head-adjunct rule, markers, and argument composition.

head-specifier rule X-bar structures at the $\bar{X}$ level are distinguished by the fact that all their valencies except for SPR valencies are satisfied. The head-specifier rule is fomulated as follows, where the subcat lists are in diamond brackets, e.g <> is an empty subcat list, and [] is a list containing one element.

$$[\text{SPR}<>] \longrightarrow \begin{array}{ll} [\text{SPR}<[]>, \text{COMPS}<>], & [] \\ \text{HEAD} & \text{SPR} \end{array}$$

In words, a sign with the feature specification SPR<>, i.e. with fulfilled SPR subcat requirements, can contain a head daughter with the feature specifications COMPS<> and a specifier daughter. In cooperation with the head feature principle and the subcategorisation principle, this rule schema makes sure that head daughter and mother are identical, and that the required SPR valency is identical to the sister of the head daughter.

head-complement rule X-bar structures at the X^0 level are distinguished by the fact that none of their valencies are satisfied. The head-complement rule is fomulated as follows, where L is a list.

$$[\text{COMPS}<>] \longrightarrow \begin{array}{ll} [\text{COMPS L}], & []* \\ \text{HEAD} & \text{COMPS} \end{array}$$

In words, a sign with the feature specification COMPS<>, i.e. with fulfilled COMPS subcat requirements, can contain a head daughter with any list in the COMPS feature, and an arbitrary number of complements. In cooperation with the head feature principle and the subcategorisation principle, this rule schema makes sure that head daughter and mother are identical, and that each of the required COMPS valencies is identical to a sister of the head daughter.

head-adjunct rule The head-adjunct rule is formulated as follows.

$$\boxed{1}\,[\text{COMPS L}] \longrightarrow \begin{array}{cc} [\text{COMPS L}], & [\text{MOD}\,\boxed{1}\,] \\ \text{HEAD} & \text{ADJUNCT} \end{array}$$

We have discussed in section 3.1.4 that as long as the relation label set can be mapped to specifiers, arguments and adjuncts, DG is identical to X-bar theory and hence these rule schemata. There are two additional rule schemat in HPSG: markers and argument composition.

markers Markers are usually treated a dependents in DG. Again, if specific relation labels can be mapped to markers, DG is equivalent to HPSG.

argument composition Argument composition extends locality. In practice, secondary labels extending trees to graphs can be used to share dependents. We use secondary labels to treat long-distance dependencies. We discuss locality, extending locality and long-distance dependencies in detail in chapter 6.

3.3.2 LFG

We discuss the relation of LFG to DG in detail in (Schneider, 2005), a summary of our findings is given in section 6.5.2.

3.4 Conclusions

We have given an introduction to DG. We have presented four conceptions of DG. We have discussed in which way the version of labelled DG that we use can be said to be functional. We have discussed that our functional concept of DG leads to representations in which all types of dependency (specifier, arguments, adjuncts), plus all markers, are available locally to the main verb. Locality naturally extends to the clause level. This is an important preparatory step for our discussion of long-distance dependencies in chapter 6 There we show that our conception of functional DG leads to a DG which has the same locality as TAG extended locality.

Chapter 4

State of the Art

4.1 Introduction

This chapter reviews a number of current successful approaches in dependency parsing and suggests to combine some of their advantages as it has been done in Pro3Gres, a low-complexity but deep-syntactic parser expressing grammatical roles. We will mainly consider current parsing approaches, which traditionally used to fall into two groups: formal grammar parsers and statistical parsers. Recent progress at combining them will be reviewed. A non-parsing approach aiming at the expression of grammatical roles will also be discussed.

Recently, some deep linguistic grammars have achieved the coverage and robustness needed to parse large corpora, as will be discussed in section 4.6. (Riezler et al., 2002) show how a hand-crafted LFG grammar scales to the Penn Treebank with Maximum Entropy probability models. Hockenmaier and Steedman (2002) acquire a wide-coverage CCG grammar from the Penn Treebank automatically, Burke et al. (2004) an LFG grammar. We suggest to combine a tag-sequence based, hand-crafted functional dependency grammar (Hajič, 1998; Tapanainen and Järvinen, 1997) with Maximum Likelihood Estimation (MLE) lexicalized probabilities extracted from the Treebank. Our approach is similar to Collins and Brooks (1995), but for a large subset of dependency relations instead of for PP-attachment only, including the majority of long-distance dependencies.

Let us first consider a number of dependency-based approaches that focus on just one dependency relation: the attachment of PPs. Then we will extend to approaches where full parsing is done by similar means. The PP-attachment relation is especially interesting because it is highly ambiguous (Church and Patil, 1982), and because it has been shown to profit considerably from lexicalized approaches (Collins and Brooks, 1995).

4.2 PP attachment disambiguation

We will consider two classical approaches that have been very influential: the unsupervised Hindle and Rooth (1993) approach and the supervised Collins and Brooks (1995) approach.

4.2.1 The question

For both of the sentences *John eats steaks with a knife* and *John eats steaks with fries*, syntactically two analyses are permissible. On semantic grounds, a human reader has no difficulties to disambiguate between attaching the PP to the verb or to the noun, but the amount of world knowledge required to be able to do so is considerable.

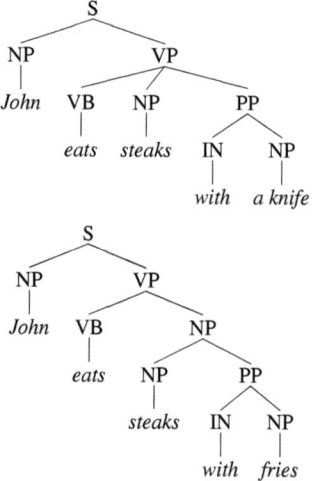

4.2. PP attachment disambiguation

Instead of the cumbersome attempt to model world knowledge, statistical approaches disambiguate by imitation of empirical evidence from correctly parsed training text material. The disambiguation is not always as clear-cut as in the above example. Inter-annotator agreement for PP-attachment is thus relatively low. Both (Hindle and Rooth, 1993) and (Collins and Brooks, 1995) considered exclusively binary ambiguous cases, where a verb is followed by an NP and a PP, and the PP-attachment is therefore ambiguous between verbal and nominal attachment. (Hindle and Rooth, 1993) report 85-88 % human performance on their experiments, in which both the human and the machine were only given the head words (the verb and the noun) of the possible attachment site and the preposition of the PP. (Ratnaparkhi, Reynar, and Roukos, 1994) report 88.2 % average human performance on experiments in which both the human and the machine were given the head words (the verb and the noun) of the possible attachment site, the preposition of the PP and the head of the noun inside the PP (which is sometimes called description noun). More context leads to better disambiguation, the verb or noun and the preposition (and the description noun) may not be enough context. (Ratnaparkhi, Reynar, and Roukos, 1994) report 93.2 % average human performance if the whole sentence is given.

There is a semantic reason why human performance and inter-annotator agreement is quite low, which is discussed in Hindle and Rooth (1993). There are semantically undecidable cases, in which the semantic difference between verb- or noun-attachment is very small.

Undecidable cases Undecidable cases can be divided into the following three groups.

Idioms: the nouns contained in many idioms cannot be conceived of as constituting a possible attachment site:

(38) I visited the zoo from time to time.

Locative ambiguity: in a locative PP, the place of the action and the real-world object are often identical – the PP-attachment ambiguity is semantically void.

(39) He searched all the bars in Paris.

Benefactive ambiguity: in a benefactive PP, an action intended for a person and the resulting real-world object is often intended for the same person.

(40) Jane wrote the report for the supervisor.

4.2.2 Hindle and Rooth

(Hindle and Rooth, 1993) is an unsupervised approach to PP-attachment disambiguation. They extracted 200'000 (V,N1,PP) triples from a tagged and partially parsed newswire corpus First, unambiguous cases are collected into what is called the sure-attachment base, because it only contains cases that are unambiguous:

1. No PP: the PP is assigned a NULL value

2. Sure verb attach 1: the PP is attached to the verb if the NP head is a pronoun. In

   (41) Peter gave it to the waitress.

   the PP certainly attaches to the verb. In English, only the pronoun *one* can be modified by a PP.

3. Sure verb attach 2: the PP is attached to the verb if the verb is in the passive.

   (42) It was given yesterday to the waitress.

   In the rare cases where nouns intervene between a passive verb and a PP, they are usually temporal adjuncts that cannot be modified by a PP.

4. Sure noun attach: if no verb that could serve as attachment site is present, the PP attaches to the noun. This is particularly the case in sentence-initial NPs followed by a PP.

Based on these unambiguous cases, an information-theoretic lexical preference score related to maximum likelihood estimation (MLE) is calculated.

The MLE for seeing a preposition given a verb is

$$P(prep|v) \cong \frac{\#(v \wedge prep)}{\#v} \tag{4.1}$$

This MLE is weighted by the general preference of the preposition for verb- (or noun-) attachment in order to fight sparse data

$$P(prep|\sum v) \cong \frac{\#\sum v \wedge prep}{\#\sum v} \tag{4.2}$$

The weighted probability estimation for seeing a preposition given a verb is then

4.2. PP attachment disambiguation

$$P(prep|v) \cong \frac{\#(v \wedge prep) + P(prep|\sum v)}{\#v+1} = \frac{\#(v \wedge prep) + \frac{\#\sum v \wedge prep}{\#\sum v}}{\#v+1} \quad (4.3)$$

The formula used is expressed as a logarithm, indicating attachment preference for verb in the numerator and for noun in the denominator. NULL (no PP after the noun) is considered to be an (indirect) verb-attachment preference indicator in an ambiguous situation.

$$LA = log_2 \frac{\frac{\#v \wedge prep + \frac{\#\sum v \wedge prep}{\#\sum v}}{\#v+1} \cdot \frac{\#n \wedge NULL + \frac{\#\sum n \wedge NULL}{\#\sum n}}{\#n+1}}{\frac{\#n \wedge prep + \frac{\#\sum n \wedge prep}{\#\sum n}}{\#n+1}} \quad (4.4)$$

Iteration: For all ambiguous cases the lexical association score (LA) is calculated. If it lies above a certain threshold, the attachment is considered to be reliable and thus asserted to the sure-attachment base. The LA is recalculated and the next iteration starts. The iteration loop exits once no new reliable attachments can be made. For the remaining cases, the default of noun-attachment is used.

4.2.3 Collins and Brooks

(Collins and Brooks, 1995) is a supervised approach to PP-attachment disambiguation. They also include the noun inside the PP (so-called description noun) in the probability model, whenever non-zero counts exist. A supervised approach, using a parsed corpus, has the advantage that noise is virtually absent and that it has full recall, hence a probabilistic model is possible. The potentially ambiguous (V,N1,PP) triples are extracted from the Penn Treebank. The PP is represented as preposition and PP-internal noun (N2). The MLE estimation for verb attachment for the resulting (V,N1,P,N2) quadruple is as follows.

$$P(\text{verb-attach}|V, N1, P, N2) \cong \frac{\#\text{verb-attach}, V, N1, P, N2}{\#V, N1, P, N2} \quad (4.5)$$

The disadvantage of using a parsed corpus is that the sparse data problem becomes even more serious. The inclusion of the PP-internal noun further aggravates sparseness. Collins and Brooks (1995) proposes a back-off method as an alternative to smoothing. We discuss backing-off and the variations that we use in detail in subsection 4.3.1 and in chapter 7.

4.3 Treebank-Based Statistical Parsers

Now we extend the discussion to all relations needed to do full parsing. The Penn Treebank, which has been used by Collins and Brooks (1995), contains full syntactic annotations, which can allow parsers to disambiguate all relations. A variety of Treebank-based statistical parsers exist, for example Collins (1999),Charniak (2000), and Henderson (2003). We will limit our discussion to one of them, the Collins parser.

4.3.1 Collins 1996

Michael Collins' PhD (Collins, 1999) is seen as a milestone in the history of lexicalized parsing approaches. Three probabilistic parsing models are introduced. Each of these three models is described here, since many of the elements of the parser presented in this thesis can be seen as versions and extensions of these models, especially of Model 1. Model 1 is a purely dependency-based model (Collins, 1996; Collins, 1997; Collins, 1999; Collins, 2003).

Collins's parsing models can be seen as an extension of his PP-attachment work, described in the previous section. Since lexicalization greatly improves PP-attachment results, it is natural to use similar approaches for all syntactic relations. Instead of taking local decisions, the probabilities of the local ambiguities are multiplied to calculate a global probability. Klein and Manning (2003) and Bikel (2004) have shown that also very weakly lexicalised approaches can perform almost as well as strongly lexicalised approaches. Their results do not, however, in any way discredit the use of a strongly lexicalised approach, such as ours, as *one* possible, successful and linguistically intuitive approach among others – a point that also Klein and Manning (2003) explicitly make.

Mapping Treebank trees to Dependencies As the Treebank is in constituency format, its structures need to be mapped to dependencies for a dependency-based model. The main components of the model are as follows.

1. Only the heads of base NPs (base NP=unnested NPs) are used (Abney, 1991;

4.3. Treebank-Based Statistical Parsers

Abney, 1995). For *This man generally eats fresh bananas with a fork* the reduced tree becomes:

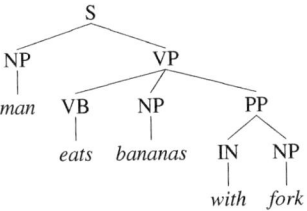

2. For each CFG rewrite rule, the head is established. For example, given the tree above, the heads are the syntactic categories indicated in boldface.

   S ⟶ NP **VP**
   VP ⟶ **VB** NP PP
   PP ⟶ **IN** NP

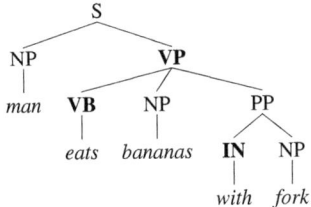

3. The dependencies are derived directly from the rewrite rules. Binary rules lead to one dependency, ternary rules to two, etc. The dependency label t is a combination of the syntactic categories of the mother and daughter node, as follows:

   Dependency = $arrow\_from$ each dep. to its head with type t:
   $t = \langle Dependent, MotherNode, Head \rangle$ if head is to the right OR
   $t = \langle Head, MotherNode, Dependent \rangle$ if head is to the left.

   For instance,

   $\langle NP, S, VP \rangle$
   man ⟶ eats $arrow\_from(loc_{man}) = (loc_{eats}, \langle NP, S, VP \rangle)$

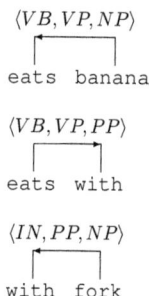

The advantage Breaking up non-binary CFG rules into individual dependencies means that data becomes considerably less sparse, and that more valuable lexical information than in a PCFG can be accessed. In early probabilistic parser implementation, all CFG rules permitted in the Penn Treebank were extracted and learnt. From his 300,000 words training part of the Treebank Charniak (1996) thus obtains more than 10,000 CFG rules, of which only about 3,000 occur more than once, leading to very serious complexity and sparseness problems. A useful method to alleviate this problem is to break down the often very flat Treebank CFG rules. (Collins, 1996) therefore suggested to use the individual dependencies between a head (LHS) and its daughters (the RHS elements), assuming independence among the individual RHS elements.

If, for example, the first three of the following rewrite rules are seen for the verb *give* during training, but the fourth one is needed at parse time, a PCFG assigns a zero-probability, or at best a smoothed, but likely too low, non-zero probability. But in Collins' approach, the data learnt from the third rule can be directly used.

(43) VP ⟶ V NP ("gives the money")
VP ⟶ V NP NP ("gives them all his money")
VP ⟶ V NP PP ("gives his money to the poor")
VP ⟶ V PP ("gives to the poor")

To give another example, flat NP rewrite rules like the one in 44 are commonplace in the Penn Treebank.

(44) NP ⟶ DT $ CD NN ("the $ 200 hat")

They lead to a big sparse data problem. In this example, the situation is aggravated by the Penn Treebank design preference for flat rules.

4.3. Treebank-Based Statistical Parsers

The Statistical Model Collins uses two models: The base NP model B, which calculates chunking probabilities, and the dependency model D, which calculates parsing probabilities. The probability of a tree is the product of both.

$$P(Tree|Sent) = P(B|Sent) * P(D|Sent) \tag{4.6}$$

The dependency model probability is

$$P(D|Sent, B) = \prod_{j=1}^{m} P(arrow\_from(j)|Sent, B) \tag{4.7}$$

Only the Dependency Model is discussed in detail here, since the Base NP Model uses standard tagging and chunking techniques.

The MLE probabilities for a relation of type t from training corpus are calculated as follows:

$$P(t|\langle depword, deptag\rangle \wedge \langle headword, headtag\rangle) =$$

$$\frac{\#(t \wedge \langle depword, deptag\rangle \wedge \langle headword, headtag\rangle)}{\#(\langle depword, deptag\rangle \wedge \langle headword, headtag\rangle)} \tag{4.8}$$

At parsetime, the expected probability for a current word w_j to have a dependency of type R_j to some head h_j, i.e. $arrow\_from(w_j) = (h_j, R_j)$, is the MLE probability $P(R_j|\langle w_j, wtag_j\rangle \wedge \langle h_j, htag_j\rangle)$

The best dependency-model parse maximises over the product of all the dependencies thus possible in the current sentence.

$$argmax_D P(D|Sent) = \prod_{j=1}^{m} P(R_j|\langle w_j, wtag_j\rangle \wedge \langle h_j, htag_j\rangle) \tag{4.9}$$

Since the denominator is constant – the words are a given and the tags are provided by the Base NP Model – the denominator can be neglected for maximising.

Extensions to the Core Model The model as presented has a few shortcomings, some of which are immediately addressed and corrected in (Collins, 1996), some in Collins (1997; Collins (1999; Collins (2003). We list and discuss them below.

- The only dependency boundary is the sentence

  In the model presented so far, longer and shorter distance dependencies have equal weights, any relation can span the whole sentence. Collins introduces distance measure heuristics based on the following four features: direction, punctuation, intervening verbs, and adjacency.

  At first sight, these heuristics may seem non-linguistic. But conditioning relation probabilities on distance considerably improves performance (see chapter 7). In fact such heuristics are well founded. They are reasonable approximations of structure: increasing distance, intervening punctuation and verbs increase the chance that a clause boundary occurs between the two words. On the other hand, they approximate psycholinguistic recency and mental load effects, which partly depend on complexity that cannot be expressed in terms of structure.

  We use a slightly different approach for each of these features. Direction is constrained by the manually written grammar (see chapter 5). The majority of English dependencies are only to one direction, or they are strongly constrained. For punctuation, we use a parsing approach that regards commas as high-level boundaries (see chapter 5). Instead of intervening verbs or adjacency, we measure real distance in chunks. 74.2% of all WSJ dependencies between chunks are adjacent, but these dependencies are also relatively easy to retrieve.

- Sparse data problems

  During parsing, very often no $\langle w_j, wtag_j \rangle \wedge \langle h_j, htag_j \rangle$ pairs exist. Collins thus backs off to tags only, according to the following back-off hierarchy (where $>$ is the precedence operator)

  $\#(\langle w_j, wtag_j \rangle \wedge \langle h_j, htag_j \rangle)$
  $> \#(\langle w_j, wtag_j \rangle \wedge \langle htag_j \rangle) + \#(\langle wtag_j \rangle \wedge \langle h_j, htag_j \rangle)$
  $> \#(\langle wtag_j \rangle \wedge \langle htag_j \rangle)$

  A hierarchy that directly steps from words to syntactic tags without an intervening back-off to semantic classes seems very coarse. The bulk of decisions is taken with only very partial lexicalisation. We discuss this topic in chapter 7.

- Independence assumptions: no probability relations across several dependencies

  Some syntactic relations span several subtrees. For example in PP-attachment, the quadruples ⟨ verb, prep, description noun ⟩ and ⟨ noun, prep, description noun ⟩, which are used for resolving PP-Attachment by (Collins and Brooks, 1995) span two subtrees. In this sense, Collins (1996), and equally (Collins, 1997; Collins, 1999; Collins, 2003) are a step backward, for which a correction is suggested in chapter 6. We will see that the majority of long-distance dependencies, dependencies that span several subtrees, can be expressed as a single dependency with a dedicated label.

Relation of Pro3Gres to Collins Model 1 Both (Collins, 1996) and Pro3Gres are mainly dependency-based statistical parsers parsing over heads of chunks. It can therefore be expected that (Collins, 1996) was a starting point for Pro3Gres. The (Collins, 1996) MLE and the main Pro3Gres MLE can be juxtaposed as follows:

(Collins, 1996) MLE estimation: $P(R|\langle a, atag\rangle, \langle b, btag\rangle, dist) \cong$

$$\frac{\#(R, \langle a, atag\rangle, \langle b, btag\rangle, dist)}{\#(\langle a, atag\rangle, \langle b, btag\rangle, dist)} \quad (4.10)$$

Main Pro3Gres MLE estimation: $P(R, dist|a, b) \cong P(R|a, b) \cdot P(dist|R) \cong$

$$\frac{\#(R, a, b)}{\sum_{i=1}^{Rels} \#(R_i, a, b)} \cdot \frac{\#(R, dist)}{\#R} \quad (4.11)$$

The following design differences can be observed:

- Pro3Gres does not use part-of-speech tag information.
    1. The first reason for this is because a licensing, hand-written grammar over Penn tags is employed, which has the advantage that the grammar size can be kept small. The grammar will be discussed in detail in chapter 5.
    2. The second reason for not using tag information is because Pro3Gres backs off to semantic WordNet classes for nouns and to Levin (or WordNet) classes for verbs instead of to tags, which has the advantage that the back-off is then more fine-grained.

- Pro3Gres uses distances measured in chunks, instead of a vector of features. While the type of relation R is lexicalized, i.e. conditioned on the lexical items, the distance is assumed to be dependent only on R. This is based on the observation that some relations typically have very short distances (e.g. verb-object), others can be quite long (e.g. Verb-PP attachment). This observation greatly reduces the sparse data problem. Chung and Rim (2003) have made similar observations for Korean.

4.3. Treebank-Based Statistical Parsers

- The co-occurrence count in the MLE denominator in equation 4.11 is not the sentence-context like in 4.10, but the sum of competing relations, as discussed in section 1.4. For example, the *object* and the *adjunct* relation are in competition, as they are both licensed by a verb chunk followed by a noun chunk. Pro3Gres models the probability of the decision to attach a given noun with an object relation or an adjunct relation in this example.

- Relations (R) have a Functional Dependency Grammar definition. Let us reconsider the reduced Tree representation for the sentence *This man eats fresh bananas with a fork*, which leads to the following Dependency Relations in (Collins, 1996) versus Pro3Gres; in the latter also non-local lexical information is considered as far as possible.

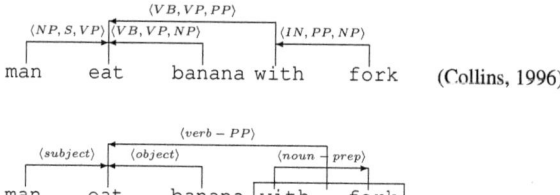

(Collins, 1996)

While Collins labels are ad-hoc heuristics, we use a principled and linguistically highly motivated conversion. While for the given example the difference may seem cosmetic, we will see in chapter 6 that it is crucial. It is one of the prerequisites for allowing us to treat the majority of long-distance dependencies locally.

Both Collins and our approach are transformations on the training trees. Johnson (1998) shows that even simple syntactic transformations for an unlexicalized PCFG model can have a significant impact on parsing performance. On ambiguous PP-attachment, a model that additionally includes parent node categories improves precision by 7% from 73 to 80%, and recall by 9% from 70 to 79%. Johnson (1998) also tested a "Chomsky-Adjunction" binarized model. It attaches several PPs in multiple steps, and is thus the model closest to our and (Collins, 1996)'s approach. Its performance is equivalent to the PCFG baseline. This should not be taken as an argument against our approach, however, for the following reason.

The assumption of independence between several PPs is too strong. For deciding if a PP attaches to a head, it is important to know whether an attaching PP intervenes. We address this shortcoming by two means. First, the grammar restricts attachment to heads that have attached other material. Second, we use a distance measure: intervening chunks between a head and a PP are mostly NPs and other PPs.

Bikel (2004) voices a frequently heard criticism on tree transformations:

> *While head-lexicalizations and other tree-transformations allow the construction of parsing models with more data-sensitivity and richer representations, crafting rules for these transformations has been largely an art, with heuristics handed down from researcher to researcher. What's more, on top of the large undertaking of designing and implementing a statistical parsing model, the use of heuristics has required a further effort, forcing the researcher to bring both linguistic intuition and, more often, engineering savvy to bear whenever moving to a new treebank.*

(Bikel, 2004, p. 91)

Although our tree transformations are specific to the treebank, we believe that its format is standardised enough to be followed by future corpora. We believe that a combination of statistical and rule-based approaches, for example a rule-based competence grammar and finite-state deep-linguistic tree transformation combined with a statistical disambiguation and pruning component is an approach worth exploring. We also believe that the linguistic insights gained are fruitful for the whole science of linguistics. We are precisely interested in descriptions of the language that are meaningful to, interpretable and editable by linguists. Finding interpretable generalisations has always been a major goal of science.

We also believe that the merit of attaining a linguistically highly motivated dependency representation outweighs the disadvantage of using a non-trivial, relatively complex and not fully complete mapping, which is detailed in the appendix.

4.3.2 Model 1, 1997

Collins states that Model 1 of (Collins, 1997) "is essentially a generative version of the model described in (Collins, 1996)" (Collins, 1997) is generative, i.e. the top-down derivation probability is modelled. Like in a PCFG, the probability of the Treebank-inherent CFG rules are calculated. In order to address sparse data issues, Collins distinguishes between the left context l and the right context r. We use Collins' original notation.

(Collins, 1997) CFG rule generation model for the rewrite rule $\mathbf{P} \rightarrow \mathbf{L}_m \ldots \mathbf{L}_1$

H R$_1$ ... R$_n$

$$P(RHS|LHS) = P_h(H|P, t(P), l(P))$$
$$\cdot \prod_{i=0}^{m} P_l(L_i, t(L_i), l(L_i)|P, H, t(H), l(H), d(i))$$
$$\cdot \prod_{i=0}^{n} P_r(R_i, t(R_i), l(R_i)|P, H, t(H), l(H), d(i))$$

where
LHS   left-hand side of rule
RHS   right-hand side of rule
P_h P of head
$P_{l:1..m}$ P of words left of head
$P_{r:1..n}$ P of words right of head

H   RHS Head Category
P   LHS Mother Category
L   Constituent Category (to the left)
R   Constituent Category (to the right)
t(H)   tag of H head word
l(H)   head word of H (l=lexical info)
d   distance measure

4.3.3 Model 2

Model 2 (Collins, 1997; Collins, 1999) extends the parser to include a complement/adjunct distinction for NPs and subordinated clauses, and it includes a subcategorisation frame model. Complements in the Treebank are identified on configurational grounds, and based on functional tags. All non-terminals that can be clearly identified as complements are added a -C suffix. For every rewrite rule, the correct subcategorisation frame needs to be selected and then processed correctly. The word probability is conditioned on the subcategorisation frame: subcategorised words are more likely to appear if they are subcategorised. Once a subcategorised word has been found, the subcategorisation frame is shortened by one element.

Let us look at an example. The *S* rewrite rule in *Last week IBM has bought Lotus S(bought)* → *NP(week), NP-C(IBM), VP(bought)*. For the subcategorisation-dependent generation of dependencies in Model 2, first the probabilities of the possible subcat frames to the right p_{rc} and to the left p_{lc} of the head are calculated, conditioned on the LHS mother category P, the RHS head category H and the lexical head h. The selected subcat frame is added as a condition to the left context l, respectively the right context r.

$$P_{head}(\text{VP}|\text{S,bought}) \cdot P_{lsubcat}(\{\text{NP-C}\}|\text{S,VP,bought}) \qquad (4.12)$$
$$\cdot P_{rsubcat}(\{\}|\text{S,VP,bought}) \cdot P_l(\text{NP-C(IBM)}|\text{S,VP,bought},\{\text{NP-C}\})$$

Once a subcategorised constituent has been found, it is removed from the subcategorisation frame, so that if *IBM* is NP-C, h=*week* has an empty subcategorisation frame.

$$P_l(\text{NP(week)}|\text{S,VP,bought}, \{\}) \tag{4.13}$$

This ensures that non-subcategorised constituents cannot be attached as complements, which is one of the two major function of a subcategorisation frame. The other major function of a subcategorisation frame is to ensure that, if possible, all the subcategorised constituents are found. In order to ensure this, the probability whether a rewrite rule should stop expanding is calculated. Importantly, the probability of a rewrite rule with a non-empty subcat frame to stop expanding is low, while the probability of a rewrite rule with an empty subcat frame to stop expanding is high.

$$P_l(\text{STOP}|\text{S,VP,bought}, \{\}) \cdot P_r(\text{STOP}|\text{S,VP,bought}, \{\}) \tag{4.14}$$

The entire probability of the phrase S(bought) → NP(week), NP-C(IBM), VP(bought) is therefore

$$P_{head}(\text{VP}|\text{S,bought}) \cdot P_{lsubcat}(\{\text{NP-C}\}|\text{S,VP,bought}) \cdot P_{rsubcat}(\{\}|\text{S,VP,bought})$$
$$\cdot P_l(\text{NP-C(IBM)}|\text{S,VP,bought},\{\text{NP-C}\}) \cdot P_l(\text{NP(week)}|\text{S,VP,bought},\{\})$$
$$\cdot P_l(\text{STOP}|\text{S,VP,bought},\{\}) \cdot P_r(\text{STOP}|\text{S,VP,bought},\{\})$$

The subcategorisation frame model of Collins Model 2 is an approximation to subcategorisation in a formal grammar. Different types of complements are not distinguished. We have decided to use a complement/adjunct distinction for NPs, and also to distinguish between different types of subcategorisation. Each type of subcategorised complement can occur maximally once per verb. Since each dependent is attached separately, subcategorisation frame selection and removing of found constituents coincide. We place strong restrictions on the co-occurrence of subcategorisation types, as we explain in chapter 5. All the examples given in support of the subcategorisation frame model in Collins (1997) are dealt with by the hand-written grammar.

4.3.4 Model 3

Model 3(Collins, 1997; Collins, 1999) extends the parser by adding a WH-movement model.

A factor for the probability of gap and filler creation and transmission is added. First, the probability of a rule's gap requirement is calculated, conditioned on the LHS mother category P, the RHS head category H and the lexical head h. A rule's gap requirement is either *head* (which means no gap), *right*, which means that a gap is required in the left or the right context, respectively. If so, the gap requirement is added to the corresponding subcat frame. Second, if a gap requirement is in the subcat frame, the probability of a (*gap*) TRACE constituent being generated is higher. Third, if a gap requirement is in the subcat frame, the probability of a (*filler*) extra constituent is also higher.

We show in chapter 6 how we treat long-distance dependencies.

4.3.5 Recovering empty nodes and functional tags with Treebank-Based Statistical Parsers

It is generally recognised that classical probabilistic parsers (Collins, 1999; Charniak, 2000; Henderson, 2003) are linguistically not convincing. They produce pure constituency data as output that does not include the grammatical function annotation nor the empty nodes annotation provided in the Penn Treebank. Many approaches thus aim to recover empty nodes or functional tags from their output in a post-processing step. Approaches to reconstruct functional tags include Blaheta (2004) and Musillo and Merlo (2005). Our approach only aims to recover a subset of the information corresponding to functional tags, we will thus not discuss them in detail. The functional tags that we aim to recover are *SBJ*, the subject dependency; *LGS*, the logical subject in passive sentences; *CLR*, PPs that are arguments; and *TMP*, NPs that act as adjuncts.

Post-processing attempts to recover empty nodes include simple approaches like Johnson (2002), and linguistically sophisticated approaches like Campbell (2004). Some approaches are based on machine-learning, for example Dienes and Dubey (2003) use a tagging approach, Jijkoun and de Rijke (2004) use memory-based learning, and Levy and Manning (2004) use loglinear classifiers. One of the best-performing approaches, Campbell (2004), is a rule-based approach using entirely hand-crafted rules. Campbell (2004) raises the question whether statistical approaches are warranted for the treatment of long-distance dependencies. He points out that empty categories follow from clear formal linguistic principles, accordingly there should be principle-based ways to recover them. Empty categories do not exist prior to the annotation, they are consciously inserted by the annotator following guidelines about linguistic configurations. The majority of empty nodes occur in configurationally clearly defined places. We describe our rule-based approach to discovering the majority of long-distance dependencies in chapter 6. It is also a largely rule-based approach, exploiting linguistic knowledge.

Recently, there have been first approaches reporting both empty nodes and functional labels integrated into the parsing stage in broad-coverage probabilistic parsing, for example Gabbard, Kulick, and Marcus (2006).

4.4 Dependency-oriented Statistical Parsers

There is a large number of dependency parsers, some of them with a probabilistic component. For space reasons we cannot discuss all of them but present an important subset. Statistical DG parsing has recently attracted a lot of interest, as is witnessed by the recent CoNLL shared tasks of multilingual dependency parsing. The first one took place at CoNLL-X (Buchholz and Marsi, 2006), the second one at and CoNLL-XI (Nivre et al., 2007). About half of the entrants of the dependency-parsing shared task of CoNLL-X used Nivre's MaltParse approach (Nivre, 2006b), which we also summarise below. Pro3Gres participated in CoNLL-XI, with average results, which are discussed in section 7.3.2.

4.4.1 Link Grammar

Link Grammar (Sleator and Temperley, 1991) is an early broad-coverage parser using a dependency-related formalism. Its parsing algorithm is context-free, that means it can only report projective structures. Nevertheless, most non-projective structures of English can be treated. A large set of labels is used in order to deliver projective analyses for structures that are inherently non-projective. In order to obtain the corresponding non-projective analyses, a considerable amount of post-processing is needed (Schneider, 1998). In practical terms, Link Grammar proves that completely projective parsing of English is possible without sacrificing long-distance dependencies.

4.4.2 Eisner

(Eisner, 1996) describes three models for probabilistic dependency parsing. The dependency structures are required to be projective, which means that since no mapping of LDDs to dedicated dependency types is used, the system is unable to express empty nodes and LDDs. The system uses only unlabelled dependencies. These two factors mean that Eisner does not use the potential of DG to express grammatical relations more directly, but just uses a version of DG equivalent to constituency. An unlabeled DG is a CFG in Chomsky Normal Form, in which the mother node and its head dependents are equivalent.

4.4.3 MacDonald et al.

McDonald et al. (2005) also use unlabelled dependencies. Their approach is one of the few really non-projective approaches. They detect discontinuous structures directly during parsing, using spanning tree algorithms from graph theory. Like in other Treebank-based approaches, most other dependency parsers are projective, some using graph rewriting in a post-processing stage. They also show that their parser increases efficiency on languages with non-projective dependencies.

4.4.4 Nivre et al.

Nivre (2003) also used unlabelled dependencies. Nivre and Scholz (2004) reports labels, but their approach is still projective. They use scores rather than probabilities and parse deterministically using an LR(n) parser. Pro3Gres differs here, as it uses a search beam on CYK instead of a sophisticated look-ahead, thus covering the middle ground between all-path parsing and deterministic parsing. Memory-based learning (Daelemans, 1999) is used for the parsing and look-ahead function in Nivre and Scholz (2004). The look-ahead is three tokens, only taking the part-of-speech tags into consideration. Nivre and Scholz (2004) reports results that are slightly below Collins (1999) and Charniak (2000).

Nivre and Nilsson (2005) use graph rewriting procedures to transform projective trees into non-projective graphs. The graph transformations are learnt from the training data in the following way: the training data for the parser is projectivized by applying and remembering lifting operations (Kahane, Nasr, and Rambow, 1998). A lifting function is a simple graph transformation, which is defined as follows: if a governor a has a dependent b, and b has a dependent c, then lifting c will make it an immediate dependent of a. When the parser is trained on the transformed data, it is also given information about lifts. After parsing, a post-processor applies the learnt lift operations inversely. Inverse lift operations correspond to our post-processing treatment of control structures. Nivre and Nilsson (2005) report that in the Czech Prague Dependency Bank (Hajič, 1998) 15 % of all sentences need at least one lifting operation, and 25 % of the sentences in the Danish Dependency Bank (Kromann, 2003). Less than one percent of the sentences in the Prague Dependency Bank need more than 3 lifting operations, and less than 3 percent of the sentences in the Danish Dependency Bank need more than 3 lifting operations. The memory-based learner reports almost correct reconstruction (99 % f-score) on perfect parses, on Czech projective parser output it improves the labelled attachment score from 72 % to 72.8 %. Such a graph rewriting task is very similar to the combined task of recovering empty nodes and antecedents in the Penn Treebank. At least for English, it could also be addressed with a rule-based approaches (Campbell, 2004), or our approach in chapter 6.

Nivre (2006a) uses a completely different parsing algorithm, in which every word is allowed to attach to any other word. The algorithm in pseudo code is as follows.

Foreach sentence $w_1, ..., w_n$ {
   for $i = 1$ up to n {
     for $j = i - 1$ down to 1 {
       LINK(i, j) }}

The link operation builds an arc with i as head and j as dependent, or j as head and i as dependent, or none, depending on the grammar rules. Such an algorithm allows the construction of arbitrarily non-projective graphs. If typical dependency constraints such as acyclicity, single-headedness and projectivity are placed as weak constraints, that can be violated under rare conditions, then we have a usable non-projective algorithm. The rest of Nivre (2006a) presents the ensuing parser and shows that the degree of violations needed on the projectivity constraint is small, corresponding to the lifting operations presented above.

Kuhlmann and Nivre (2006) have further investigated the context-sensitivity in the Danish Dependency Bank and the Czech Prague Dependency Bank. They describe that context-sensitivity constraints of the class that the grammar formalism of Tree-Adjoining Grammar (TAG) belongs to has almost complete coverage, 99.89 %, on these two Treebanks, and that the remaining uncovered data is partly due to the properties of the annotation scheme. They conclude that TAG mild context-sensitivity is a very attractive extension of projectivity. We discuss in chapter 6 that for English, TAG mild context-sensitivity is needed to analyse complex WH-questions. We have followed (Kuhlmann and Nivre, 2006)'s suggestion and implemented a simple dependency version of TAG based mild context-sensitivity, which we present in chapter 6.

Nivre's work is summarised in Nivre (2006b). Throughout the several versions of his parser, MaltParse, deterministic parsing with an oracle and a limited lookahead of typically 3 words is used. It is well known that such a short look-ahead is not sufficient for many cases, that local maxima may differ from global maxima for much longer sequences.

> *The Efficiency criterion is achieved by the deterministic and greedy (non-ambiguitypacking) nature of the shift-reduce parser. One could argue that even at a word level, deterministic, non-packing parsing is not always possible ... .* (Samuelsson, 2007)

Our approach using a full-path parser combined with a beam-search is an important difference. Whether these different architectures have an impact in terms of linguistic performance has not been evaluated, however.

More arguably, Nivre's mapping from the Penn Treebank to a dependency representation is, like Collins' (Collins, 1999), relatively surface-oriented and has not been accepted by all scholars (see, e.g. Samuelsson (2007)). We discuss some of the inconsistencies and errors that Nivre (2006b)'s mapping introduces in the evaluation in subsection 7.3. More research on dependency schemes such as Carroll, Minnen, and Briscoe (2003) and de Marneffe, MacCartney, and Manning (2006) is needed, as also one of the conclusions of Nivre et al. (2007) expresses:

> *Increasing our knowledge of the multi-causal relationship between language structure, annotation scheme, and parsing and learning methods probably remains the most important direction for future research in this area.* (Nivre et al., 2007, 929)

Our own representation has been based on the functional considerations in Lexical-Functional Grammar (LFG), it is close to Carroll, Minnen, and Briscoe (2003), and uses some of the extension advocated in marneffe-ea06, for example *appos*. Haverinen et al. (2008) have mapped the output of Pro3Gres to the Stanford scheme and shown that Pro3Gres achieves state-of-the-art performance. The Stanford scheme (de Marneffe, MacCartney, and Manning, 2006) is a recent extension of Carroll, Minnen, and Briscoe (2003) and is a widely used dependency representation.

Our representation originally left chunk-internal relations underspecified, which also allowed us to side-step some areas of gradience and focus on predicate-argument relations, which has been the original spirit of dependency grammar (see chapter 3). Versions of the parser that report all chunk-internal relations are now available. We will see in chapter 6 that using a linguistically highly motivated, functionally oriented approach is crucial.

4.4.5 Yamada and Matsumoto

Yamada and Matsumoto (2003) is very similar to Nivre and Scholz (2004). Important differences are they use a different parsing algorithm (a shift-reduce version), Support Vector Machines, and that they report slightly better performance.

At first sight, one would expect previous DG work to be a major source of influence on a DG parser such as Pro3Gres. But it turns out that, first, the recognition that Functional DG is so expressive because of its functional labels (Covington, 1994; Schneider, 2005) has not yet had a big impact. Second, there is only relatively little work on long-distance dependencies in DG, as Nivre (2006a, 73-74) points out. Third, our application of mild context sensitivity is more closely related to TAG and LFG approaches than to DG work. In fact we offer a DG-based simplification to the TAG and LFG approaches to mild context-sensitivity. Fourth, also DG research is turning to the class of extension of context-sensitivity that TAG offers. Kuhlmann and Nivre (2006) have investigated naturally occurring context-sensitivity in two corpora in dependency format (the Danish Dependency Bank and the Prague Dependency Bank) and conclude that TAG mild context-sensitivity is a very attractive extension of projectivity.

4.5 Data-Oriented Parsing (DOP)

Data-Oriented Parsing (Bod, 1992; Bod, Scha, and Sima'an, 2003) is a model in which the basic units to which probabilities are assigned are subtrees. The probability of a subtree is not the product of all its local subtrees (trees spanning two generations), but recursively the sum of the probabilities of all the subtrees – local or bigger than local – it can be composed of. (Bod, 2001) shows that subtrees as deep as 14 levels still contribute to parsing performance. These results show that lexical and structural dependencies span a large number of levels.

Pro3Gres takes the assumption that this property is strongly present in the following two configurations. First, deeply nested phrases of the same type, where the lexical head appears several levels below its maximal projection. Second, in long-distance dependencies, where lexical information needs to be shared between the gap and the filler. Collapsing LDDs into local dependency relations as Pro3Gres is related to a version of DOP in which the depth of subtrees expressing certain types of long-distance dependencies are known.

4.6 Statistical Formal Grammar Parsers

We have mentioned that state-of-the-art probabilistic parsers (Collins, 1999; Charniak, 2000; Henderson, 2003) are linguistically not convincing.

> Before the advent of statistical methods, regular and context-free grammars were considered too inexpressive for serious consideration, and even now the reliance on stochastic versions of the less-expressive grammars is often seen as an expedient necessitated by the lack of an adequate stochastic version of attribute-value grammars.
>
> (Abney, 1997)

It is recognised, for example in Kaplan et al. (2004b), that formal grammar parsers, without using the insights into statistics gained from probabilistic parsing, cannot achieve the robustness, coverage, accuracy and speed required for large-scale application. We discuss some of the successful approaches to integrate statistical disambiguation in formal grammar based parsers. The discussion is ordered by linguistic theory.

4.6.1 Lexical-Functional Grammar (LFG)

Lexical-Functional Grammar (LFG) can be seen as the outcome of the debate about the prevalence of constituency or dependency (see e.g. Schneider (1998)) LFG grammars use constituency rules that are annotated for building up functional structures (Bresnan, 1982). The functional structures of LFG are closely related to our dependency output, as we will argue in section 6.5.

Riezler et al., Maximum Entropy Modelling

Riezler et al. (2002) was he first approach scaling up an LFG parser to the entire Penn Treebank. They used Maximum Entropy Modelling, which we briefly discuss in the following. Maximum Entropy Modelling is by no means restricted to be used in the LFG theory only. It has also been used in HPSG syntax, and for many other natural language processing tasks. We discuss Maximum Entropy here because of the historical importance of Riezler's approach.

Log-linear and Maximum Entropy models A central theory on which statistical Formal Grammars are based is log-linear and Maximum Entropy modelling.

4.6. Statistical Formal Grammar Parsers

Log-linear models are models in which the log probability is a linear combination of feature values (plus a constant). Maximum Entropy models and Random Fields, but also PCFG, are examples of log-linear models.

PCFGs are a particular, simple version of log-linear models in which the sequence of features is the sequence of production rules traversed for a derivation. It is simple to get a probability model, the probabilities of all productions of the same LHS sum to 1. This useful property is lost in a straightforward extension of PCFGs to a structure-sharing, re-entrant Formal Grammar, as the re-entrancies introduce additional probability mass (Abney, 1997).

Stochastic Attribute-Value Grammar (SAVG) introduced in Abney (1997) is the general name for what can be seen as PCFG for attribute-value grammars. An attribute-value grammar rule is a rewrite-rule equipped with features that constrain each other, and that can express co-references. Rules are assigned weights in a fashion similar to PCFG or lexicalized PCFG. Because the co-references (also called re-entrancies) introduce interdependencies by adding to the probability mass in more than one place, SAVG loses the PCFG property of being probabilistic. PATR and PATR-II are attribute-value grammars. HPSG and GPSG often implemented as attribute-value grammar, although then only an important subset of HPSG can be implemented.

Abney (1997) originally suggests to base SAVG on *Markov Random Fields*. But no tractable exact parsing algorithm is known. Because of the dependencies among substructures, dynamic programming is impossible. This means that no efficiently implementable random-field approach exists yet.

Johnson et al. (1999) suggests to use Maximum Entropy models for SAVGs. Maximum Entropy modelling allows one to stochastically weigh discrete features to maximise the probability of a model, typically of an initially non-probabilistic model. One does not need to know if the features are independent and one can maximise the probability of a model that has many features by maximising each feature individually. Weight estimation is easy because the entropy function is convex. This means that it has one maximum, that no other point than the maximum is flat, and that all paths towards the maximum go upwards.

Entropy In Shannon's information theory, information I is a measure of surprise at an individual outcome given previous experience of outcomes. The less likely an outcome, the more informative. Information is measured in bytes, hence the logarithm with base 2.

4.6. Statistical Formal Grammar Parsers

$$I = log_2 \frac{1}{p} \tag{4.15}$$

Entropy H can be described as the average expected surprise, the average information of an outcome. It is simply the information weighted by its probability, as indicated in 4.16

$$H = p \cdot log_2 \frac{1}{p} \tag{4.16}$$

This function has two important properties. First, it is convex. Second, the entropy of a function is maximised at the point where the parameter probabilities fit the data best. This means that the probability of a complex function, for instance the product of weighted features, can be maximised by maximising the entropy.

Scored Features The score of an outcome a, for example a syntactic analysis given a sentence, is the product of features f weighted by α. Of all possible binary features from the feature space $1..n$, a feature f_i is either true (1) or false (0) for an outcome.

$$Score(a) = \prod_{i=1}^{n} \alpha_i^{f_i} = \prod_{i=1}^{n} \begin{cases} \alpha_i & \text{if } f_i = 1 \\ 1 & \text{if } f_i = 0 \end{cases} \tag{4.17}$$

In order to get the probability distribution, the score has to be re-normalized by a factor Z. For maximising or comparing probabilities, Z does not matter and is often not actually calculated.

$$p(a) = \frac{1}{Z} \prod_{i=1}^{n} \alpha_i^{f_i} \quad \text{where} \quad Z = \sum_{\Omega} \prod_{i=1}^{n} \alpha_i^{f_i} \tag{4.18}$$

Partial Information Maximum Entropy modeling is used where only partial information is available. The features for which training data is available get their probabilities from simple counts over the training corpus from which the weights follow directly. The automatic weighting of the features for which no information is available makes sure that they get highest entropy weights. The automatic weighting uses methods like iterative scaling. If entropy increases for a small weight change, then it is moving towards the maximum.

Riezler's approach Riezler et al. (2002) is probably the first large-scale application of Maximum Entropy models combined with a formal grammar. An LFG is scaled to parse the Penn Treebank. Sections 02-21 are used for training. Many of the features used in LFG are not expressed in the Treebank, therefore a Maximum Entropy model was used. Around 1000 features expressing information about c-structure, f-structure and lexicalization are employed. 74.7 % of the sentences in section 23 receive a full parse, in 23.5 % partial results are collected. The evaluation is done on 700 randomly selected sentences from the Penn Treebank section 23, and on 500 random sentences annotated with dependency information from the Suzanne corpus (Carroll, Minnen, and Briscoe, 1999).

Cahill, van Genabith, Burke

The Penn Treebank is currently the largest available syntactically parsed corpus for training formal grammar parsers. In order to be able to use it, one must address the fact that it leaves some features underspecified although they are used in formal grammars. One possible approach is to use Maximum Entropy, as Riezler et al. (2002) have done for LFG. Another approach used in LFG is to devise a approximative mapping from the Penn Treebank to LFG rules. While (P)CFG rewrite rules are expressed directly, such a mapping is needed in order to approximate the functional annotations that form a vital part of each LFG rule. For this purpose, Cahill et al. (2002) and Cahill et al. (2004) have developed a mapping method. The CFG rules extracted from the Penn Treebank are automatically annotated with functional annotations. Two parsing architectures are compared: a *pipeline* architecture in which the automatic f-structure annotation is done on the actual output of PCFG-trained parser; and an *integrated* architecture in which the automatic f-structure annotation is done on the gold-standard, and then an LFG parser is used. It is shown that the integrated architecture outperforms the pipeline architecture. In relation to Pro3Gres, the pipeline architecture corresponds to an approach in which Johnson (2002) patterns are used on the output of a classical probabilistic parser (Collins, 1999; Charniak, 2000), while the integrated architecture corresponds to our approach of using extended Johnson (2002) patterns on the gold standard and parsing with Pro3Gres.

Burke et al. (2004) extends on Cahill et al. (2002) by extracting paths between co-indexed constituents, thus also taking non-local information into consideration. For each of the modelled LDD types t (they mainly involve topicalization: TOPIC, TOPIC-REL, FOCUS) the path p probability is estimated

$$P(p|t) = \frac{\#(t,p)}{\sum_{i=1}^{n} \#(t,p_i)} \qquad (4.19)$$

4.6.2 Head-Driven Phrase Structure Grammar (HPSG)

Head-Driven Phrase Structure Grammar (HPSG) is close to dependency in spirit (Pollard and Sag, 1994). It also aims at a functional, even at a semantic orientation. It is certainly deep-linguistic. But due to its reliance on very complex attribute-value structures, on unification, and on pervasive use of long-distance dependencies, HPSG can suffer from enormous search spaces. Although HPSG systems are now achieving relative robustness (Miyao, Ninomiya, and Tsujii, 2003; Miyao, Ninomiya, and Tsujii, 2005), their inherent complexity is much higher than what is needed to express natural language. (Sarkar, Xia, and Joshi, 2000) state that the theoretical bound of worst time complexity for HPSG parsing is exponential.

Alpino

Alpino (Bouma, van Noord, and Malouf, 2001) is a wide-coverage HPSG grammar for Dutch trained on a Dutch corpus. It is hand-written, but uses maximum-entropy dependency probabilities (and some heuristics) for the disambiguation task, which are shown to drastically increase the accuracy of the system. The hand-written heuristics are, each of them compared to Pro3Gres, as illustrated in table 4.1.

Their statistical model is based on dependency relations. The probability of a parse y given a sentence x, where R is the relation, is modelled as:

$$P(y|x) = \frac{1}{Z(x)} \prod_{dependent_y} P(R, dependent|head). \qquad (4.20)$$

Z(x) is a normalisation factor; since the probabilities are used for comparing and maximising, and since x is fixed, Z is ignored. Like in (Collins, 1996), *dependent* and *head* is a <word, tag> tuple. Unlike in (Collins, 1996) or Pro3Gres, not only the relation R, but also the dependent is generated. For parameter estimation, the usual backoff (Collins, 1999) is used, as well as unsupervised learning: the results from parsing a large corpus.

Alpino	Pro3Gres
Complementation is preferred over modification	Left underspecified
Subject topicalization is preferred over object topicalization	Object topicalization is severely restricted, currently to questions only. More marked in English than in Dutch
Long-distance dependencies are dispreferred	Relations expressing LDDs get appropriate low probabilities from the training corpus
Certain rules are dispreferred	Similarly: some of the unmodelled rules are given low pseudo-probabilities
Certain lexical entries are dispreferred	Rely on tagger output
Certain guesses for unknown words are preferred over others	Rely on tagger output

Table 4.1: Alpino 2001 in comparison to Pro3Gres

Miyao and Tsujii et al.

Miyao, Ninomiya, and Tsujii (2003) present a probabilistically consistent model for predicate-argument structures, i.e. deep-linguistic structures as they are output by formal grammars like HPSG, LFG or Functional DG. It is discussed that the probability of a complete sentence can be calculated in a tractable parse forest, while a naive tree enumeration computation is intractable. Then it is shown that predicate-argument structures can be represented as parse forests. The conducted parsing experiments on Penn Treebank section 23 reveal that the employed HPSG parser is only relatively robust, as it fails to output structures in almost 20 % of the sentences, and that sentences longer than 40 words had to be cut.

Miyao, Ninomiya, and Tsujii (2005) improves robustness to above 95 % of Penn Treebank section 23, but also with limitations: first, sentences longer than 40 words still needed to be excluded, secondly the predicate-argument information – the HPSG SEM feature had to be neglected: "predicate-argument structures (SEM features) cause exponential explosion in the search space. The SEM feature was thus ignored in the parsing experiments." Using HPSG without its SEM feature leaves many of the aspects for which HPSG has been designed unexpressed.

Miyao and Tsujii (2004) use an HPSG system for the task of PropBank predicate-argument discovery, including predicate-argument relations that involve long-distance dependencies. Their completely rule-based approach outperforms most machine learning approaches on the task. This confirm the intuition that voiced by Campbell (2004) that linguistic knowledge is a good alternative to advanced machine-learning approaches for the task of detection and resolution of long-distance dependencies.

4.6.3 Combinatory Categorial Grammar (CCG)

Combinatory Categorial Grammar (CCG) has been successfully applied to probabilistic large-scale parsing in Hockenmaier (2003). Performance is very competitive, and with its combination of a relatively simple grammar formalism with a proper treatment of long-distance dependencies, it is a close relative to our approach. Differences are, however, that CCG is constituency-oriented and that search spaces are enormous. As a practical solution, super-tagging is used. Like TAG, CCG is a mildly context-sensitive grammar. We discuss TAG and its relation to our approach in chapter 6.

Constituency orientation of CCG and search-spaces CCG and categorial grammars (CG) generally are, like DG, valency oriented lexicalized grammars. The category assigned to a word encode its valency requirements. For example, the transitive verb *love* has a category $((S\backslash NP)/NP)$ which means that if its category requirements for an NP to the right $(/NP$, typically the *object* in DG) and then an NP to the left $(\backslash NP$, typically the *subject* in DG) are satisfied then we have an S node. But while DG is typically *functionally* oriented, taking nouns and gerunds and subordinated sentences alike as potential objects, categorial grammars are constituency-oriented. While (at least our) DG does not express valency requirements but licenses attachments, which means that unsatisfied valencies never pose problems, CGs even need to express adjunction as an artificial valency (e.g. $((S\backslash NP)/NP)$ $((S\backslash NP)/NP)$ is an adverb of a transitive verb). Also, there is no unique class for all verbs (intransitive, transitive, (di)transitive with PP, (di)transitive with subordinated S etc.), but all of them are treated separately. In practice, this means that the number of possible categories per word is large. On Treebank section 00, each word token has on average 22 categories. Inflated word category ambiguity in turn inflates parsing search spaces, to several orders of magnitude more than in other formal grammars.

Super-Tagging   As a practical solution, a super-tagging approach has been implemented (Curran and Clark, 2004). Super-tagging has been described as "almost parsing" (Bangalore and Joshi, 1999) because a partial parse tree is assigned to a word. Originally applied to TAG, super-tagging is highly suitable for CG, where each word category expresses its valency requirements in the form of sister and parent node requirements very similar to TAG. (Curran and Clark, 2004) have shown that aggressive super-tagging strategies drastically reduces search spaces and turns CCG systems into probably the fastest current parser ((Clark and Curran, 2004)). The super-tagger initially assigns a small number of CCG categories to each word, and the parser only requests more categories from the super-tagger if it cannot provide an analysis. Super-tagging is related to the carefully designed non-local restrictions that we place in our hand-written grammar. Super-tags express partial trees and therefore restrict, or even predetermine the parsing process to a large degree. We will show in an evaluation in section 7.8 that constraints have even a bigger impact on parsing time than pruning.

4.6.4   Tree-Adjoining Grammar (TAG)

The grammar formalism of Tree-Adjoining Grammar (TAG) and its relation to Functional Dependency Grammar are discussed in detail in chapter 6. TAG belongs to the class of mildly context-sensitive grammars. This class is described as being sufficiently expressive for all linguistic phenomena in natural language (Frank, 2002; Frank, 2004). As context-sensitivity is restricted, worst-case parsing complexity for TAG is $O(n^7)$ or $O(n^8)$, depending on the implementation (Eisner, 2000). We discuss in 6 that Functional Dependency Grammar inherently expresses TAG's extended domain of locality (Carroll et al., 1999; Frank, 2002; Sarkar and Joshi, 2003). Only a minimal extension to CYK-based CFG parsing, which has complexity $O(n^3)$, is needed for parsing a Functional Dependency Grammar that is akin to TAG: adjoining to the main verb.

4.7   Shallow Parsing, Finite-state Cascading

There is a popular, robust, very fast alternative to full parsing: be it by a probabilistic approach, which is typically fast but fails to express long-distance dependencies, or a formal grammar, which typically expresses long-distance dependencies but is often slower and less robust: shallow parsing. Typically, the text to be analysed is run through a sequence of finite-states machines, which build up a partial structure in a bottom-up fashion. Each finite-state machine corresponds to a level of syntactic processing: tagging for POS disambiguation, chunking for Base-Phrase recognition (in some systems followed by a PP-chunker for PPs), a verbal (and sometimes nominal) attacher for the phrase level. Super-phrasal attaching is rarely done, long-distance dependencies are usually neglected. Because of the sequential processing, each finite-state transducer taking as input the output of the previous transducer, they are often called cascaded finite-state transducers.

While this approach is highly promising and reliable for the low-level cascades, tagging and chunking, the performance for high-level chunking, at the phrase level, drops off. Briscoe and Carroll (2002) take a critical viewpoint. They state that shallow parsing output is neither as complete nor as accurate as state-of-the-art statistical parsers, and that it is unlikely that they will achieve the same level. A major problem for the development of accurate shallow parsers is that heuristics like longest match interact in complex ways with the large number of manually coded rules required in a wide-coverage system. This makes effective development of additional rules increasingly difficult, it is thus difficult to scale up. A second problem is the pipeline approach, which requires that the output from each phase of processing is deterministic, thus many decisions need to be taken too early in the processing chain, favouring local maxima. A third problem is that many such systems achieve much of their domain independence by basing rules as much as possible on part-of-speech (PoS) tags, rather than specific lexical items, in order to limit the number of rules required. Therefore, they cannot profit from the increased performance that lexicalisation offers (Collins, 1999).

4.7.1 Tag-Based Chunking and Partial Parsing Grammars

Abney (1991) and Abney (1996) describe a well-known tag-based chunking system. While the application of a finite-state chunker for the entire parsing process is controversial, Abney (1991) points out that such chunkers are very fit tools for low-level tasks.

> First, one of the most difficult problems for context-free parsing techniques is attachment ambiguities. But within chunks, (syntactic) attachment ambiguities do not arise, and simple context-free parsing techniques are very effective. By having separate chunker and attacher, we can limit the use of expensive techniques for dealing with attachment ambiguities to the parts of the grammar where they are really necessary – i.e., in the attacher.
>
> Another motivation is modularity. Since the chunker is insensitive to

> *the state of the attacher, we can develop and debug it separately from the attacher. The chunker also simplifies the task the attacher faces: many lexical ambiguities can be resolved within chunks, relieving the attacher of that task, and there is less clutter to deal with at the level of words.*
>
> *A related motivation is that the chunker-attacher division keeps attachment ambiguities from being multiplied with chunk ambiguities. The chunker evaluates chunks as well as it can on its own, instead of taking decisions relative to one or another branch of the attacher's non-deterministic computation.*
>
> (Abney, 1991, 17)

Abney (1991) is a full parser, unlexicalized, disambiguating by means of subcategorization frames and built-in preferences for argument-attachment, verb- attachment and low attachment. Abney (1991)'s scientific merit is now mainly seen that it introduces the notion of *chunk* and the division of labour between the chunker and the attacher – a division that is still valid today, and used by many parsing systems, Collins (1996), Daelemans, Buchholz, and Veenstra (1999), and also by Pro3Gres.

Abney (1995) suggests a model that mixes chunking and dependency grammar. Based on the observation that finite-state chunking approaches are unsuitable for analysing ambiguous structures such as PP-attachment it is suggested to step back from a full finite-state parsing approach to using chunking only for unambiguous sub-structures. In addition to the standard structural definition of chunks as being unnested NPs (so-called Base-NPs) and verb-groups, Abney gives chunks a functional, pragmatic definition: "We can define chunks as the parse tree fragments that are left intact after we have unattached problematic elements" (Abney, 1995) As to the definition of "problematic" cases, Abney argues that they are post-head sisters, i.e. arguments, modifiers and conjuncts that follow their head, plus pre-head elements of the *S* constituent only.[1] Due to these findings, the structural and Abney's pragmatic definition largely coincide.[2]

---

[1] The constraint that only the S constituent can contain pre-head ambiguities may be true for English, but closely related languages, e.g. German, also allow noun or even adjective pre-head ambiguities, for example *der auf der Bank beim Brunnen/beim Zeitungslesen sitzende Mann* where the PP is ambiguous between attaching post-head to the noun *bank* or pre-head to the adjective *sitzend*. This entails that chunking approaches, and constituency approaches in general, are considerably more problematic for languages like German

[2] As a notable exception we can mention NPs like *some of the people*, which is assumed to be one chunk with *people* as head, while syntactically we have two base-NPs, the superordinate *one* with

After thus "unattaching" all ambiguous cases, Abney goes on to suggest to re-attach them by a thematic, valency-based, grammar-role centred approach.

> *... essential information is clearly lost by "unattaching" chunks. Fortunately, we can re-introduce the deleted information, without losing the phrase boundaries we require to account for processing facts, by including the severed attachments as a relation distinct from immediate constituency. Since post-head sisters are canonically licensed by θ-role assignment, it is natural to reintroduce the severed attachments as relations between post-head sisters and their governors, rather than their immediate dominators. Such a move would lead us to what is essentially a mixed immediate-constituency/dependency structure, in which dependency relations contribute to semantic interpretation and syntactic constraints involving binding and movement ...*
>
> (Abney, 1995, 6)

This is the syntactic model adopted for Pro3Gres.

4.7.2 Grefenstette, Brants

There are a number of other systems based on cascaded finite-state transducers, for example Grefenstette (1996). After standard tagging, a chunker that differs from traditional approaches by including verb arguments and modifiers into the verb group, and noun arguments and modifiers, and prepositions, into the noun group. A second transducer extracts the heads of the chunks, distinguishing between PPs and NPs for the noun chunks, and between active, passive and copular verbs for the verb chunks. Brants (1999) is a successful cascaded finite-state transducer that has been tested on English and German. It is claimed to be psycholinguistically adequate.

4.8 Memory-Based Grammatical Relation Finding

Daelemans, Buchholz, and Veenstra (1999) and Buchholz (2002) are memory-based cascading approaches extending on the finite-state automaton idea. While Daelemans, Buchholz, and Veenstra (1999) deals with subjects and objects only,

---

some as head. This is one of the major sources of the Pro3Gres parsing errors that appear under the *grammar assumption* label in section 7.2.2.

4.8. Memory-Based Grammatical Relation Finding 98

Buchholz (2002) extends to all verbal arguments. Memory-based Learning (MBL) is a similarity-based supervised learning approach in which a memory-based learning algorithm builds a classifier by storing a large set of examples. From each training example, a vector of manually defined features, including the target feature, is extracted. When used on a new feature-vector at application time, the classifier assigns a class to the new feature vector, based on the most similar feature vectors in memory. Which similarity measure to use can be automatically or manually adapted to the classification task.

A large number of distance metrics have been suggested in the literature. On numerical values, the dot product, which is equivalent to the cosine measure of two vectors since normalised vectors are used, is the most obvious metric. On symbolic features, the edit distance is the simplest. The MBL software (Daelemans, Buchholz, and Veenstra, 1999) also uses many advanced algorithms, based on information gain, χ-square goodness of fit tests, Kullback-Leibler divergence in order to weigh features according to their importance, and makes use of decision-trees to abstract generalisations and reduce the data load.

4.8.1 Daelemans et al. 1999

After standard tagging and chunking a feature vector is extracted from each training instance. The following features are used:

The distance from the verb to the argument head (measured in chunks); the number of base VPs between the verb and the argument head (maximally 1 allowed); the number of commas between the verb and the argument head; the verb; the part-of-speech tag; the first left argument head context word; the first left argument head context tag; the second left argument head context word; the second left argument head context tag; the first right argument head context word; the first right argument head context tag;

As a realistic baseline for the combined subject and object assignment f-measure, 66% is given: "[u]sing the simple heuristic of classifying each (pro)noun directly in front of resp. after the verb as *S[ubject]* resp. *O[bject]* yields a ... baseline of 66%" (Daelemans, Buchholz, and Veenstra, 1999) . The best MBL algorithm used for this task improves just above 10 % over this baseline to 76.2 %. While the improvement over the baseline is impressive, the baseline seems surprisingly low. Our own baseline experiments for unlexicalized parsing with Pro3Gres (see chapter 7), admittedly done on a different corpus (Carroll, Minnen, and Briscoe, 1999), show a baseline of 85 % combined precision and 75 % combined recall. Shallow parsing approaches probably miss something very important: the parsing context.

Let us consider the simple example sentence *the report issued by the commission in 1986 has shown that* ...: While the parsing context disambiguates the local ambiguity of *report* as a subject (unless no parse spanning the very short distance from *report* to *shown* can be found), in the case of shallow parsing the disambiguation has to rely on lexical and tagging context information, which is much less reliable than parsing context. Although parsing is highly ambiguous, only a small minority of locally possible parses manage to combine to globally possible parses; a piece of information that shallow parsing misses. We will give an indication of the extent to which this can affect performance in section 7.7.2.

4.8.2 Buchholz 2002

Buchholz' work starts with Daelemans, Buchholz, and Veenstra (1999) and carefully extends the system, first by optimising the MBL algorithm parameters, then by testing and adding new features to the vector, and finally by including long-distance dependency features.

We will not discuss the MBL parameters. New features that are tested are first a bigger observation window, and the Penn Treebank functional labels. It is shown experimentally that the argument head-centred observation window performs better if it is larger to the left than to the right, which is to be expected from Abney's observation that all non-S ambiguities are post-head sisters. It is found that the observation window to the right need not even include any lexical information, whereas the best-performing observation window to the left includes chunk type and lexical information for the two previous chunks.

In order to approximate the missing parsing context, the derivation-history in history-based approaches, (Buchholz, 2002) introduces features for elements before the verb (*front material*), elements between the verb and the argument/adjunct (*intervening material*) – the chunks that can or cannot be attached to the verb, which leads to the parsing-based disambiguation – and the part of the sentence following the argument/adjunct (*back material*) – a sort of a parser look-ahead.

Buchholz (2002) finds that the *intervening material* feature does indeed make a significant difference, correcting an important shortcoming of Daelemans, Buchholz, and Veenstra (1999)'s approach. Unlike most statistical parsers, Buchholz (2002) next extends her features that deal with long-distance dependencies. Structure-shared arguments are given a complex dependency label composed of the two labels of the gap and the filler position. For example, a passive subject is assigned a <*NP-Subj; T-NP-Obj*> label. After these linguistic extensions, (Buchholz, 2002) is a competitive system, according to (Preiss, 2003) possibly better than state-of-the art statistical parsers.

4.9 Conclusions

We have summarised the state of the art and shown in which ways Pro3Gres is related to current approaches. We suggest a parsing architecture that combines the advantages of formal grammars and of probabilistic context-free parsers.

Kaplan et al. (2004a) compare speed and accuracy of a successful probabilistic context-free parser (Collins, 1999) to a robust LFG system based on (Riezler et al., 2002). They show that the gap between probabilistic context-free parsing and deep-linguistic full LFG parsing can be closed. On a random test set of 560 sentences from the Penn Treebank (4/5th of the PARC700 corpus[3]) their full LFG grammar gives an overall improvement in F-score of 5% over (Collins, 1999) at a parsing time cost factor of 5. They also show that a limited LFG grammar (so called core system) still achieves a considerably higher f-score at a parsing time cost factor of only 1.5: about 200 seconds for (Collins, 1999) and about 300 seconds for the LFG core system. A conclusion that can be drawn from their results is that research in simplifying, restricting and limiting formal grammar expressiveness is bridging the gap between probabilistic parsing and formal grammar-based parsing, between shallow parsing and full parsing.

The resulting system that we have implemented is hybrid at many levels. It carefully combines successful elements from a variety of approaches, while avoiding elements that are either too unreliable or too complex. The philosophy is to stay as shallow as possible while getting deep-linguistic analyses and using a functionally oriented, linguistically highly motivated dependency representation. We aim to obtain complete analyses for the majority of real-world sentences, and meaningful partial analyses for the remaining cases.

Our approach reduces the vast majority of long-distance dependencies to a more shallow, less complex task by expressing the majority of long-distance dependencies in a context-free way, thus offering on the one hand a parsing complexity as low as for a context-free probabilistic parser, but on the other hand delivering a deep-syntactic analysis as with a formal grammar. We have followed (Kuhlmann and Nivre, 2006)'s discovery that the mild context-sensitivity which TAG expresses is a suitable extension to context-sensitivity. We thus implement a simple dependency version of TAG based mild context-sensitivity, which we present in chapter 6.

---

[3] www2.parc.com/istl/groups/nltt/fsbank/

Chapter 5

Grammar Engineering

Pro3Gres is a Formal Grammar parser in many senses, because it follows a formalized and established grammar theory, because it treats the phenomena for which formal grammars were invented, for example long-distance dependencies, and because it analyzes for the entities defined in Formal Grammars such as LFG: deep-syntactic functions. At the same time, it is a robust parser, and it integrates lexicalized statistics obtained from the Penn Treebank. One of the aspects that Pro3Gres shares with many systems based on formal grammars is its use of a hand-written grammar, which we explore in this chapter.

We describe the design principles and the hand-written grammar in detail. It is explained why we have decided to use a hand-written grammar and which governing principles we have followed during the development. The individual rule types are then presented and discussed in detail.

5.1 Introduction

Before the success of probabilistic parsers such as Collins (1999) and Charniak (2000) the use of hand-written grammars was commonplace, in formal grammar based systems it still is. Grammar writing and grammar engineering proved to be a feasible, but very labour-intense and complex task.

5.1. Introduction

> *Grammar writing is much more difficult than rule writing. The intricate interrelations of the individual rules of a grammar make grammar writing a complex and error-prone process, much like computer programming.*
>
> (Friedman, 1989, 254)

The majority of classical probabilistic approaches learns the grammar from the corpus, obviating the need for a cumbersome hand-written grammar, but the amount of manual work for annotating a large corpus manually is considerable. Recently, hand-written formal grammars are combined with statistical data (Riezler et al., 2002) or formal grammars are learnt from syntactically annotated corpora (Hockenmaier and Steedman, 2002; Burke et al., 2004; Hockenmaier and Steedman, 2002) (see chapter 4). Miyao, Ninomiya, and Tsujii (2005) develop an interesting semi-automatic grammar acquisition algorithm. They state the traditional wisdom on hand-written grammars as follows: *"Although a few studies could apply a hand-crafted grammar to a real-world corpus, (Riezler et al., 2002), these required considerable effort that lasted over a decade."* (Miyao, Ninomiya, and Tsujii, 2005, 684). We follow the hand-written option and combine a hand-written rule-based grammar with lexicalized statistical data obtained from the Penn Treebank.

We have experienced that the amount of work needed to write a broad-coverage grammar manually is manageable, as we describe in subsection 5.1.2. The grammar, once written, can be ported without or with only small changes across most domains. What changes between domains is terminology and lexicalization probabilities. We discuss in chapter 7 that the former has a large, but the latter only a small impact. Before describing the grammar, we need to introduce the tagset on which it is based: the Penn Treebank tagset. We do so in subsection 5.1.1.

Writing a grammar manually can have benefits. For example, sentence types that are underrepresented in the Penn Treebank training corpus, notably questions, are difficult to learn. Pro3Gres has been employed for question parsing at a TREC conference (Burger and Bayer, 2005).

5.1.1 The Penn Treebank

The Penn Treebank is a large collection of syntactically annotated sentences (Marcus, Santorini, and Marcinkiewicz, 1993b; Bies et al., 1995). It is annotated with morphosyntactic part-of-speech information, and with syntactic constituency information. The tagset for the part-of-speech annotation is very small, it only uses 36

5.1. Introduction

tags. They are summarised in figure 5.1. Notable idiosyncrasies of this tagset are that the word *to* is never disambiguiated (it can e.g. be a preposition or an infinitive marker), and that no distinction is made between complementizer and preposition. The latter requires disambiguation for parsing.

The syntactic annotation is as theory-independent as possible. This has led to the following design decisions. No X-bar theory, no intermediate categories are annotated. The functional GB categories CP, IP, DP are not used. Auxiliary - main verb relations are expressed by VP reduplication. The top node of a sentence is S or a derivative of S (such as SQ for yes/no questions, SBARQ for wh-questions), not a verbal projection as in HPSG, LFG, or DG. Functional roles known form LFG and functional DG are only partially annotated. Specifically, subjects are annotated, objects are not, some PPs are functionally or semantically annotated. Functional and semantic tags are summarised in table 5.2. Structurally, all PPs modifying verbs are attached in under the VP, thus appearing as arguments, while all PPs modifying nouns are Chomsky-adjoined. Also the functional annotations do not always deliver argument or adjunct status in a consistent way. For example, the functional label LOC is both used for location adjuncts (e.g. *sit on a bench*) and adjuncts (e.g. *a rise in interest rates*).

Careful use of empty categories and co-indexation expressing long-distance dependencies is made in the Penn Treebank. We discuss empty categories and co-indexation in detail in chapter 6.

5.1.2 The Difficulty of Writing Grammars

While automatically or semi-automatically acquiring grammars is a very promising approach, we maintain that the expense needed for writing a large-scale dependency grammar over Penn tags is sufficiently small and that grammars are quite domain-independent. The broad-coverage English Functional Dependency grammar described in this chapter was developed in about a person-month. Despite the apparent simplicity of Dependency Grammar, we show in chapter 6 that Functional Dependency Grammar is a formal deep-linguistic grammar that does not make linguistic compromises.

The Penn tagset consists of 36 tags (plus some punctuation tags). Considering that dependency rules are always binary, that there are about 20 rule types and 2 possible dependency directions, the upper bound – both on rule writing and parsing

5.1. Introduction

Count	Tag	Legend
1.	CC	Coordinating conjunction
2.	CD	Cardinal number (N.B. ordinal numbers are adjectives)
3.	DT	Determiner
4.	EX	Existential *there*
5.	FW	Foreign word
6.	IN	Preposition or subordinating conjunction
7.	JJ	Adjective
8.	JJR	Adjective, comparative
9.	JJS	Adjective, superlative
10.	LS	List item marker
11.	MD	Modal verb
12.	NN	Noun, singular or mass
13.	NNS	Noun, plural
14.	NNP	Proper noun, singular
15.	NNPS	Proper noun, plural
16.	PDT	Predeterminer (*such* a good time, *both* the girls)
17.	POS	Possessive ending (John *'s* idea)
18.	PRP	Personal pronoun
19.	PRP$	Possessive pronoun
20.	RB	Adverb
21.	RBR	Adverb, comparative
22.	RBS	Adverb, superlative
23.	RP	Verbal particle (give *up*)
24.	SYM	Symbol
25.	TO	*to*
26.	UH	Interjection
27.	VB	Verb, base form
28.	VBD	Verb, past tense
29.	VBG	Verb, gerund or present participle
30.	VBN	Verb, past participle
31.	VBP	Verb, non-3rd person singular present
32.	VBZ	Verb, 3rd person singular present
33.	WDT	Wh-determiner (*which*, relative pronouns)
34.	WP	Wh-pronoun (*what, who, whom*)
35.	WP$	Possessive wh-pronoun (*whose*)
36.	WRB	Wh-adverb (*how, where, why*)

Table 5.1: The Penn Treebank Tagset

5.1. Introduction

Label	Legend	Example or Explanation
Grammatical Functions		
-CLF	true cleft	[S-CLF it was Casey who ...]
-NOM	non NP in NP function	heard of [S-NOM asbestos being dangerous]
-ADV	clausal and NP adverbial	reaches 10,000 barrels [NP-ADV a day]
-LGS	logical subject in passive	done by [NP-LGS the president]
-PRD	non VP predicate	is [NP-PRD a producer]
-SBJ	surface subject	[NP-SBJ Peter] walks.
-TPC	topicalised constituent	[S-TPC-1 I agree, he said [SBAR [S-1]]
-CLR	closely related	"open class of other cases"
Semantic Roles		
-VOC	vocative	Close the door, [NP-VOC John]!
-DIR	direction & trajectory	attention [PP-DIR to the problem]
-LOC	location	declines [PP-LOC in interest rates]
-MNR	manner	happy [PP-MNR like a kid]
-PRP	purpose and reason	[PP-PRP (in order) to ...]
-TMP	temporal phrase	shares rose [NP-TMP yesterday]

Table 5.2: Penn Treebank Functional Labels

search space complexity – is about 50,000 rules. In a realistic scenario, assuming on average one direction and relation type per possible tag combination (36^2) we get about 1000 rules. We only need grammar rules containing lexical information for closed classes. For example, a small class of gerunds, such as *including* and *excluding* can serve as a preposition, or a closed list of temporal expressions serving as adjuncts is used. For all open word classes, the Penn tags provide enough generalisation to deliver syntactically correct analyses in the vast majority of cases. The task of the lexicalized disambiguation is to select the semantically most convincing among all syntactically possible analyses.

The current Pro3Gres grammar has about 1200 rules and is 140 KBytes long. The number of rules may seem high because of tag combinatorics leading to many almost identical rules. A subject relations is e.g. possible between the 6 verb tags and the 4 noun tags. The grammar has been written from scratch, writing and debugging it took about a person month. Although it is probably not entirely error-free error-reports have become increasingly rare. The supplied Pro3Gres grammar does not aim at covering all phenomena of the English language. The decision of which phenomena to exclude depends on "armchair linguistics" intuition, followed by many test cycles to supplement the necessary empirical evidence. This decision also depends on the amount of ambiguity and errors rare rules introduce. The perspicuous rules of a hand-written dependency grammar build up the possible syntactic structures, which are ranked and pruned by calculating lexical attachment probabilities for the majority of the dependency relations used in the grammar (see chapter 2). The grammar rules contain the dependent's and the head's tag, the direction of the dependency, lexical information for closed class words, and context restrictions. The rules are described in detail in the following section 5.3.

The task of grammar writing is further simplified because we follow the Dependency-based broad architecture suggested by (Abney, 1995), which uses chunking for the base phrase level, thus making it unnecessary to write base NP grammars. This approach naturally integrates chunking and dependency parsing and has proven to be practical, fast and robust (Collins, 1996; Basili and Zanzotto, 2002). Tagging and chunking are robust, finite-state approaches, parsing only occurs between heads of chunks.

The most time-consuming aspect of manual grammar writing is the practice of incremental engineering across a large number of test cycles. Incremental engineering is a classical, well-established principle for bottom-up development. We first consulted Quirk et al. (1985), a comprehensive and very carefully written grammar of English. A small set of simple rules is tested first, the missing rules are then added in a large number of development cycles. There is a constant quality feedback from the development set corpus at each development cycle. Rules that are found to create more errors than correct analyses are refined or eventually discarded. We have trained over Penn section 2-22 and used section 0 as development corpus. Evaluations (see chapter 7) have been made on John carroll's 500 sentence test corpus, and 100 random sentences form the GENIA corpus.

5.1.3 Benefits of a Hand-Written Grammar

Writing a grammar manually is more time-consuming than applying a machine learning algorithm to learn the rules from a corpus. Still, there may be potential benefits from writing a grammar manually.

Parsing Questions Sentence types that are underrepresented in a training corpus are difficult to learn. In the Penn Treebank, this is the case for questions, which are crucial for Question Answering applications. (Hermjakob, 2001) shows that question parsing considerably improves if a grammar is enriched with additional question parsing knowledge. In section 6 we show that Pro3Gres is highly capable of parsing both simple and complex questions. Pro3Gres has been employed for

5.1. Introduction   108

question parsing at a TREC conference (Burger and Bayer, 2005).

Correcting Tagging Errors In a hand-written grammar, some typical parsing errors can be corrected by the grammar engineer, or rules can explicitly ignore particularly error-prone distinctions. Examples of rules that can correct tagging errors without introducing many new errors are allowing *VBD* to act as a participle, or the possible translation of *VBG* to an adjective. Most taggers perform poorly in the distinction between verb past tense *VBD* and participle *VBN*. But the distinction can usually be made in the parsing process. Therefore, the grammar leaves this tag distinction underspecified for a number of constructions, for example the *modpart* relation. A second example of ignoring error-prone distinctions is the distinction between prepositions and verbal particles, which are known to be particularly unreliable – and also human inter-annotator agreement is quite low. The grammar has therefore been designed to make no distinction between verbal particles and prepositions.

The Power of Linguistic Constraints Linguistic knowledge allows us to place strong non-local restrictions on the co-occurrence of different relation types. Verbs that have attached adjuncts cannot attach complements, since this would violate X-bar constraints. Verbs that have no object cannot attach secondary objects. The application of dependency rules can often be lexically restricted: for example, only temporal expressions occur as NP adjuncts. We have noticed during the development that these restrictions play a crucial role for the improvement of the parser's performance. We will assess the huge impact on speed and performance of these constraints in section 7.8. History-based parsers learning a sufficiently large number of subtree generations, such as in data-oriented parsing (Bod, Scha, and Sima'an, 2003), inherently learn these linguistic constraints, while we concisely express them in the grammar rules. The fact that the majority of these non-local constraints become local in DG makes it easy to express them in a DG grammar, and reduces search spaces.

Almost Complete Grammar A practical system, such as the one devised in this work, can choose to rule out linguistic constructions that are possible, but very marked and rare, and that often introduce more errors than improving the coverage. For example, while it is generally possible for nouns to be modified by more than one PP, only nouns seen in the Treebank with several PPs are allowed to have several PPs in the best-performing grammars used in Pro3Gres. Or, while it is generally possible for a subject to occur to the immediate right of a verb (*said* *she*), this is only allowed for verbs seen with a subject to the right in the training corpus, typically verbs of utterance, and only in a comma-delimited or sentence-final context.

Grammar Teaching and Learning A hand-written grammar offers the possibility to the user to inspect, edit and experiment with the grammar. Although this possibility does not give any scientific advantage, it is useful for learning and teaching purposes. On a personal level, manually writing and testing a grammar has considerably improved our knowledge of English grammar.

5.2 Subcategorisation and Lexicalisation

Collins (1999, 7) identifies subcategorization and lexical restrictions as the major problems for hand-written grammars. We model lexical restrictions by means of lexicalized statistical data. As for subcategorization, which is a robustness problem for hand-written grammars if subcategorized elements are absent, (Collins, 1999) uses a subcategorisation probability model in his Model 2, which we introduced in chapter 4. I We have decided to use a complement/adjunct distinction for NPs, and also to distinguish between different types of subcategorisation. We distinguish them by using a dedicated dependency type for each subcategorisation type (subject, object, secondary object, subordinate clause), and by grammar rules which only allow one dependency per subcategorised dependency type. The attachment probabilities are probabilities for attaching a dependent as a specific subcategorisation type: subcategorisation frame selection and removing of found constituents coincide. The only way in which a verb that has its valencies filled can continue attaching is to attach adjuncts, which increasingly gets unlikely due to the distance measure.

The task of the lexicalized disambiguation is to select the semantically most convincing among all syntactically possible analyses. During the development of the grammar, we have observed that the amount of ambiguity a rule creates, its scope of application and thus the amount of semantically absurd readings that are possible for a sentence, is beyond imagination. The fact that humans can reliably make precision judgements (deciding whether an analysis or an utterance is correct or finding one example) but are unreliable at recall judgements (finding all analyses for a sentence or utterances of a certain type) has been a major motivation for corpus linguistics, where rational decisions are supported by vast amounts of empirical data. Everybody who has developed and tested grammars knows how unreliable human capabilities are when it comes to predicting syntactically well-formed but semantically nonsensical readings of everyday sentences. The "intricate interrelations" that Friedman (1989) identifies have turned into every grammar engineer's nightmare. Here, a statistical disambiguator which ranks all syntactically possible readings is vital.

Since (Charniak, 1996) and (Collins, 1999) it is commonplace that a very powerful method to disambiguate between all syntactically well-formed analyses of a given sentence is to respect lexical preferences learnt from annotated corpora. Klein and Manning (2003) partly revise this commonplace by showing that a rich set of unlexicalized, i.e. structural, features is sufficiently complementary to lexicalisation, so that performance of a parser using them can almost equal the best lexicalized systems. As a first step, all tags are subdivided by adding the parent category to each tag occurrence. This takes a tag's into consideration and was the step that increased performance most. As a second step, closed class words are subdivided into linguistically meaningful subclasses, for example expressing the distinction between the tag IN as complementizer or preposition. As a third step, selected functional annotation from the Penn Treebank, for example $-TMP$, is preserved. As a fourth step, head annotation is added to the constituents. In distinction to lexicalisation, where the head word is added, the head tag, or aspects of it, is added. Aspects that Klein and Manning (2003) noted as crucial are the distinction between finite and infinite verbs, and the distinction between possessive and other NPs. Applying all of these steps leads to a model whose performance is almost equal the best lexicalized systems. Klein and Manning (2003) stress that it is not their goal to argue against lexicalisation, but to show that carefully used structural features can lead to a very high unlexicalized baseline. We have taken the choice to largely opts for lexicalisation.

5.3 The Rules in Detail

We now describe the rules in detail. Each rule has four arguments and a restriction part. The arguments are the tag of the head, the tag of the dependent, the tag of the projection, and the direction. The tag of the projection is usually identical to the head tag, according to the endocentricity principle, which most head-driven formalisms, for example HPSG, X-bar or Dependency Grammar use. There are a few exceptions, for example a preposition and a noun project into a prepositional phrase, the projection tag is PP. The direction can be left underspecified, like in an ID/LP grammar. The restriction part allows one to place arbitrary restrictions on the application of a rule. Some rules are lexically restricted. For example, there is a postposition rule forming a PP from a preposition and a preceding noun (i.e. the direction of the dependency is to the right), but this rule is restricted to a closed class of words like *ago*. Other rules express non-local restrictions on the co-occurrence of different dependency types. For example, a verb that already has attached an adjunct cannot attach a complement, since this would violate X-bar constraints.

We distinguish between the following three classes of dependency types:

1. Major types: these are the classical dependency types like subject and object. For each of them, statistical data has been extracted from the Penn Treebank, and an appropriate version of our probability model is used. This class consists of the following dependency types: *subj, obj, obj2, adj, sentobj, pobj, modpp, modpart, prep, compl* and *adjtrans*. Examples of these types are found in table 5.3.

2. Minor types: minor types are not probabilistic. They have auxiliary functions, such as building up noun chunks that the chunker has missed. Not all of them can be semantically interpreted. The adverb relation attaches to any noun or verb without aiming at a meaningful interpretation. Some relations are in this class because they give rise to very little ambiguity and thus do not warrant a probabilistic treatment: the *modrel* relation that attaches relative pronouns and the *predadj* relation that attaches predicative adjectives.

3. Unconventional types: there are a number of types that are each very different from any other type. Conjunctions, a classical DG problem, are split into two binary rules and leave ambiguities underspecified. WH-rules receive a simple treatment as real long-distance dependencies (see chapter 6). Commas have an important function in structuring the sentence and are treated in a special way, as will be discussed in subsection 5.3.3.

5.3.1 Major Types of Grammar Rules

All major verb types are probabilistic. They comprise the relations given in table 5.3.

Subject

There are 145 subject rules, the high number is due to tag combinations: Any verb tag, corresponding to the regular expression *VB[ZPGDN]?* can combine with any

5.3. The Rules in Detail

RELATION	LABEL	EXAMPLE
verb–subject	$subj$	he sleeps
verb–direct object	obj	sees it
verb–second object	$obj2$	gave (her) kisses
verb–adjunct	adj	ate yesterday
verb–subord. clause	$sentobj$	saw (they) came
verb–pred. adjective	$predadj$	is ready
verb–prep. phrase	$pobj$	slept in bed
noun–prep. phrase	$modpp$	draft of paper
noun–participle	$modpart$	report written
noun–preposition	$prep$	to the house
verb–complementizer	$compl$	to eat apples
noun–gerund-adjective	$adjtrans$	developing countries

Table 5.3: The major Pro3Gres dependency types

noun tag, corresponding to the regular expression *(NN[P]?[S]? or EX or IN or WP or DT or CD or PRP or RB or VBG)*. Each rule exists in a version with and without a comma between the verb and the subject. The subject relation is the only relation to have two probability models: one for active verbs and one for passive verbs.

General restrictions:

- Maximally one $subj$: The subject candidate is only allowed to attach if the verb does not already have a subject.

- Verb-chunk is not *to* followed by an infinitive: infinitival verbs are assumed not to take subjects. This entails a GPSG-style treatment of control, where the matrix verb takes both a nominal and a clausal object.

Special restrictions:

- Plural nouns: verb chunk does not contain *VBZ*. This is a simple method to ensure agreement.

- if the verb tag is *VBG*: verb chunk length>1. Present participles (gerunds) are not allowed to take a subject.

5.3. The Rules in Detail

- if the noun tag is *VBG*: noun chunk length=1, only with copula verb. Gerunds acting as nouns (e.g. *Swimming_VBG is fun*) are only allowed to attach to copular verbs (**Swimming_VBG likes fun*). The length restriction on gerund chunks is redundant for the current parser.

- Relation to right: only verbs seen in training corpus (in assertive sentences) are allowed to have verb-subject inversion (e.g. *says she* The restriction to seen material is an intermediate step between a rule- and probability-based model. It restricts the application of rare rules to attested cases. This measure can reduce search spaces considerably. The chunk distance is restricted to one, which means that no intervening elements are permitted (**says quickly she*).

- if the noun tag is *EX*: no noun conjunction is allowed. Expletives are not allowed to participate in conjunctions (**there and it seems to be a problem*).

- Noun tag *RB* for pronouns: The pronouns *this, that, it* are tagged *RB*. Only this closed lexical class is permitted to be subject.

Object

There are 78 object rules, the high number is due to tag combinations. Any verb tag, corresponding to the regular expression *VB[ZPGDN]?* can combine with with any noun tag, including lonely determiners, numbers, or WH-words, pronouns, gerunds and symbols, corresponding to the regular expression *NN[P]?[S]?* or *IN* or *WP* or *DT* or *CD* or *PRP* or *VBG* or *SYM* or *RB*. Verb-object dependencies are not allowed to overstep commas.

General restrictions:

- Maximally one *obj*: the 2nd, ditransitive object is labeled *obj*2. This ensures proper subcategorization.

- Verb has no adjunct to the right yet (all objects are closer to verb than adjuncts to the right). According to X-bar theory, case and θ-role assignment, complements need to be closer than adjuncts. In the CYK derivation history, this means that a verb can only attach complements before it attaches adjuncts. There can be rare and marked violations of X-bar theory in real-world language (*?they will ask today John*), which we explicitly intend not to cover in our parsing approach.

5.3. The Rules in Detail

- Verb has no *sentobj* (all objects are closer to verb than subordinate clauses): this assumption is based on the closeness of the object to the verb, and on the observation that considerably longer constituents are usually placed further than short constituents.

- Verb has no *pobj* (almost all objects are closer to verb than verb-PPs). This assumption, based on the same observations, is occasionally flouted *?they prescribed to John this dangerous stuff that had relieved generations of previous death candidates from unbearable pain*. While missing some readings, the restriction disambiguates for instance *she donated to the poor every Sunday* to an adjunct reading for *every Sunday*

- Verb has no *predadj* (predicate adjective): verbs cannot have a predicative adjective and an object simultaneously.

Special restriction: noun tag RB for pronouns: The pronouns *this, that, it* are tagged *RB*. Only this closed lexical class is permitted to be object.

Assumptions: In order to facilitate parsing, two assumptions are made:

- The predicate of a copular verb is considered to be *obj* (also in the lexicalized probability model). This does not mean that the complement of a copular verb (e.g. *president* in *Mary became president*) is really an object, but it allows a uniform syntactic treatment of verbs. Since copular verbs are a closed and unambiguous class, a simple mapping to e.g. a *complement* label would always be possible.

- In a ditransitive verb, *obj* is the indirect object (also in the lexicalized probability model).

Object2

There are 24 second object rules. Any verb tag, corresponding to the regular expression *VB[ZPGDN]?* can combine with any noun tag, corresponding to the regular expression *NN[P]?[S]?*. Other *obj2* tags are rare but possible, the grammar is thus potentially still incomplete. The tags *CD* and *WP* seem possibple, *DT* and *PRP* seem unlikely, as the following examples illustrate.

(45) She gave him 23_CD.

(46) ? She gave him what_WP ?

(47) ?? She gave him this_DT.

(48) * She gave him it_PRP.

The indirect objects in these examples tend to be expressed rather by means of a *to*-PP.

General restrictions:

- Maximally one *obj2*. The second, ditransitive object is labeled *obj2*. This ensures proper subcategorization.

- Verb already has an object.

- Only verbs seen in the training corpus or from a licensing list: this restricts *obj2* to verbs attested as ditransitive.

- No temporal expression noun: temporal expressions are excluded. This can lead to a few errors but reduces the search space.

- Verb has no adjunct to the right yet (all objects are closer to verb than adjuncts to the right): according to X-bar theory, case and θ-role assignment, complements need to be closer than adjuncts.

- Verb has no *sentobj* (all objects are closer to verb than subordinate clauses), similar to the object relation.

- Noun has no *modpart*: this heuristic constraint is prone to introduce errors, for instance in *He gave her the roses bought in the shop*, which is rare, but not impossible. It was introduced to correct frequent misanalyses of sentences such as *He reported her the roses sold in the shop*. In other words, a structural constraint that prefers a superordinate zero-complementizer to a subordinate zero-relative has been implemented. While structural soft constraints are not in the spirit of a statistical system, the very successful constraint grammar (CG) approaches rely on elaborate versions of such constraints. Hybrid combinations of such different approaches are a promising field of research.

5.3. The Rules in Detail   116

Adjunct

There are 50 adjunct rules. Any verb tag, corresponding to the regular expression *VB[ZPGDN]?* can combine with any noun tag, corresponding to the regular expression *NN[P]?[S]?*. Adjunct relations are allowed to overstep commas.

General restrictions:

- Only nouns seen in the training corpus or from a list of temporal expressions. Temporal expressions are a closed class. This step greatly reduces the search space.
- Noun has no *modpart* relation.
- Verb has no *sentobj*: this heuristic constraint forces a low attachment in (*stocks were said [to rise] Friday*).

Special restriction: The direction of the adjunct relation is possible to the left only if the verb has subject (*Friday they said ...*)

Sentobj

There are 130 sentential object rules. Any verb or noun tag, corresponding to the regular expression *VB[ZPGDN]?* or *NN[P]?[S]?* can combine with any verb tag, corresponding to the regular expression *VB[ZPGDN]?*. *sentobj* relations are allowed to overstep commas.

General restrictions:

- Maximally one *sentobj*: this ensures proper subcategorization.
- The subordinate clause is generally required to have a subject. This constraint is however subject to the following special restrictions.

Special restrictions:

- Infinite subordinate clauses with *to* are allowed not to have a subject: these are typically control structures, which get their object at the post-parsing predicate-argument stage.

- Comma-involving *sentobj* requires the subordinate verb to have a complementizer or the superordinate verb to be a verb of utterance: this helps us to restrict ambiguities arising from zero-complementizers. Zero-complementizers are rare if there is a comma between the matrix and the subordinate clause, except when the matrix verb is a verb of utterance.

    (49) She said, the winners have arrived.

    (50) ?She believed, the winners have arrived.

- Nouns can have subordinate clauses, but only subjectless ones, and only if the noun was seen in the training corpus. These are mostly relational nouns, e.g. *tendency to go*. The fact that they need to be attested greatly reduces the search space and eliminates many incorrect analyses.

Pobj

There are 30 verb-PP attachment rules. Any verb or adjective tag, corresponding to the regular expression *JJ or VB[ZPGDN]?* can combine with any prepositional phrase, corresponding to the regular expression *PP. pobj* is allowed to overstep commas. Attachment to left is allowed if a PP is fronted to the beginning of a sentence.

General restrictions:

- No verb-PP attachment if there is a predicative adjective (**she grew [tired] from too much walking, she grew [tired from too much walking]*)
- Unlimited number of PPs possible: no distinction between PP-arguments and adjuncts is made, an unlimited number of PP-attachments is thus allowed.

Special restrictions:

- *According* as verb is disallowed, because it is analysed as a preposition.
- Adjective-PP attachment is restricted to small distances only.
- The verb *be* is not allowed to attach PPs unless it has no object: this heuristic was introduced to correct a large number of incorrect analyses.

Modpp

There are 10 noun-PP attachment rules. Any noun tag, corresponding to the regular expression *NN[P]?[S]?* can combine with any prepositional phrase, corresponding to the regular expression *PP*. *modpp* is allowed to overstep commas.

General restrictions:

- Noun has no *modrel*: this restriction does not allow a full analysis of *she has a problem [which annoys her] with computers*, but it eliminates attachment ambiguities in *she has a problem [which annoys people with computers]*.

- Only relational nouns are allowed to have more than one PP (relational noun recognition is approximated by Wordnet). This heuristic is a rather crude approximation. It leads to errors with nouns that have several adjunct PPs. But we have empirically seen on the development corpus that the error rate increases considerably if we eliminate this restriction.

Modpart

There are 30 modification by participle rules. Any noun tag, corresponding to the regular expression *NN[P]?[S]?* can combine with gerunds, corresponding to the regular expression *VB[NDG]*. *modpart* is allowed to overstep commas. VBD is included (because this is a very frequent tagging error), in order to exclude at least the perfect tense under the restriction that it is the first element in the verb chunk (unless an adverb precedes).

General restrictions:

- Maximally one *modpart* per noun.
- Verb has no subject.
- Noun has no apposition (*appos*): a heuristic that rules out possible but rare readings: *the report, 60 pages, issued yesterday, shows that ...* but considerably increases performance on the development corpus.
- Verb has no object, unless it is an *appoint class* verb.
- Noun is no temporal expression.

- The distance is very short.

Special restrictions:

- If the tag is VBD then the verb chunk is checked in order to exclude verbs that are not participles.

Prep

There are 72 preposition rules. Any noun tag, including lonely determiners, adjectives, numbers, symbols, or PPs, corresponding to the regular expression *NN[P]?[S]? or PP or DT or CD or SYM or JJ[RS]?* can combine with preposition tags and verbal particle tags, corresponding to the regular expression *IN or TO or RP*. PPs can attach prepositions to treat multi-word prepositions, for example in *from under the bed*. Some rules need access to lexical items. For example,

- *including_VBG* is analyzed as a preposition contrary to its verb tag.
- The adverbs *ago, later, before* are considered to be real postpositions.
- *that_IN* and *because_IN*, if allowed as prepositions, lead to many incorrect analyses.

General restrictions:

- The distance needs to be very short distance. Adjacency is thus enforced.
- *that_IN* is not a preposition.
- *because_IN* is not a preposition.

Special restrictions:

- The direction allowed to the right only for the English postpositions *ago, later, before*.
- *Including_VBG, involving_VBG* can be prepositions.
- *Because of, according to* is a multi-word preposition. The attachment of *because* to an *of*-PP is thus allowed, although *because* is otherwise no preposition. The present participle *according* is allowed to attach an *to*-PP.

Compl

There are 24 complementizer rules. Any verb tag, corresponding to the regular expression *VB[ZPGDN]?* can combine with tags and closed class words expressing complementizers, corresponding to the regular expression *IN or WRB or whether_CC or but_CC)*. An example for *WRB* is the following.

(51) While many of the risks were anticipated *when_WRB* Minneapolis-based Cray Research first announced the spinoff ...

General restriction:

- The subordinated clause verb needs to have a canonical subject.

Adjtrans

There are 12 adjective translation rules. Any noun tag, corresponding to the regular expression *NN[P]?[S]?* can combine with verb gerund tags, corresponding to the regular expression *VB[DNG]*, as shown in the following example.

(52) Longer maturities are thought to indicate *declining_VBG* interest rates

Gerunds that can act as verbs or adjectives are a major source of ambiguity. The chunker does not include them in the noun chunk, which means that the parser has to decide. The gerund cannot be an adjective if the noun chunk contains a determiner. The local ambiguity created by gerunds often survives up to the sentence level: *He likes developing countries.*

Restrictions:

- Short distance. Adjacency is enforced.
- The noun chunk does not contain a determiner.
- No verb of utterance is allowed: in order to avoid conflicts with verb-subject inversion, verbs licensing this inversion cannot act as adjectives.

  (53) Share prices will fall, stock brokers kept quoting.

  (54) ? Share prices will fall, kept quoting stock brokers.

5.3.2 Minor Types

All minor types do not have a probability model.

Nountrans

"Lonely" adjectives, i.e. adjectives outside noun chunks (for example *the same*, *the poor*) can have noun function. There are 3 noun translation rules.

Restriction: Only an adjacent determiner can trigger the translation.

Adv

There are 51 adverb rules. Any verb or noun tag, corresponding to the regular expression *VB[ZPGDN]?* or *NN[P]?[S]?* can combine with any adverb tag, corresponding to the regular expression *RB[RS]?*. *adv* is allowed to overstep commas. Proper adverb-attachment is often not ensured. There is no probability model, the main purpose of the adverb-relation is to attach adverbs somewhere, so that an adverb does not fragment the parse into two parts. This is an area where Pro3Gres can be improved in the future.

Restrictions:

- Short distance

- The preposition *about* can be analysed as an adverb (*about 200 people came.*)

Modrel

There are 65 modification by relative clause rules. Any noun tag, including WH-words, corresponding to the regular expression *(NN[P]?[S]?* or *WP* can combine with any verb tag, corresponding to the regular expression *VB[ZPGDN]?*. *modrel* is allowed to overstep commas. No distinction between restrictive and non-restrictive relative clauses is made, although that would be easy to integrate.

5.3. The Rules in Detail
122

General Restrictions:

- The relative clause has a subject
- This subject is a pronoun: the rel. pronoun or a personal pronoun
- The relativized noun does not have a modpart

Special restriction: if the subject of the relative clause is a personal pronoun, the relative pronoun (zero-relative object) may be absent. The restriction of zero-relatives to the pronoun case is a pragmatic simplification.

Adjective

This auxiliary relation covers a number of noun-adjective modification including an adjective equivalent to *modpart*. There are 2 rules. Examples for the *adjective* relation are the following.

(55) ... for the purpose of keeping *[the_DT prices_NNS] reasonable_JJ*

(56) We have demonstrated that triggering delivers *[signals_NN] capable_JJ* of activating the NF-AT transcription factor

Predadj

This rule is used to attach predicative adjectives to the verb. There are 18 rules. Any verb tag, corresponding to the regular expression *VB[ZPGDN]?* can combine with any adjective tag, corresponding to the regular expression *JJ[RS]*.

Restrictions:

- Short distance
- Verb has no object, except if it is a verb of the *elect class*: (*consider them incompetent*). This is a consequence of our treatment of copular and *elect* verb complements as objects.

Comp

comp is used to build up comparison constructions involving an adverb *RBR* or an adjective *JJR* in the comparative.

Gen, Pos

gen and *pos* are used to build up the Saxon genitive. The *gen* relation attaches the *'s_POS* or *'_APOSTR* marker to the noun, which can then be attached to its head noun. The head noun cannot be a proper noun.

5.3.3 Unconventional Types

This class contains a number of relation types which are each quite different from all other relations.

Conj

Conjunctions have always been a problem for DG. At least three elements, two conjoined elements and the conjunction, need to be combined into a structure. This is difficult in a grammar that knows binary rules only. Also, on a semantic level, it cannot be said that any of the conjoined elements governs the other. In order to treat conjoined and non-conjoined phrases on a par, it is also not desirable to have the conjuction as the governor. As a pragmatic solution, we use binarized conjunction rules. In a first step, a word of a given word class can govern a preceding conjunction. In a second step, that word (it is checked that it governs a conjunction) can be governed by a preceding word of the same part-of-speech tag. As a consequence, the following simplification is made for lexicalization: only the lexical item of the first conjoined element is respected.

Enumerations: A comma is allowed to be a conjunction if the enumeration is terminated by a conjunction. Enumerations are a case where commas are easily disambiguated.

Apposition and other relations stepping across commas

Commas are generally ambiguous. Three cases are distinguished: Enumerations (see above), appositions and boundaries. Appositions are (often) identifiable as starting and ending with a comma, the head of the apposition is a noun or an adjective, and appositions modify nouns.

Boundary commas are commas which have structuring information. They do not alter relation types but mark a separation a high level in the syntax tree. In a first parsing step, only the apposition and conjunction relations are allowed to span across commas. When parsing finishes, i.e. all possible reductions have been made, all other syntactic relations that can span across commas (e.g. subject, PP-attachment, but not object) are allowed to do so and parsing continues, finding new reductions that overstep commas. This procedure implements the intuition that commas are a strong boundary.

Nchunk

$nchunk$ corrects some chunking insufficiencies involving $adjtrans$, currencies, percent signs, numbers, etc. For example, in *the corresponding_VBG solution* the chunker does not deliver a chunk. The $adjtrans$ relation attaches the present participle to the noun, then an $nchunk$ relation can attach the determiner. There are 51 rules of this type.

Aux and wh-preparsing

The aux relation is needed to attach auxiliary verbs in questions. Since DG does not distinguish internal and external arguments, the auxiliary verb can attach locally to the matrix verb. WH-relations the are only real long-distance dependencies. Chapter 6 discusses their treatment in detail.

5.4 Conclusion

We hope to have shown that the expense needed for writing a large-scale dependency grammar over Penn tags is sufficiently small. We have motivated our use of a hand-written grammar and discussed the bottom-up design of our grammar involving many incremental development cycles. Then we have discussed the grammar rules in detail, and we have explained the linguistic constraints that we use.

Chapter 6

Extended Locality: Treatment of Long-Distance Dependencies in Functional Dependency Grammar

6.1 Introduction

We have discussed in chapters 1 and 4 that there are broad-coverage probabilistic parsers with good performance (Collins, 1999; Charniak, 2000; Henderson, 2003), but they typically have context-free grammars, which means that they produce pure constituency data as output that does not include the grammatical function annotation nor the empty nodes annotation provided in Treebanks such as the Penn Treebank (Marcus, Santorini, and Marcinkiewicz, 1993b; Bies et al., 1995). Very recently, there have been first approaches reporting empty nodes and functional labels in broad-coverage probabilistic parsing (Gabbard, Kulick, and Marcus, 2006). We have also seen that context-sensitive DG parsing is now being used (Nivre, 2006a).

Context-free grammars are appealing as they allow a parser to use fast parsing algorithms. From a DG perspective, projectivity is a very powerful constraint which reduces the search space tremendously at a relatively small loss in performance. The loss in performance is due to the fact that context-free grammars cannot express non-local information, so-called long-distance dependencies. We will explore in this chapter how we extract long-distance dependencies from the Penn

Treebank, how the majority of long-distance dependencies can be expressed in a context-free way, and how we treat the few remaining long-distance dependencies.

A simple way to find long-distance dependencies and empty nodes is to try to reconstruct them from the output of a context-free syntactic parser. Johnson (2002) presents a pattern-matching algorithm for post-processing the output of a parser that can process the Penn Treebank (Charniak, 2000). The algorithm adds empty nodes to its parse trees. Encouraging results are reported for gold standard parses, but performance drops considerably when using trees produced by the parser. Johnson (2002) notes that if the parser makes a single error anywhere in the tree fragment for which the pattern has been conceived, the pattern fails to match. Errors are frequent, especially as the statistical parsing models are more local than the span that long-distance dependencies have. Johnson (2002) concludes that performance may be improved by generating parsing, empty node recovery and antecedent finding in a single system.

Pro3Gres offers a response to this suggestion by combining a statistical approach with a rule-based approach in Dependency Grammar (DG). Instead of Johnson (2002)'s pipeline system, we offer an integrated treatment which uses extended locality and an approach based on the treatment of mild context-sensitivity in Tree-Adjoining Grammar. We extend locality by (1) using and modelling dedicated patterns across several levels of constituency subtrees partly leading to dedicated but fully local dependency syntactic relations, and by (2) using non-local but bounded syntactic constraints, combining lexicalized statistics and syntactic knowledge. We model mildly context-sensitive phenomena in DG, and our DG approach profits from the fact that some non-local dependencies are artefacts of the grammatical representation.

For selected phenomena where post-processing approaches promise good results, we keep a post-processing approach, like Johnson (2002). These are notably control and raising, where the appearance of a control verb in the matrix clause and a subjectless infinitive with *to* in the subordinate clause trigger a sharing of constituents on the deep-syntactic level.

After Johnson (2002), there have been a number of approaches trying to recover empty nodes from the output of broad-coverage probabilistic parsers (Collins, 1999; Charniak, 2000; Henderson, 2003). Some approaches are based on machine-learning, for example Dienes and Dubey (2003) use a tagging approach, Jijkoun and de Rijke (2004) use memory-based learning, and Levy and Manning (2004) use loglinear classifiers. One of the best-performing approaches, Campbell (2004), is a rule-based approach using entirely hand-crafted rules. Campbell (2004) points out that empty categories follow from clear formal linguistic principles, accordingly there should be principle-based ways to recover them. Empty categories do not exist prior to the annotation, they are consciously inserted by the annotator following guidelines about linguistic configurations. The majority of empty nodes occur in configurationally clearly defined places.

We first show how we extract grammatical relations from the Penn Treebank. For grammatical relations involving long-distance dependencies, their boundedness is discussed, illustated by a quantitative analysis. We discuss that in English most long-distance dependencies are bounded, and the few unbounded long-distance dependencies, for example WH-questions, are cyclic. The former class can be treated with extended locality and post-processing, the latter class needs mild context-sensitivity.

We then present our treatment of recursive long-distance dependencies. Mildly context-sensitive constructions known from Tree-Adjoining Grammar (TAG) can be naturally implemented in a DG framework. We discuss examples and suggest that our approach has fundamental implications for Lexical-Functional Grammar (LFG).

6.2 The Boundedness of Long-Distance Dependencies

In order to be able to train a DG on constituency data such as the Treebank, a conversion is necessary. Such conversions are described in Covington (1994) or Basili, Pazienza, and Zanzotto (1998).

A conversion is either *full*, if the constituency trees are entirely translated into DG structures, or *selective*, if a set of dependency relations are converted, without enforcing that connected DG structures are possible. For the purpose of extracting relations, irrespective of whether they are local relations or non-local subtree relations involving long-distance dependencies, a selective conversion is sufficient, so we will restrict ourselves to introducing a selective conversion.

We have used *tgrep* for the conversion task, a popular query language for syntactically annotated corpora[1]. The discussion will stay as general as possible, but the detailed extraction patterns we use are listed in the appendix. This will allow the interested reader to individually test the conversion patterns in detail.

---

[1] tgrep is shipped as part of the Penn Treebank from LDC. The online man page is http://www.ldc.upenn.edu/ldc/online/treebank/man/cat1/tgrep.1 . For tgrep2, see http://www.cs.cmu.edu/dr/Tgrep2/

Relation	Label	Example
verb–subject	subj	*he sleeps*
verb–first object	obj	*sees it*
verb–second object	obj2	*gave (her) kisses*
verb–adjunct	adj	*ate yesterday*
verb–subord. clause	sentobj	*saw (they) came*
verb–prep. phrase	pobj	*slept in bed*
noun–prep. phrase	modpp	*draft of paper*
noun–participle	modpart	*report written*
verb–complementizer	compl	*to eat apples*
noun–preposition	prep	*to the house*

Table 6.1: Important Pro3Gres Dependency types

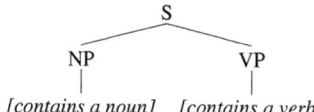

[contains a noun]   [contains a verb]

Figure 6.1: Prototypical subject configuration

6.2.1 Local Relations

Before turning to long-distance dependencies, we illustrate the extraction of local dependencies from the Penn Treebank. We will discuss two examples, subjects and objects. Table 6.1 gives an overview of important dependencies extracted from the Treebank and subsequently used by our parser.

Subjects

Local relations are between a mother node and immediate daughter nodes. A prototypical *active subject* relation holds between and NP and a VP that are dominated by an S node, as shown in figure 6.1.

In the Penn Treebank II (Marcus, Santorini, and Marcinkiewicz, 1993b) some syntactic relations are now made explicit. Subjects are given an explicit SBJ functional label.

Dependency relations are always between lexical items, so that the lexical

6.2. The Boundedness of Long-Distance Dependencies

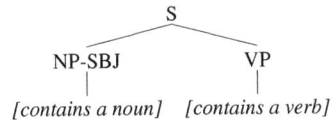

Figure 6.2: Explicit Penn-II subject relation

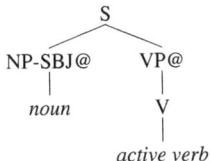

Figure 6.3: Extraction pattern for active subject-verb relations

heads need to be extracted from the Treebank. We thus use patterns that descends into the subject noun, following the possibly nested NPs to the head noun, and into the VP, following down the possibly nested VPs to the head verb. We symbolise the possible nestedness by using an '@' symbol in fig. 6.3. Thus, like in lexicalized PCFGs, the lexical information of local relations becomes non-local.

A base NP head is assumed to be a noun ($NN*$), a pronoun (PRP), a WH-element (WDT,WP), a number (CD), or an existential (EX). At the terminal level, the rightmost element falling into any of these categories is assumed to be the base NP head. A VP head is assumed to be the verb ($VB*$) at the lowest level. This restriction is necessary in order to exclude auxiliaries. The lowest level verb is a verb that has no VP sister. The pattern thus conceived can be expanded to a set of tgrep queries or pattern instances. A comprehensive list of the patterns can be found in the appendix in fig. A.

Objects

The extraction of other local relations, e.g. objects, is analogous. While it is common for all verb to have a subject in English, whether a verb has objects or other types of complements largely depends on the verb subcategorisation. Quirk et al. (1985) describe the following three types of nominal verb complementation:

6.2. The Boundedness of Long-Distance Dependencies

First, copular complementation: complements of copular verbs, such as *be, remain, stay, appear, become*. Second, monotransitive complementation: verbs taking one object. Third, ditransitive complementation: verbs taking two objects. The object closer to the verb (in English) is the indirect object, the object further away from the verb can be referred to as the secondary object.

The nominal complement of a copular verb is called subject complement. They are expressed in the Penn Treebank by means of the functional label PRD.

(57) Mr. Vinken [VP is [NP-PRD chairman of Elsevier, the Dutch publishing group]].

Monotransitive verbs and copular verbs are in disjoint distribution; monotransitive and copular subcategorisation are mutually exclusive. For convenience, we can therefore use the dependency label obj for subject complements, the verb semantics are unambiguous. The comprehensive list of tgrep extraction pattern instances for objects, including subject complements, can be found in the appendix in fig. A.

As for ditransitive complementation, the tgrep extraction instances match verbs with two objects. The second object is extracted and obtains the relation label $obj2$, which stands for secondary object. The comprehensive list is shown in the appendix in fig. A.

6.2.2 Nonlocal Relations

We now discuss nonlocal relations, also called long-distance dependencies. Before doing a quantitative analysis of nonlocal relations, we consider two common examples of nonlocal relation: the relation between subjects and passive verbs, and control constructions.

Passive Verb Subject

A Treebank example of a passive sentence is illustrated by the following sentence.

(58) [NP-SBJ-2 Preliminary findings] [VP were [VP reported [NP NONE *-2] more than a year ago]].

In passive verbs, a movement involving an empty constituent is assumed. An extraction pattern for the above example is in figure 6.4, where again VP@ is an arbitrarily nested VP, and NP-SBJ-X@ the arbitrarily nested surface subject. X

6.2. The Boundedness of Long-Distance Dependencies

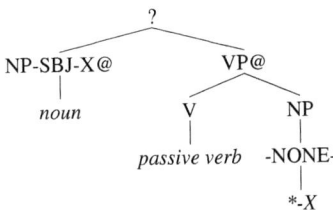

Figure 6.4: Extraction pattern for passive subjects

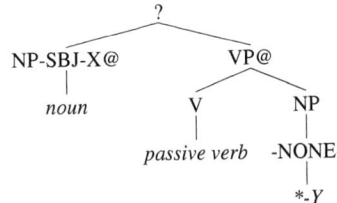

Figure 6.5: First experiment pattern for passive subjects: Coreference is not enforced

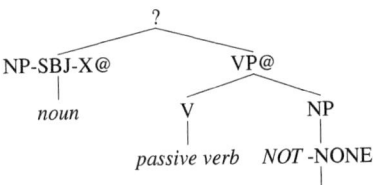

Figure 6.6: Second experiment pattern for passive subjects: Forcing *no* trace in the object position

6.2. The Boundedness of Long-Distance Dependencies

represents the numerical counter of the co-indexed, moved element. The passive pattern expanded into comprehensive tgrep queries can again be found in the appendix in figure A.

As an initial assumption, movements can be of arbitrary length. It has been widely investigated that the majority of movements is subject to local restrictions (Ross, 1967; Chomsky, 1986). Passive movement is very restricted. The rigid pattern 6.4, in which the movement is of fixed length, would otherwise miss subject-passive-verb relations. We now show that we do not miss any case in the Penn Treebank and confirm that passive movement is of fixed length.

Since it is not possible to express long-distance dependencies directly in *tgrep*, our arguments are indirect. The following questions are relevant.

How many filler and gap indices coincide in our fixed pattern?

The pattern 6.5 differs from 6.4 as it does not enforce the identity of the filler and gap index. In our tests listed in the appendix no case in which patterns 6.4 and 6.5 return different results was found.

How many fillers do not find their gap in the passive verb sister?

In a second experiment, we test in how many cases a filler occurs without a gap position in the position expected by our fixed pattern, i.e. the passive verb object position. In order to exclude some mismatches when using the negation, we restrict ourselves to cases where the gap immediately follows the verb sister. Our experiment, detailed in the appendix, shows that pattern 6.4 occurs about 30 times more often than pattern 6.6. None of the tested cases of pattern 6.6 involves a passive verb form.

These tests, though small and potentially incomplete, indicate that passive movement is locally fixed. It can therefore be replaced by a single, local, but uniquely labelled dependency, for example $psubj$, which always allows a re-conversion into a constituency-based format including the correct LDD indices.

Since the verb form already allows a clear identification of passive structures, we have decided to use the same relation label as for the active subject, $subj$, but to use separate probability estimations for the active and the passive case.

There is a class of verbs, following Levin (1993) often called *dub* verbs, which take a noun phrase as object complement. Examples of dub verbs are *name, appoint, consider*, like in *the queen appointed William Cecil her personal secretary*. As dub verbs are in disjoint distribution with ditransitive verbs, we can give the object complement the secondary object label $obj2$. Dub verbs are very frequently in the passive voice. The (slightly different) extraction pattern for them, involving

6.2. The Boundedness of Long-Distance Dependencies 134

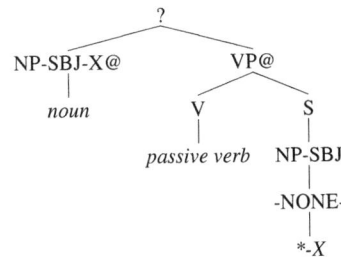

Figure 6.7: Extraction pattern for passive *dub* verb subjects

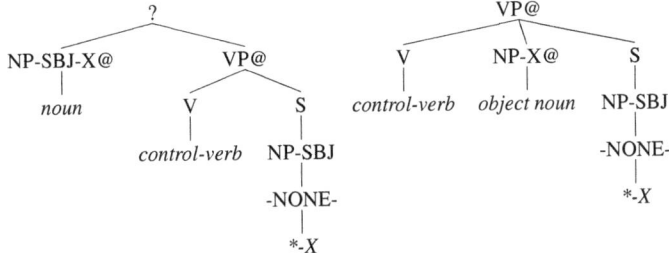

Figure 6.8: Extraction pattern for subject control (left) and object control (right)

a small clause, is shown in figure 6.7.

Control

Control is another course-book example of long-distance dependency. The extraction pattern for control is in fig. 6.8.

Control and raising coreferences can be reconstructed successfully from the context of the matrix and the subordinate clause. If the matrix clause contains a control verb, a raising verb, or a control adjective, and if the subordinate clause contains a verb in the infinitive with *to* and a corresponding unfilled argument position, then coreference is assumed. This is the assumption expressed by our fixed extraction pattern.

6.2. The Boundedness of Long-Distance Dependencies

How many filler and gap indices coincide in our fixed pattern?

Filler and gap indices coincide in our fixed pattern to a high degree. Comparing the counts with enforced and relaxed filler identity analogous to the experiment on passives, we get 98 % identity for subject-control. In the 320 cases tested, 7 had no identity of gap and filler. An example of these 7 sentences where the subject-control pattern goes astray is:

```
(NP-SBJ-1 (DT Some)
          (NNP Golenbock)
          (NNS lawyers))
(VP (MD wo)
    (RB n't)
    (VP (VB be)
        (VP (VBN invited)
            (NP-2 (-NONE- *-1))
            (S (NP-SBJ (-NONE- *-2))
               (VP (TO to)
                   (VP (VB join)
                       (NP (NNP Whitman)
                           (CC &)
                           (NNP Ransom)))))
            (, ,)
            (PP (VBG according)
                (PP (TO to)
                    (NP (NP (NNS partners))
                        (PP-LOC (IN at)
                                (NP (DT both)
                                    (NNS firms)))))))))
```

Complex interaction between different types of long-distance dependencies, in this case between passive and control, means that the extraction pattern can make errors. While this affects the recall of the pattern on the Penn Treebank for obtaining lexical statistics, reconstruction of the control relation during parsing remains unaffected.

We obtain above 99 % identity for object-control. Of the 264 cases tested in the appendix, one failed to have identity.

How many fillers do not find their gap in the subordinate subjectless clause?

In this experiment, we tested in how many cases a filler occurs without a gap position in the position expected by our fixed pattern, i.e. the subordinate clause subject position. Our experiment, detailed in the appendix, shows that the control pattern occurs 37 times more often than an (otherwise identical) pattern explicitly requiring a no-trace subordinated subject.

The 8 tested subject-control cases where no gap occurs in the subordinate clause subject position include a conjunction that triggers a mismatch, an annota-

6.2. The Boundedness of Long-Distance Dependencies

tion error, a complex interaction between passive and control, and one case where the movement is longer than what the pattern matches, but not a typical case of control:

```
(NP-SBJ-1 (PRP we))
(VP (MD should)
    (VP (VB be)
        (VP (VBG helping)
            (S (NP-SBJ (NNP U.S.)
                       (NNS companies))
                (VP (VB improve)
                    (NP (VBG existing)
                        (NNS products))
                    (PP (RB rather)
                        (IN than)
                        (S-NOM (NP-SBJ (-NONE- *-1))
                               (ADVP-TMP (RB always))
                               (VP (VBG developing)
                                   (NP (JJ new)
                                       (NNS ones)))))))))))
```

For object control, the control pattern is only 22 times more frequent than an (otherwise identical) pattern explicitly requiring a no-trace subordinated subject. But the tested 15 object-control cases where no gap occurs in the subordinate clause subject position include 13 cases where the pattern erroneously matches a temporal expression in the object position.

As a tentative conclusion we can say that control is almost as clearly fixed as passive subject movement. Although there are a few exceptions and fixed patterns fail when several movements interact, we only lose very few cases when extracting relations with a fixed pattern. While the extraction of long-distance dependencies may fail when several movements interact, the impact on lexical statistics used for parsing and thus the impact on parsing success is very small, and the post-processing step after parsing delivers the correct result unless there are intervening parsing errors.

The trace of both a passive and a control relation is expressed by an *NP** constituent in the Penn Treebank. Campbell (2004) uses a single, purely configurational rule to recover *NP** from Treebank trees where they have been removed. Campbell (2004) reports similar rules for other long-distance relations.

We have written structural patterns corresponding to such rules. Each long-distancce dependency type corresponds to a pattern or a set of patterns. Grammatical role labels, empty node labels and tree configurations spanning several local subtrees are used as integral part of long-distance dependency patterns. This leads to much flatter trees, as typical for DG, which has the advantages that (1) it helps to alleviate sparse data by mapping nested structures that express the same dependency relation[2], (2) fewer decisions are needed at parse-time, which reduces complexity and the risk of errors (Johnson, 2002), (3) the costly overhead for dealing with unbounded dependencies can be partly avoided. It is ensured that the lexical information that matters is available in one central place, allowing the parser to take one well-informed decision.

While these dependency relations covering empty nodes and several levels of subtrees express some non-local dependencies and reduce parse tree depth and complexity, the questions about their quantitative and qualitative coverage must be answered. We discuss quantitative coverage in section 6.3, and qualitative coverage in section 6.4.

6.3 A Quantitative Analysis of Types of Empty Nodes

We have seen that passive and control movements are of bounded length, now we would like to investigate all major types of movement.

6.3.1 Overview

The ten most frequent types of empty nodes cover the vast majority, more than 60,000 of the approximately 64,000 empty nodes of sections 2-21 of the Penn Treebank. Table 6.2, reproduced from Johnson (2002) (row numbers and counts from the whole Treebank added), gives an overview.

Empty units, empty complementizers and empty relative pronouns (rows 4,5,9,10) pose no problem for our functional DG as they are optional, non-head material (see section 3.1.3). For example, a complementizer is an optional dependent (or in HPSG a marker) of the subordinated verb (see chapter 5).

Fronted constituents (row 6) are mostly PPs or clausal complements of verbs of utterance. Only verbs of utterance allow subject-verb inversion in affirmative clauses (row 8). The linguistic grammar provides rules with appropriate restrictions for all of these. In an ID/LP framework, none of them involve non-local dependencies or empty nodes. Moved constituents (row 6) and empty clauses (row 8) have rules in our functional DG that allow an inversion of the dependency direction, loosening linear precedence constraints, under well-defined conditions.

---

[2]Data sparseness also depends on the probability model. As an alternative to collapsing the structure in the annotation as we do, it could also be collapsed in the statistical model

6.3. A Quantitative Analysis of Types of Empty Nodes

	Antecedent	POS	Label	Count	Description/Example
1	NP	NP	*	22,734	NP trace *Sam* was seen *
2		NP	*	12,172	NP PRO * to sleep is nice
3	WHNP	NP	*T*	10,659	WH trace the woman *who* you saw *T*
(4)			*U*	9,202	Empty units $ 25 *U*
(5)			0	7,057	Empty complementizers Sam said 0 Sasha snores
(6)	S	S	*T*	5,035	Moved constituents *Sam had to go*, Sasha said *T*
7	WHADVP	ADVP	*T*	3,181	WH-trace Sam explained *how* to leave *T*
(8)		SBAR		2,513	Empty clauses *Sam had to go*, said Sasha (SBAR)
(9)		WHNP	0	2,139	Empty relative pronouns the woman 0 we saw
(10)		WHADVP	0	726	Empty relative pronouns the reason 0 to leave

Table 6.2: The distribution of the 10 most frequent types of empty nodes and their antecedents in the Penn Treebank (adapted from Johnson 2002). Row numbers in parentheses indicate cases that are inherently local in our functional DG

Type	Count	prob-modeled	Treatment
passive subject	6,803	YES	local relation
indexed gerund	4,430	NO	Tesnière translation
subject control, raise, semi-aux	6,122	YES	post-parsing processing
object control	333	YES	post-parsing processing
others / not covered	5,046		
TOTAL	22,734		

Table 6.3: Coverage of the patterns for the most frequent NP traces [row 1]

6.3. A Quantitative Analysis of Types of Empty Nodes

Type	Count	prob-modeled	Treatment
modpart	5,656	YES	local relation
non-indexed gerund	3,095	NO	Tesnière translation
adverbial of verb	1,598	NO	no loss of information
adverbial of noun	268	NO	no loss of information
others / not covered	1,555		
TOTAL	12,172		

Table 6.4: Coverage of the patterns for the most frequent NP PRO [row 2]

6.3.2 NP Traces

A closer look at NP traces (row 1 of table 6.2) reveals that the majority of them are recognised by the grammar. Except for the indexed gerunds, they participate in the probability model. In control, raising and semi-auxiliary constructions, the non-surface semantic arguments, i.e. the subject-verb relation in the subordinate clause, are created based on lexical probabilities at the post-parsing stage, where minimal predicate-argument structures are output.

Unlike in control, raising and semi-auxiliary constructions, the antecedent of an indexed gerund cannot be established easily. The fact that almost half of the gerunds are not indexed in the Treebank indicates that information about the unexpressed participant is rather semantic than syntactic in nature, much like in anaphora resolution. The parser does not try to decide whether the target gerund is indexed or not, nor does it try to find the identity of the lacking participant in the latter case. This is an important reason why recall values for the subject and object relations are lower than the precision values, and constitutes one of the cases where real information is lost by our conversion into a local DG representation.

6.3.3 NP PRO

As for the 12,172 NP PRO (row 2 of table 6.2) in the Treebank, 5,656 are recognised by the *modpart* pattern (which covers reduced relative clauses), which means they are treated as a local relation covered in the probability model. The extraction patterns for the *modpart* relation are presented in fig. A. The dedicated *modpart* relation typically expresses object function for past participles (*the report issued*) and subject function for present participles (*a sum totalling*). The full tgrep extraction pattern instances for the *modpart* relation are listed in the appendix in section A.

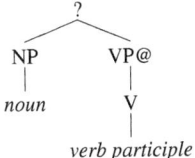

Figure 6.9: The extaction pattern for the *modpart* relation. The NP is explicitly a non-subject NP

A further 3,095 NP PRO are recognised as non-indexed gerunds. Infinitives and gerunds may act as subjects, which are covered by Tesnière (1959)'s translations (see section 3.2.3), although these rules do not participate in the probability model. For example, a translation allows a verb to act as a noun upwards in the tree. In *to read books is great*, *read* takes an object dependent *books* like a regular verb, but acts as a noun dependent for the copula *be*.

Many of the structures that are not covered by the extraction patterns and the probability model are still parsed correctly, for example adverbial clauses are treated as unspecified subordinate clauses. Non-indexed adverbial phrases of the verb account for 1,598 NP PRO, non-indexed adverbial phrases of the noun for 268. As the NP is non-indexed, the identity of the lacking argument in the adverbial is unknown anyway, thus no semantic information is lost if the empty node remains underspecified.

6.3.4 WH Traces

Only 113 of the 10,659 WHNP antecedents in the Penn Treebank (row 3 of table 6.2) are actually question pronouns. The vast majority, over 9,000, are relative pronouns. We first discuss our treatment of relative pronouns, and then we discuss in which way question pronouns require a different treatment.

Relative Pronouns

In subject relatives, the relative pronoun is analysed as a subject. The post-processing module of the parser resolves the relative pronoun. Post-processing links are thick, labels in bold font in the following pictures.

(59) *boys who saw girls*

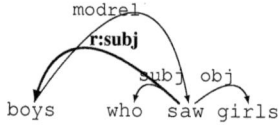

In object relatives and prepositional object relatives, an inversion of the direction of the relation they have to the verb is allowed if the relative pronoun precedes the subject.

(60) *boys who girls saw*

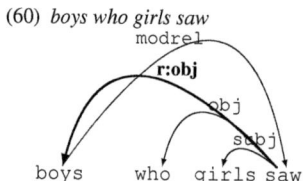

(61) *boys to whom girls gave presents*

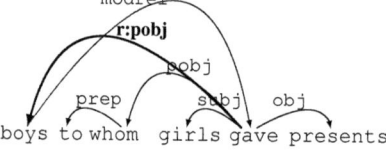

This method requires non-standard assumptions for stranded prepositions. The dependency is localized to the relativized matrix noun, which is in correspondence to our general treatment of prepositions as a marker-type dependent of the noun. A post-processing step, similar to the one used for control structures, delivers the dependency between the verb and the preposition. In practice, stranded prepositions are thus treated as if they were a long-distance dependency of the second class of the classes introduced in section 6.4.

(62) *boys who girls gave presents to*

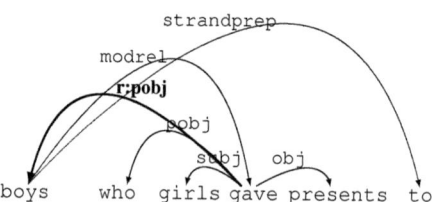

6.3. A Quantitative Analysis of Types of Empty Nodes

Relative clauses with stranded prepositions appear frequently as zero-relative clauses (row 9 of table 6.2).

(63) *boys 0 girls gave presents to*

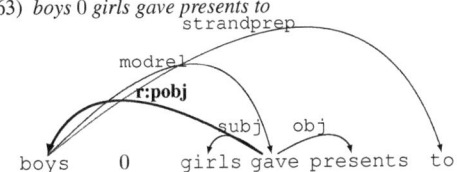

Relative clauses, like WH-questions, can be embedded, as illustrated in sentences 64 and 65.

(64) William got a present$_1$ [to which Peter believes [I will contribute $\_1$]]

(65) William got a present$_1$ [Peter believes [I will contribute to $\_1$]]

The output of Pro3Gres for these sentences is given in figures 6.10 and 6.11.

The recursive clauses of an embedded relative clause are traditionally assumed to be introduced by complementizers rather than relative pronouns. This assumption is supported by the semantic fact that, unlike in control structures, the relativized constituent does not act as an implicit argument of the verbs of the intervening clauses. A recursive version of the post-processing step for the resolution of relative clause anaphora has been implemented. Because the relativized constituent does not act as an implicit argument of the verbs of the intervening clauses, this version of the post-processing step traverses embedded relative clauses without leaving coreferences in the intervening relative clauses. This is different from the post-processing of raising and control, where a coreference is introduced in every subordinate clause, and where an explicit recursive call is thus not necessary (it is not necessary since each of the newly introduced coreferences is again subject to post-processing).

As it is expected from a robust parser, also sentences exhibiting gradience and low acceptability are treated.

(66) ? William got a present$_1$ [I believe [which$_1$ suits Peter]]

(67) ? William got a present$_1$ [I believe [that Peter likes $\_1$]]

Figures 6.12 and 6.13 show the actual parser output for sentences 66 and 67. The analysis of sentence 67 is correct, but as needs to be expected when delivering input of low acceptability, the analysis of sentence 66 is debatable.

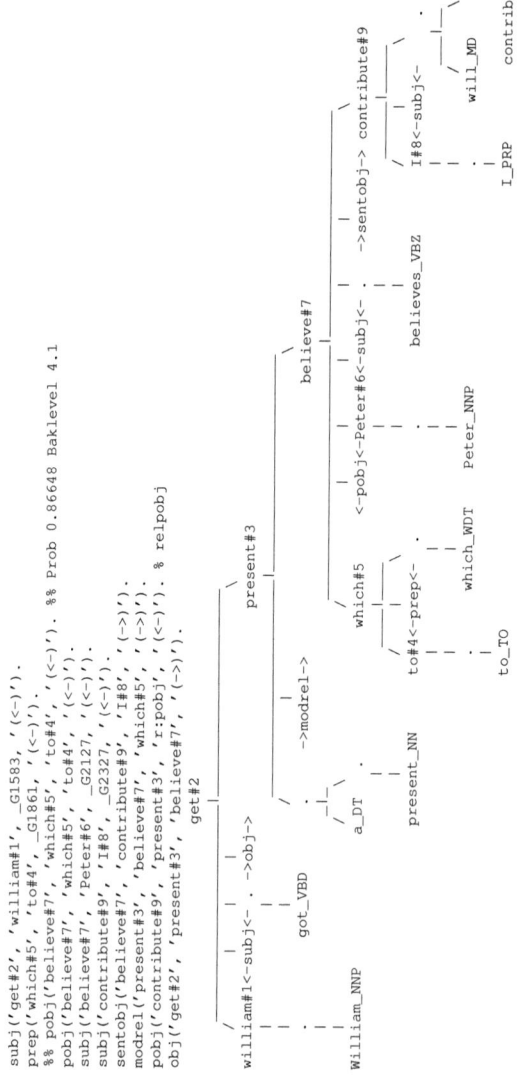

Figure 6.10: Actual parser output for example sentence *William got a present to which Peter believes I will contribute*

6.3. A Quantitative Analysis of Types of Empty Nodes

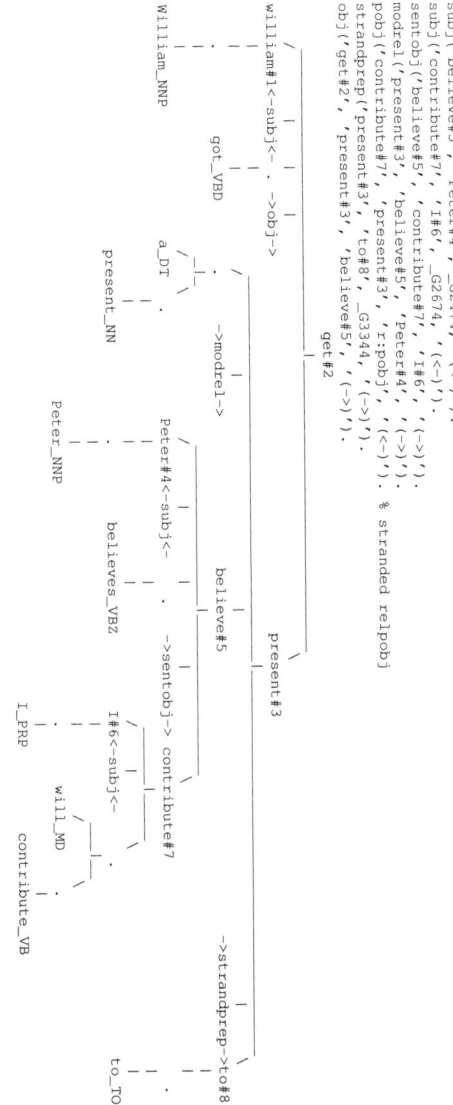

Figure 6.11: Actual parser output for example sentence *William got a present Peter believes I will contribute to*

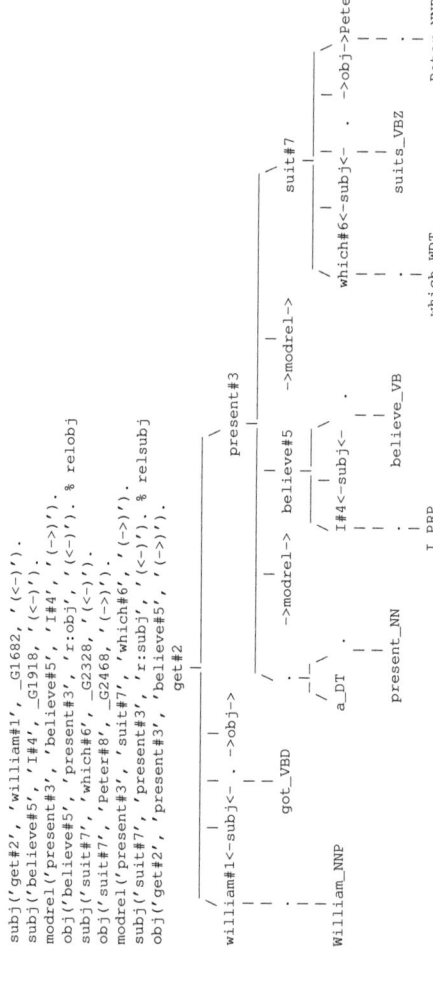

Figure 6.12: Actual parser output for example sentence *William got a present I believe which suits Peter*

6.3. A Quantitative Analysis of Types of Empty Nodes   146

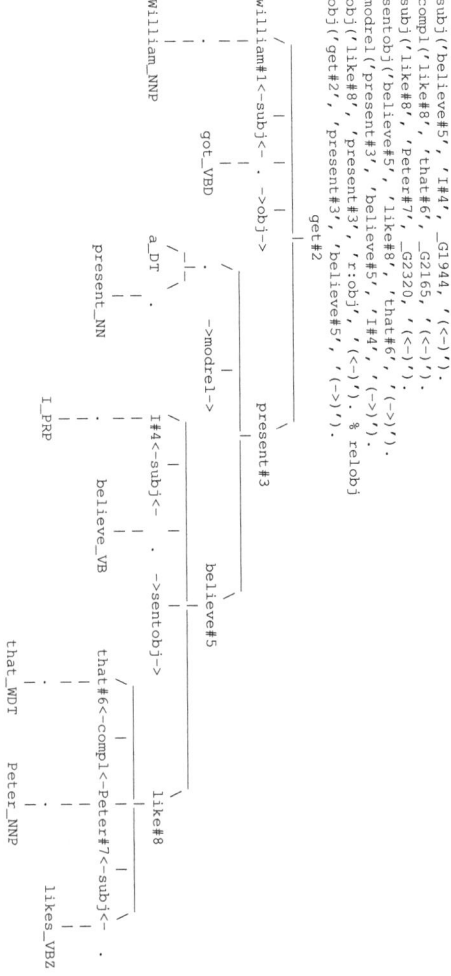

Figure 6.13: Actual parser output for example sentence *William got a present I believe that Peter likes*

Embedded WH-questions

A second nonlocal dependency that can stretch across embedded clauses is the dependency from a verb in a question to its WH pronoun. This type of dependency is fundamentally different in nature, from all dependencies we have discussed so far. While so far all dependents appeared in a canonical "surface" syntactic position, including the relativized matrix noun in a relative construction, the WH-question pronoun does not.

(68) William got a present$_1$ [Peter believes [I will contribute to $\_1$]]

(69) What$_1$ do you think [Peter believes [I will contribute to $\_1$]] ?

In example 68, *present* is a canonical argument of *get*, but in example 69, *what* is not an argument of *think*. *What* refers to *a present*, but the answer to a question *What do you think?* can hardly be *present* since this would lead to a selectional restriction violation. The object of *what* is an epistemological fact, in example 69 the entire subordinated clause that depends on *think*.

The fact that WH-pronouns in embedded clauses are not arguments to the matrix verb entails that while context-free parsing suffices to analyse the canonical position of the matrix noun in a relative construction, and the successive post-processing does not need to revise context-free parsing decisions, such a pipeline approach has to fail on WH-questions. Unlike all other non-local relations we have discussed so far, they warrant a treatment as really unbounded dependencies. We discuss our treatment in the following section: a Tree-Adjoining Grammar (TAG) approach leading to mild context-sensitivity is investigated and a DG version of it is implemented.

6.4 A Qualitative Analysis of Types of Empty Nodes

Long-distance dependencies are traditionally grouped into two classes. In the first class, there is an overt constituent in a nonargument position that can be thought of as strongly associated with (or filling) the gap or trace. As the type of movement associated with this class is to a non-argument position it is called $\bar{A}$-movement (Chomsky, 1981). In this class we find topicalisations, WH-questions, WH-relative clauses and pseudo-cleft constructions. Pollard and Sag (1994, p. 157) give the following examples:

(70) Kim$_1$, Sandy loves$\_1$. (topicalization)

(71) I wonder [who$_1$ Sandy loves$_{-1}$] . (*wh*-question)

(72) This is the politician [who$_1$ Sandy loves$_{-1}$]. (*wh*-relative clause)

(73) It's Kim [who$_1$ Sandy loves$_{-1}$]. (*it*-cleft)

(74) [What$_1$ Kim loves$_{-1}$] is Sandy. (pseudocleft)

An additional important construction of this class is the use of support verbs in questions:

(75) Does$_1$ Sandy $_{-1}$ love Kim? (fronted auxiliary verb)

In the second class, there is no overt filler in a nonargument position, instead there is a constituent in an argument position that is interpreted as coreferential with the trace. As the type of movement associated with this class is to an argument position, it is called A-movement (Chomsky, 1981). In the second class, we find control and raising (e.g. purpose infinitive or tough movement), relative clause and it-cleft constructions. Pollard and Sag (1994, p. 157) give the following examples:

(76) I bought it$_1$ for Sandy [to eat $_{-1}$]. (purpose infinitive)

(77) Sandy$_1$ is hard [to love $_{-1}$]. (*tough* 'movement')

(78) This is the politician [Sandy loves $_{-1}$]. (relative clause)

(79) It's Kim$_1$ [Sandy loves $_{-1}$]. (*it* cleft)

In the first class (examples 70 to 75), the coreference is local inside a single clause. If we can define an extended notion of locality in which locality means local inside the clause, this class may only have context-free complexity despite its long-distance character. In DG, locality naturally extends to the clause level. Let us illustrate this point with two examples. First, in a grammar representation where both inner and outer arguments depend on the verb, topicalized constituents and support verbs – in fact all clause-internal constituents – are available locally to the main verb. Example 80 receives a context-free analysis.

(80) *Who did you see ?*

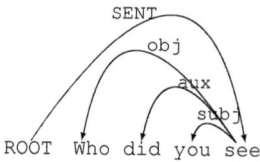

Second, in a grammar representation where immediate dominance and linear precedence are distinct (often called ID/LP grammars), structures involving non-canonical word order do not require us to resort to non-locality. The subject dependency is allowed to go the right in selected contexts, for example in questions involving verb-subject inversion, as in example 81.

(81) *Are you sure ?*

While extending locality to the clause level allows us to treat simple WH-non-subject questions, embedded WH-questions are not covered. Embedded WH-question are the only class 1 construction in which the dependency is not local to the clause.

In the second class, the coreference is not local to one clause, but the overt constituent in the matrix clause appears in an argument position. The coreference is between two subjacent clauses in the above examples, but it can also stretch across several subclauses.

(82) Sandy$_1$ is believed [$\_1$ to be hard [to love $\_1$]].

If the coreferenced constituent can be said to appear covertly in each of the intervening clauses, then the movement is cyclic, it can be modelled step by step from clause to clause, from argument position to argument position.

In our quantitative analysis of the Penn Treebank in section 6.3, we have seen five types of English long-distance dependencies that are not local to their clause: (1) indexed gerunds (see 6.3.2), (2) control structures including raising (see 6.3.3), (3) relative clauses (see 6.3.4), (4) stranded prepositions (see 6.3.4), and (5) WH-question dependencies (see 6.3.4). If all these long-distance dependencies were cyclic, then context-free parsing would be sufficient, because the coreference of the argument position can be resolved at the post-processing stage.

Indexed gerunds are a special case: theoretically, they can be treated with a pronoun resolution approach. We believe that they are rather semantic than syntactic in nature. We leave them underspecified and will not discuss them further. Control structures are cyclic, the movement proceeds from clause to clause across argument positions. Relative clauses are not cyclic, because the relativized noun does not necessarily appear in argument positions in intervening clauses. Since the overt appearance of the relativized noun is in argument position, however, context-free parsing followed by a recursive post-processing module which does not leave traces in the intervening clauses is sufficient. We have presented our recursive treatment of relative clauses and of stranded prepositions in section 6.3.4. We have discussed that WH-question dependencies are the only long-distance dependency that belongs to the first class and that is not local to one clause. Long-distance dependencies of the first class are characterised by the fact that the overt appearance of the moved constituent is in a non-argument position. While extending locality to the clause allows us to use a context-free approach by underspecifying the distinction between the overt, non-argument position appearance and the covert argument appearance if they both are in the same clause, this approach has to fail for embedded WH-questions, because they are not in the same clause. A different, context-sensitive, approach is thus needed. Either we selectively and carefully extend locality further than to the clause, or we resort to the classical context-sensitive treatment of long-distance dependency as filler-gap constructions for this case, attaching the overt non-argument dependent with a purely syntactic, non-functional label which is accessible from all subordinate clauses.

The first option would mean that WH-question pronouns can directly access a large context, up to the entire sentence. The second option could follow classical approaches to treating long-distance dependencies as gap-filler constructions. From a GPSG perspective, a gap feature is shared across all intervening clauses. From a GB perspective, the WH-constituent moves to the CP-specifier position, which typically serves as an 'escape hatch' through which the WH-constituent can cyclically move up, clause by clause until it reaches its overt non-argument CP-specifier position. Option 2 would require syntactically empty nodes and non-functional, purely syntactic dependency relations for attaching the overt non-argument WH-constituent. Both are undesirable in a deep-syntactic, functional representation which should maximally abstract away from surface configurations and directly express grammatical roles, as functional DG aims to deliver. Since we use a monostratal grammar theory, there is no classical movement operation available. Instead we need to allow some form of context-sensitivity, allowing dependencies to cross (which is also referred to as *non-projectivity*). Complete non-projectivity leads to NP-complete parsing complexity (Neuhaus and Bröker, 1997). Non-projectivity needs to be severely constrained. Nivre (2006a) has shown that also for a practical parser restricting non-projectivity leads to shorter parsing times.

In his parser, the number of edges constructed with unrestricted projectivity is about quadratic to the number of words per sentence, when allowing maximally two non-projective dependencies per sentence it is almost linear.

Tree-Adjoining Grammar (TAG) follows the first option. TAG extends locality beyond the clause under clearly defined conditions, it does not use movement between clauses, and it maximally restricts non-projectivity while staying expressive enough to treat natural language phenomena, particularly embedded WH-questions. This approach is mildly context-sensitive (Joshi, 1985). It has been argued that mild context-sensitivity is expressive enough for natural language processing (Frank, 2002). Kuhlmann and Nivre (2006) have investigated naturally occurring context-sensitivity in two corpora in dependency format (the Danish Dependency Bank and the Prague Dependency Bank). They confirm that context-senstivity constraints of the class that TAG belongs to has almost complete coverage, 99.89 %, on these two Treebanks, and that the remaining uncovered data is partly due to the properties of the annotation scheme. They conclude that TAG mild context-sensitivity is a very attractive extension of projectivity.

6.4.1 Tree-Adjoining Grammar

The TAG formalism (Joshi, 1985; Joshi and Kroch, 1985) has developed a mathematically restrictive formulation of phrase structure grammar. In contrast to the string-rewriting systems of the Chomsky hierarchy, TAG is a system of tree-rewriting. Structural representations are built up from pieces of phrase structure, so-called *elementary trees*, which are taken as atomic. These trees can be combined by using one of two operations: *Substitution* and *Adjoining*.

Substitution involves the rewriting of a non-terminal node at the frontier of one elementary tree as another elementary tree with the requirement that the rewritten node must have the same label as the root of the elementary tree that rewrites it. Substitution can be understood as a traditional rewriting operation. Substitution accomplishes effects similar to those of the Merge operation (Chomsky, 1995): it inserts XPs into the argument positions of syntactic predicates. Crucially, it is a context-free operation: context-free elementary trees combined by substitution only yield context-free structures. An example of Substitution is given in fig. 6.14. Elementary trees are context-free by definition. "Every syntactic dependency is expressed locally within a single elementary tree" (Frank, 2002, p. 22)

The Adjoining operation rewrites a non-terminal node anywhere within an elementary tree as another elementary tree. Unlike substitution, which rewrites or expands trees only along the frontier, Adjoining uses a special class of recursive

6.4. A Qualitative Analysis of Types of Empty Nodes

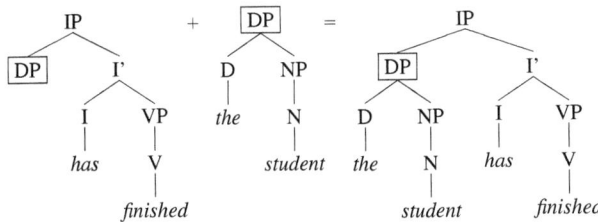

Figure 6.14: An example of the Substitution operation. The rewritten node is boxed.

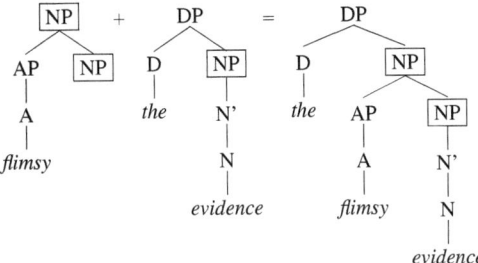

Figure 6.15: An example of the Adjoining operation. The foot node is boxed.

trees, so-called *auxiliary trees*. The root of an auxiliary tree is labelled identically to some node along its frontier, the *foot node*. Given an auxiliary tree A with foot node X, Adjoining rewrites as A a node N that is labelled as X in an elementary tree T, and attaches the node that was under N in T at the foot node of the auxiliary tree. Adjoining thus works by rewriting some node of an elementary tree as a recursive piece of structure (the auxiliary tree). An example is seen in figure 6.15. Trees that have undergone Adjoining can be subject to subsequent Adjoining operations, such as in 6.16.

6.4.2 TAG Adjoining and mild context-sensitivity

We will now describe how TAG Adjoining can be a context-sensitive operation.

The Adjoining operation can be used for Chomsky adjunction. In this case, the root node immediately dominates the foot node, as in 6.15 and 6.16.

6.4. A Qualitative Analysis of Types of Empty Nodes

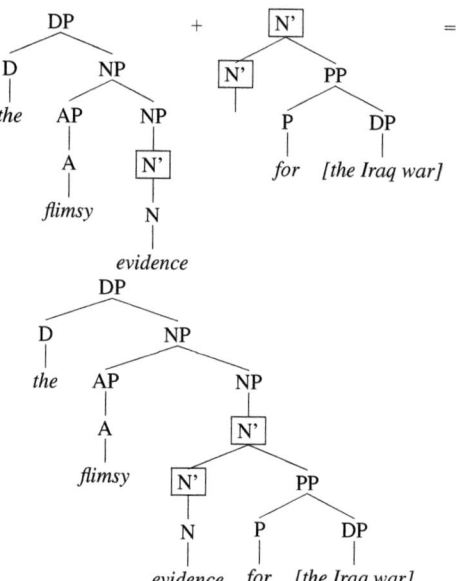

Figure 6.16: An example of the Adjoining operation. The foot node is boxed.

6.4. A Qualitative Analysis of Types of Empty Nodes

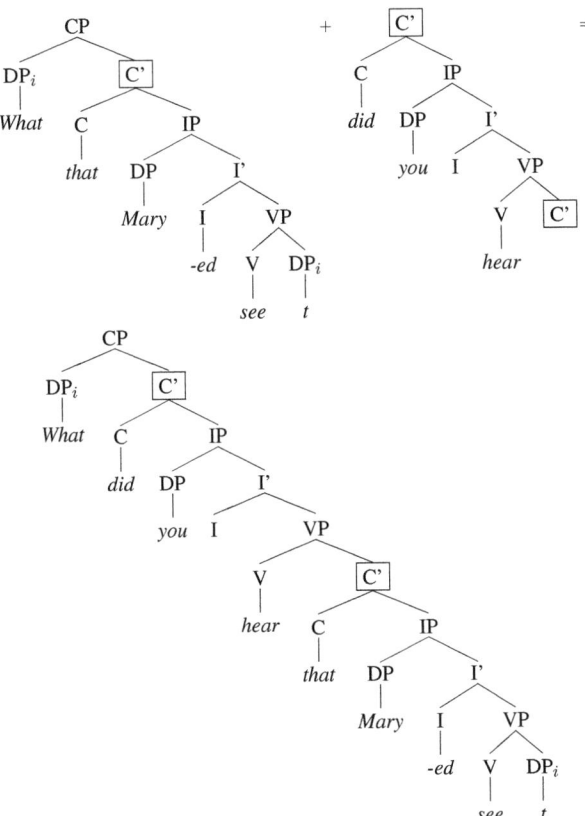

Figure 6.17: Adjoining for WH-questions. The deep recursion of the auxiliary trees introduces mild context-sensitivity. The foot node is boxed.

But TAG also allows the use of auxiliary trees in which the root node does not immediately dominate the foot node, where a number of nodes intervene between the root node and the foot node, in other words : the recursion stretches across several nodes. In this case, auxiliary trees that contain terminal nodes can be inserted into elementary trees and thus stretch out local dependencies. Question 83, analysed in fig. 6.17, provides an example.

(83) What did you hear that Mary saw ?

TAG treats this sentence as follows: First, the dependency between the WH-element and its base position is established locally, within a single elementary tree, according to TAG principles. The effect of dislocating the WH-element into a higher clause is accomplished by means of Adjoining in fig. 6.17. Further embedding of instances can be derived analogously by further Adjoining operations.

Such stretching by Adjoining with recursive auxiliary trees is the one and only way in which context-sensitive constructions can be generated in TAG. This fact is known as the nonlocal dependency corollary: "Nonlocal dependencies always reduce to local ones once recursive structure is factored out." (Frank, 2002, p. 27). Research in TAG argues that the severely restricted type of context-sensitivity generated by Adjoining, so-called *mild context-sensitivity*, accurately characterises the non-locality present in natural language (Frank, 2002).

6.4.3 The Nature of Elementary and Auxiliary Trees

While the basic operations over elementary and auxiliary trees have been outlined now, nothing has been said about the nature of these trees. We will follow Frank (2004) and "assume that elementary trees are built around a single lexical element, that is, a semantically contentful word like a noun, verb or adjective" (Frank, 2004, p. 11).

This means that elementary trees are similar to DG nuclei or chunks (if we allowed attributive adjectives to be part of elementary trees). Elementary trees are assumed to provide argument slots and are closely related to predicate-argument structure:

> *A great deal of work in syntactic theory has assigned a privileged status to the syntactic analogue of predicate argument structure. Such a domain, which we call a thematic domain, consists of a single lexical predicate along with the structural context in which it takes its arguments. This notion takes a variety of forms and names, but the*

6.4. A Qualitative Analysis of Types of Empty Nodes

> *same idea seems to underlie kernel sentences in Harris (1957) and Chomsky (1955; Chomsky (1957), cyclic domains in Chomsky (1965), strata in Relational Grammar (Perlmutter, 1983), F-structure nuclei in LFG (Bresnan, 1982) and governing categories in Government-Binding Theory (Chomsky, 1981).*
>
> (Frank, 2002, p. 38)

DG parses directly for a predicate argument structure and DG structures have been described as the F-structure part of LFG (Bröker, Hahn, and Schacht, 1994). DG and TAG thus take a very similar stance on the inherent aims and structures of syntactic theory. Following work by Grimshaw (1991), elementary trees are assumed to include extended projections (Frank, 2002, p. 43).

Auxiliary trees are defined as elementary trees that show the recursive characteristics described. TAG uses transformations to generate elementary trees. Grimshaw (1991) and Frank (2002) discuss that in head movement the base position and the ultimate landing site lie within a single extended projection. This entails that head-movement generally is not unbounded, but local to a clause. We have shown in subsection 6.2 how finite-state patterns can be used to cover most head-movements in English. This approach obviates the need for using costly transformations for creating elementary trees. If every elementary tree can be mapped to a dedicated dependency label then they are equivalent. Therefore, many dependencies (for example head-movement) that stretch across more than one mother-daughter node relation and are thus non-local for PSG remain local in TAG, as they only involve a single elementary tree. The extended projections of a TAG elementary tree (Grimshaw, 1991) are also called *extended domain of locality* (Carroll et al., 1999).

6.4.4 Sketching TAG Adjoining in DG

In the following, we illustrate how TAG Adjoining can be implemented in DG. We do not provide a formal proof of our method nor claim that our method and TAG adjoining are always equivalent in arbitrarily complex cases. We evaluate the usefulness and coverage of this approach experimentally in chapter 7 below.

DG shares important characteristics of extended domain of locality with TAG. All arguments and verbal modifiers of a clause are available locally to the verb. We will first show that the foot node corresponds to a DG verbal projection. Then we discuss that the foot node is the pre-maximal projection in which a WH-element is

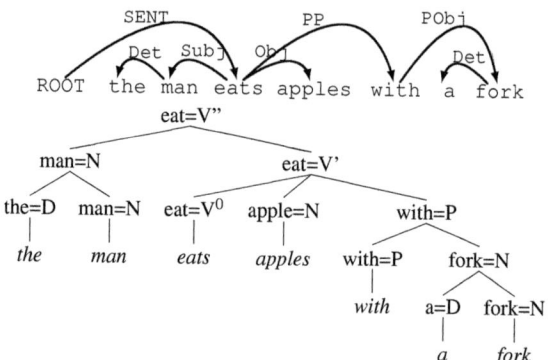

Figure 6.18: An unlabelled DG representation and its X-bar equivalents

not attached. Finally we show how the Adjoning operation can be implemented in DG.

We have discussed in chapter 3 that in LFG F-structure, HPSG and our Functional DG, where functional projections are dependents of the content-word head (HPSG calls this type of dependent markers), the elementary tree of a content word and its maximal projection coincide. All bar-levels are isomorphic to the head word W in DG (Schneider, 1998; Miller, 2000)[3]. The suggested algorithm to convert between DG and X-bar described in Covington (1994), is illustrated again in figure 6.18, where X^0 equates to a word without dependents, X' to a word with a subclass of dependents, and X'' to a word with all its dependents attached.

Let us annotate a TAG elementary tree with the same algorithm. The resulting structure is given in fig. 6.19.

Since functional words are attached as markers, all DG equivalents of functional projections (the combination of a content word and a function word) are governed by the content word. As figure 6.19 illustrates, all mother nodes of the main verb are governed by the main verb within the same clause – they are all ver-

---

[3]The important difference between different bar-levels is that they have attached a smaller or larger number of dependents. Different projections of a content word can be seen as different stages of derivation, with more or less dependents already attached in the parsing process. A possible conversion from DG to X-bar for example distinguishes between a projection or derivation state of V with all dependents except subject attached (V', internal arguments), and a projection or derivation state of V with all dependents attached (V", including the external argument).

6.4. A Qualitative Analysis of Types of Empty Nodes

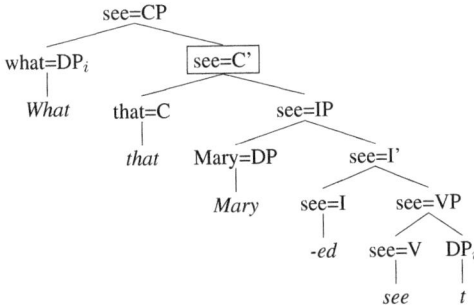

Figure 6.19: An unlabelled DG representation and its TAG equivalents. The foot node is boxed.

bal projections. The only possible foot node in DG is therefore a projection of the content word.

Adjoining inserts a recursive structure at some projection of the content word which is called the foot node. Adjoining inserts new governors into an existing structure and thus breaks up the context-freeness. In a nutshell, the DG difference between Substitution and Adjoining is: Substitution inserts dependents, Adjoining inserts governors.

In DG, Adjoining inserts an auxiliary tree into a partial projection of a content word. From a process-oriented perspective, partial projections correspond to a stage of derivation where only a subset of all dependents have been attached to a governor. Adjoining to maximal projections (in which all dependents are attached) is pointless, because then Adjoining A to B is equivalent to Substituting B to A. The auxiliary tree is inserted at a derivation stage in which not all dependents have been attached. In particular, a partial projection in which the CP-specifier (the position that traditionally serves as an 'escape hatch' for constituents to move up) is not yet attached, corresponds to C', the foot node.

While in the example of 6.18 derivation order coincides with the internal/external argument ordering, that is not the case when WH-question arguments are attached. Consider what would happen if a standard CYK algorithm is employed for the sentence in 84.

(84) *Who did you see ?*

The subject (external argument) is attached before the object (internal argu-

6.4. A Qualitative Analysis of Types of Empty Nodes

ment, moved to CP-Spec), as can also be seen in fig. 6.19. At the stage where all dependents except for the object are attached, Adjoining can occur.

84 *Who did you see ?*

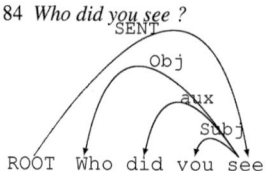

The Adjoining operation can be described in Functional DG as the following example shows.

(85) *Who did you say that Mary saw ?*

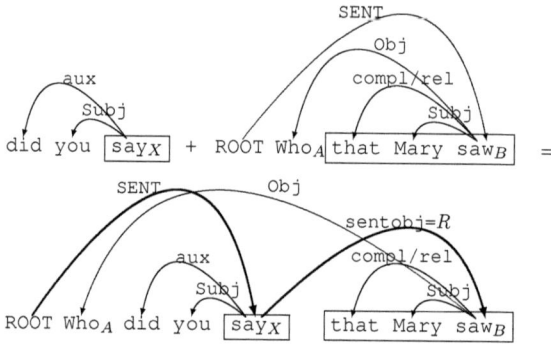

Given a local dependency (of a type falling inside a TAG elementary tree, hence non-clausal) from a main verb B to dependent A in the elementary tree, if there is a maximal projection equivalent to a TAG auxiliary tree X, and if the grammar licences a dependency both from X to A and also from X to B such that

1. the relation type R from X to B is across elementary trees, hence expressing a subclause relation,

2. the governor of B is also licensed of be governor of X, and has the same relation type

then the auxiliary tree X can adjoin to the elementary tree formed by A and B. Adjoining inserts X between A and B, thus stretching the dependency from B to

A, by (1.) constructing a relation R from X to B, and by (2.) making the governor of B become the governor of X. As a result, the Adjoining operation attaches A to the subordinate verb B instead of to the local verb X. It can also be seen as an operation that delegates a WH-pronoun to a lower clausal level, similar to Nivre and Nilsson (2005).

Unlike in TAG, also the equivalent of elementary trees are constructed without transformations in DG. The verb has local access to the fronted object in the elementary tree, i.e. in a non-embedded WH-question, like in LFG F-structure, where all arguments appear flat under the verb predicate.

6.4.5 An Implementation at the Functional Level

An important theoretical consideration should be made first. In GB theory, the internal argument explicitly moves to the non-argument CP-Spec position, and is thus attached farther (procedurally speaking later). In our illustration above, we exploit the coincidental fact that the WH-object in its non-canonical position is attached farther (procedurally later) due to its position. This may appear as a confusion of design and coincidence, and of grammar formalism and parsing algorithm. The DG grammar formalism per se leaves the procedural order of attachment and formal grammar bar-level ordering completely underspecified (see chapter 3). We may attach WH-pronouns at any time during the parsing process, as long as we recognise them, and as long as the WH-pronoun and its governor are accessible. After a subordinate clause has been attached to the matrix clause, the subordinate clause is no longer accessible. There is one obvious moment when all phrase-level constituents are accessible: before parsing starts all chunks form a flat sequence of minimal constituents. At this moment our implementation temporarily suspends the adjacency constraint (which normally ensures that only adjacent phrases can be combined), allowing sentence-initial WH-pronouns to attach to any verb[4].

In non-subject WH-questions, the WH-pronoun appears at the front of the sentence rather than in its usual post-verbal position. The first implemented approach is based on pre-parsing: In WH-question sentences, before the main parsing is started, the WH-pronoun pre-parses as subject, object, adjunct, or PP-attachment with each verb, and as complement with each stranded preposition (which will modify a verb or a noun).

---

[4]This pre-parsing approximation to Adjoining cannot always guarantee that only mildly context-sensitive structures are generated. Also, island constraints are not checked. The latter restriction is defended in section 6.4.8

6.4.6 Ambiguous WH-attachment

The attachment of the WH-pronoun is sometimes ambiguous, since it can be be unclear from which clause the WH-pronoun originates. Compare the following examples.

(86) What$_1$ do you think (that) Peter believes I contribute to t_1 ?

(87) ? What$_1$ do you eat (that) Peter believes I contribute to t_1 ?
? What$_1$ do you eat t_1 (that) Peter believes I contribute to ?

Example 86 has a matrix clause verb *think* that prefers a sentential complement over an NP object complement. Example 87, in contrast, has a matrix clause verb *eat* that prefers an NP object complement over a sentential complement and seems infelicitous. The empirical question [1] has to arise whether sentences like 87 are really much less frequent than sentences like 86, which would support our assumption that 87 is infelicitous. If the answer is positive then we can restrict the movement to a closed class of verbs that licence movement.

The matrix verb seems to play an important role for the decision whether the WH-pronoun attaches locally to the matrix clause or originates from a subordinate clause, but there may be other factors. Consider the following sentences:

(88) What$_1$ did you say that Mary eats t_1 ?

(89) Why$_1$ did you say t_1 that Mary eats ?

Example 89 has a WH-pronoun that typically refers to an adjunct. Already Ross (1967) observed that extraction from inside adjuncts is impossible and formulated the adjunct island constraint.

(90) *Who$_1$ did John fire Bill [after he met t_1] ?

Huang (1982) describes that extraction of adjuncts out of a WH-island is usually impossible.

(91) *How$_2$ do you wonder [which problem$_1$ John could solve t_1] t_2

But extraction of adjuncts is in general thought to be possible, although adjuncts are less easily extractable than objects (Ouhalla, 1999, 269) One may be tempted to think that WH-pronouns referring to adjuncts usually do not move, since adjuncts can attach to every verb; no subcategorisation errors or selectional restriction violations would occur that trigger human parsers to expect the WH-pronoun to originate from a subclause. The empirical question [2] has to arise whether in examples like 91 there are really much fewer cases in which the adjunct originates from a subordinate clause. If the answer is positive then we can exclude adjunct WH-pronouns *why*, *where*, *when* from licencing movement in a robust parser.

There is ample theoretical linguistics literature based on introspection to answer both questions [1] and [2]. A simple answer to [1] is that *think* does not have the right subcategorisation frame. A possible answer to [2] is that extraction of adjuncts is in general thought to be possible, although adjuncts are less easily extractable than objects (Ouhalla, 1999, 269). Since introspection can on the one hand lead to the invention of complex grammatical examples that people never produce, and on the other hand important examples may be forgotten, the use of a corpus linguistics approach in complementation to a theoretical linguistics approach is recommendable, supplementing psycholinguistic research with empirical data. The scientific methodology of descriptive linguistics based on corpora is a key component for an empirical science approach to linguistics.

A corpus-based survey of ambiguous WH-pronoun attachment

We answer the two questions raised with a corpus-based approach and compare our results to rationalist approaches.

Since the Penn Treebank does not have many questions, we needed to use a bigger corpus, the British National Corpus, henceforth BNC (Aston and Burnard, 1998). We have searched the BNC using BNCWeb CQP (Evert and Hoffmann, 2006) with two word-tag pair queries. The two queries are 6 resp. 7 words long. They are identical except for the presence versus absence of a complementizer Word 1 is the WH-pronoun. Word 2 is the auxiliary verb (although auxiliary status is not enforced). Word 3 is the pronoun *you*. Word 4 is the main matrix verb. Word 5 is a complementizer in the first query. The last two words are the subject and the main verb of the subordinate clause. The subordinate clause subject was restricted to be a pronoun in order to exclude some mismatches in which the *that* was a determiner.

The first query delivers 28 matches. The second query delivers 862 matches. This reveals that the version with a non-zero complementizer is marginal.

We have manually checked the 28 matches of the first query. 8 were accidental hits, mostly involving a causative verb at word 2. The remaining 20 matches are few to answer questions [1] and [2]. 10 matches have the argument WH-pronoun *what*, 8 have the adjunct WH-pronoun *why*, 2 have the adjunct WH-pronoun *when*. Of the 10 argument WH-pronouns *what*, 6 attach in the matrix clause (5 of which involve relativisation, e.g. *So what have you got that I've not seen ?* (CE0 573)), 4 originate from subordinate clauses. There is a strong tendency to allow movement for argument WH-pronouns. Of the 10 adjunct WH-pronouns *why, when*, 9 attach in the matrix clause, only 1 probably originates from a subordinate clause.

(92) Why do you think that he said said to court he was gon na go for? (JNT 61)

Still, there is a strong tendency to block movement for adjunct WH-pronouns. These findings seem to answer question [2] positively, but data is sparse. As for question [1], in all cases where the main matrix verb is *think*, *say*, or *suggest*, the WH-pronoun originates from a subordinate clause, and otherwise not. This seems to answer question [1] positively, but data is sparse.

We have manually checked a 50 item random sample of the 862 matches of the second query. There are 5 accidental hits, mostly involving a causative verb at word 2. 24 matches have the argument WH-pronoun *what*, 5 matches have the argument WH-pronoun *who*, 8 have the adjunct WH-pronoun *when*, 5 have the adjunct WH-pronoun *why*, 2 have the adjunct WH-pronoun *when*.

Addressing question [2], we were surprised to see that almost all matches, irrespective of whether they have an argument or adjunct WH-pronoun, originate from a subordinate clause. There is only one match where attachment in the matrix clause is semantically possible.

(93) "Well," I said, "I thought you were in the Mafia, but it's not much of a Mafia name." *"Why do you think I was* in the Mafia?" "Because you're a landlord, I suppose," I said, ...(FRH 2018-2020)

The evidence suggests that question [2] needs to be answered negatively when a zero-complementizer is used. Zero-complementizers are a stronger indicator of movement than the question whether a WH-pronoun refers to an argument or adjunct. There is a significant semantic difference between a complementizer and a zero-complementizer.

As far as the extraction of subjects is concerned, it is well known in theoretical linguistics that subjects, unlike objects, cannot be extracted if the subordinate clause has an overt complementizer, the so-called *that*-trace effect.

(94) Who$_1$ did you think t_1 would fix the car ?

6.4. A Qualitative Analysis of Types of Empty Nodes

(95) *Who$_1$ did you think that t_1 would fix the car ?

(96) What$_1$ did you think John would fix _1 ?

(97) What$_1$ did you think that John would fix t_1 ?

This subject-object asymmetry led to a reformulation of the Empty Category Principle (ECP) in GB. ECP states that non-pronominal empty categories need to be governed. It is based on the observation that objects of verbs are governed by a lexical category, while subjects of finite clauses are governed by the non-lexical category I. Subsequently, lexical government is assumed to be a stronger form of government, so-called proper government[5]. The ECP is then reformulated to state that non-pronominal empty categories need to be properly governed.

But extraction of adjuncts is thought to be insensitive to the presence or absence of a complementizer. It is admitted that adjuncts are generally less easily extractable than objects (Huang, 1982), but it is generally assumed that adjunct-extraction differs from subject-extraction, with only the latter being sensitive to the presence or absence of the complementizer (Rizzi, 1995, 46), (Ouhalla, 1999, 269). Our small corpus investigation reveals that although adjuncts may theoretically pattern like objects, in practice they usually pattern like subjects: empirically, most WH- adjuncts with a zero complementizer subclause have moved, most WH- adjuncts with a non-zero complementizer subclause have not moved. In practice, non-zero complementizers typically block WH-movement. This object-adjunct asymmetry cannot be explained in terms of proper government.

Turning to question [1], a small number of matrix verbs, mostly epistemic verbs, especially *think* dominate the matches. Over the 862 matches, we find 619 think, 59 say, 52 mean, 32 know, 17 suggest, 16 suppose, 16 imagine, 15 reckon, 15 let, 10 have, 10 feel. Other types occur less than 10 times.

This supports our assumption that a sentence like 99 may be infelicitous – although to draw a reliable correlation from rareness to infelicity would be difficult.

(98) What$_1$ do you think (that) Peter believes I contribute to t_1 ?

(99) ? What$_1$ do you eat (that) Peter believes I contribute to t_1 ?
    ? What$_1$ do you eat t_1 (that) Peter believes I contribute to ?

---
[5]Proper government also includes antecedent-government

6.4. A Qualitative Analysis of Types of Empty Nodes

Before we describe the implementation, let us summarise our findings. We have seen that embedded WH-questions with a non-zero complementizer are very rare. This has no direct impact on our implementation. We have seen that with regard to question [1] our assumption holds: a very small group of matrix verbs occurs, dominated by *think*. We conclude that restricting movement to a closed class of matrix verbs, epistemic verbs, is a good approximation to real-world occurrences. We call these verbs licensing verbs. With regard to question [2], we have seen that in non-zero complementizer cases, our assumption also holds: adjunct WH-pronouns seem to block movement. Then we have discovered that zero-complementizers show a different behaviour: almost all adjunct WH-pronouns have moved, i.e. originate from a subordinate clause.

Now we describe our implementation. We have considered the answer to question [1] by restricting our algorithm to allowing movements to stretch only across clauses whose main verb has more clausal complements than NP object complements in the Penn Treebank. Figures 6.20 and 6.21 show the actual parser output for sentences 98 and 99.

As a consequence of the answer to question [2], we have extended our algorithm to block movement of an adjunct WH-pronoun across a complementizer.

(100) Why$_1$ do you think t_1 that Peter believes ?

(101) Why$_1$ do you think Peter believes t_1 ?

Figures 6.22 and 6.23 show the actual parser output for sentences 100 and 101.

We have said that our first implemented approach was based on pre-parsing: In WH-question sentences, before the main parsing is started, the WH-pronoun pre-parses as subject, object, adjunct, or PP-attachment with each verb, and as complement with each stranded preposition (which will modify a verb or a noun). Such an approach had the disadvantage that some necessary knowledge about the sentence structure is not available before the parsing starts. For example, non-licensing verbs may occur linearly but not structurally between licensing verbs and the attaching verb. For example, in *What do you think the car which stands in my garage may cost?* the verb the non-licencing verb *stand* would block the attachment of *what* to *cost*.

We have therefore made a second implementation in which in online version of the above pre-processor, a module similar to the recursive relative clause post-processor is used. At the moment where the WH-element and the matrix verb are reduced, it checks if the matrix verb has (possibly recursive) *sentobj* relations, whose head(s) fulfil the verb-chain requirement, i.e. whose verbs are all licensing.

6.4. A Qualitative Analysis of Types of Empty Nodes

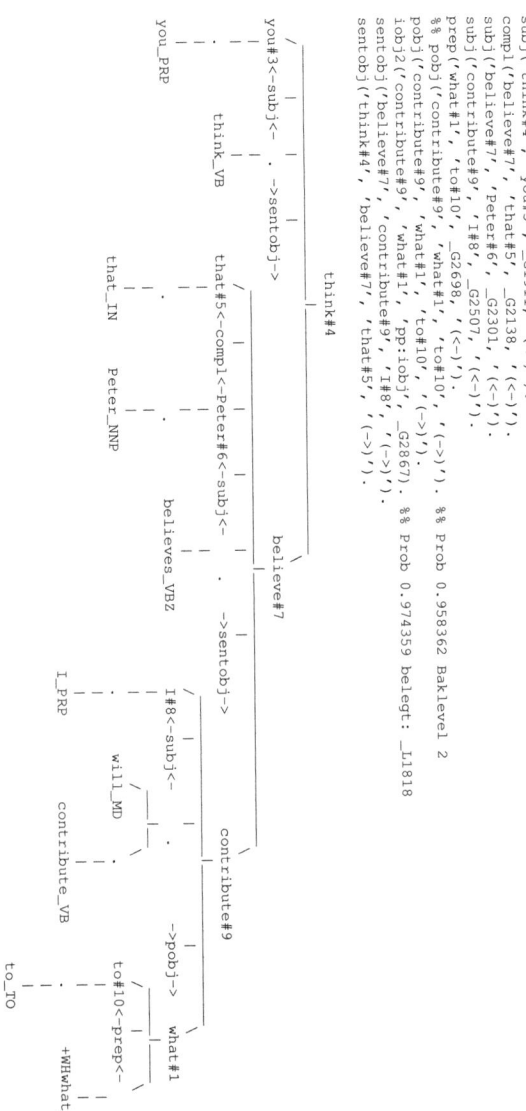

Figure 6.20: Actual parser output for example sentence *What do you think that Peter believes I will contribute to*

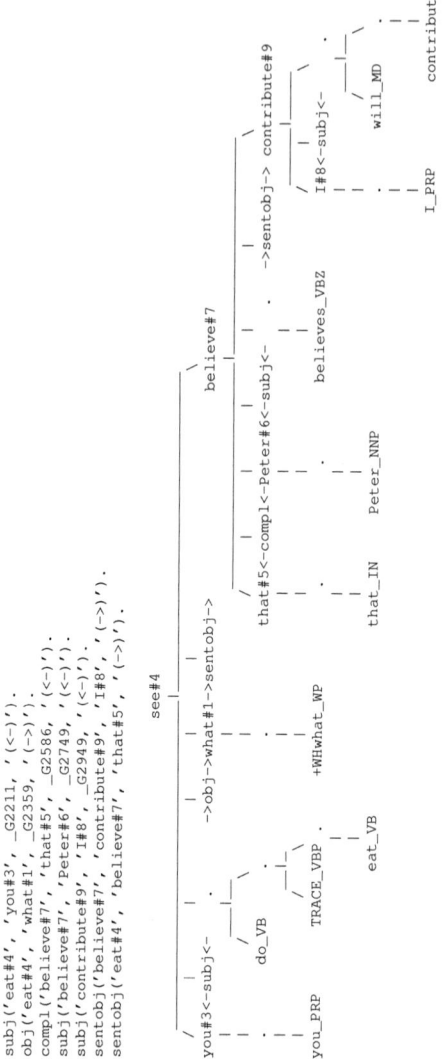

Figure 6.21: Actual parser output for example sentence *What do you eat that Peter believes I will contribute to*

6.4. A Qualitative Analysis of Types of Empty Nodes 168

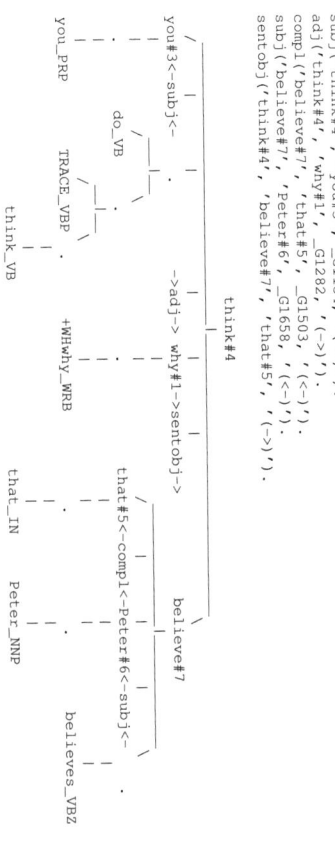

Figure 6.22: Actual parser output for example sentence *Why do you think that Peter believes*

6.4. A Qualitative Analysis of Types of Empty Nodes

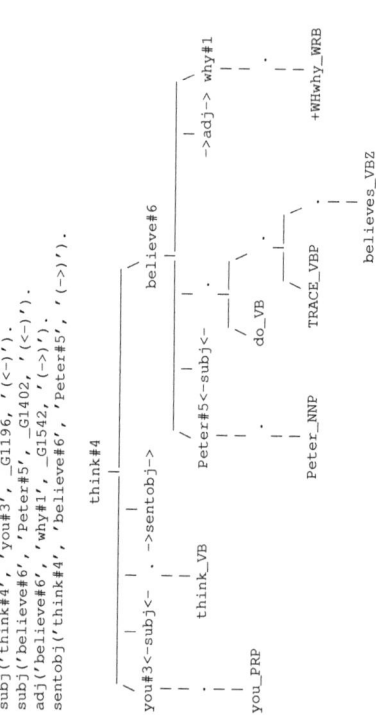

Figure 6.23: Actual parser output for example sentence *Why do you think Peter believes*

6.4.7 Subjacency and Barriers

A potential shortcoming of our approach is that barriers (Chomsky, 1986) are not checked. For example the Subjacency condition restricts how far one movement step across a clause level can go (Chomsky, 1981).

(102) Which book$_1$ did Ruth report [$\_1$ that Judith damaged $\_1$].

The Subjacency condition says that the locality of WH-movement is restricted to the number of certain types of nodes, so-called bounding nodes, that can be crossed. Traditionally, NP and IP are assumed to be bounding nodes [6]. Subjacency requires exactly one bounding node to intervene between each stepwise movement. This licenses 103 but not 104, in which two bounding nodes (an IP and an NP) intervene.

(103) Which book$_1$ did Ruth report [$\_1$ that [$_{IP}$ Judith damaged $\_1$]].

(104) *Which book$_1$ did Ruth believe [$_{NP}$ the report] [$\_1$ that [$_{IP}$ Judith damaged $\_1$]].

A robust system does not aim at deciding if given input is acceptable or not, but analyses naturally occurring text, which may also contain partly but not really completely unacceptable utterances. The purpose of Pro3Gres is the analysis of naturally occurring language, it is neither a language generator nor a grammar checker. Analysis of naturally occurring language requires disambiguation if several analyses are possible, as we have seen in the case of the attachment of the WH-pronoun. We have found out that the matrix verb and the presence or absence of a complementizer are major factors for the resolution of this ambiguity. We have implemented our findings. Checking for acceptability constraints such as barriers is largely an irrelevant task for a robust parser[7].

It is relevant, however, if such constraints disambiguate, as we have seen in 6.4.6. In WH-questions across several clauses, the WH-pronoun can attach to any potential verb governor. GB theory has developed the concept of Minimality, which is part of Barriers theory, to licence some structures and rule out others, and thereby disambiguates in situations where several governors are possible.

---

[6] Some cross-linguistic variation is assumed. Cinque (1990) argues that in Italian CP is a bounding node

[7] If desired, a post-processing module that traverses the syntactic tree, accepting or rejecting it if barrier violations are encountered, can be employed.

6.4.8 Minimality and Relativized Minimality

The concept of Minimality has been introduced by Chomsky (1986) and revised by Rizzi (1995). The Minimality condition is a locality constraint which specifies that a potential governor is ruled our from governing inside the domain of another governor. Informally speaking, in a configuration [XP ... X [YP ... Y ... ZP] ...] X is ruled out from governing ZP, because Y already governs ZP. It is a condition on chains.

We have discussed in section 3.1.2 that GB government and DG dependency are largely equivalent. Disambiguation between different possible governors thus seems a typical attachment and hence parsing problem. GB distinguishes between two kinds of government: head-government and antecedent-government. Head-government is similar to DG dependency, but what about antecedent-government?

Antecedent-government licences or rules out coreferences. From a DG perspective, antecedent-government is not a relation between a head and a dependent, but a relation between peers, between an overt and a covert dependent. Head-government and antecedent-government together form a triangular relation expressing long-distance dependencies by connecting a governor to its surface dependent via its deep dependent. We have seen that the large majority of long-distance dependencies can be underspecified and the relation from the governor to its surface dependent can be expressed directly if it is clause-internal or by post-processing if it crosses clause-boundaries. The one exception are WH-dependencies across clause boundaries, because the WH-element cannot attach in a functionally correct way in the matrix clause. Every such configuration is syntactically ambiguous, because the WH-pronoun could also attach to the matrix clause. In fact, if attachment to the matrix clause is plausible, human parsers will attach it there, choosing the most local plausible attachment. This is the central insight of Minimality and Relativized Minimality.

The difference between Minimality and Relativized Minimality is that Relativized Minimality distinguishes between the three types of movements: head movement, A movement and A-bar movement. Only intervening movements of the same type block antecedent government.

(105) How$_1$ do you expect [to solve the problem t_1?]

(106) *How$_1$ do you expect [which problem$_2$ [to solve t_2 t_1 ?]]

In 106 the intervening NP specifier, blocks *how* from antecedent-governing its trace, because a more local antecedent governor, *which problem* is available. This means that only a reading in which *how* is attached to the matrix verb *expect* can be licensed.

(107) *How$_1$ do you expect [which problem$_2$ [to solve t_2 t_1 ?]]

(108) How$_1$ do you expect [(that) [Peter solves the problem t_1 ?]]

The A movement of the subject from V-Specifier to I-Specifier does not affect antecedent-government of the trace. Minimality in its original formulation would not have licensed 108.

Let us now turn to the situation in our parser. We have seen that A movement can be treated with post-processing, because the surface position attaches to the local clause. Head movement is clause internal (see e.g. Frank (2002)). Disambiguation for these cases, if several readings are possible, is thus a context-free parsing problem, treated by the lexicalized disambiguation model. The only case that we explicitly disambiguate is the case where several A-bar movements are involved. In example 107 the intervening A-bar element blocks the pre-parsing step, an alternative reading in which *how* attaches to the matrix verb *expect* is attempted, which does not lead to a full analysis. In 108 pre-parsing successfully attaches the WH pronoun to the subordinate verb if no complementizer is present, and to the matrix verb if a complementizer is used.

6.5 TAG Adjoining and LFG

Tesnière (1959)'s original Dependency Grammar (DG) concept aims at being a proto-semantic, monostratal, Älanguage-independent theory rather than merely a syntactic theory[8]. In LFG terms, he always challenged the need for C-structure. His strategy is to parse surface text (*ordre linéaire*) directly to F-structure (*ordre structurale*) in which word order plays no primary role, but may of course help disambiguating in a secondary role, for example by preferring projectivity. Bröker, Hahn, and Schacht (1994) refers to DG as an LFG that only knows f-structure.

6.5.1 Functional Uncertainty

Functional uncertainty allows long-distance dependencies to extend across an unlimited, recursive path in LFG f-structures. Subordinate clauses appear as a COMP

---

[8] An extended version of the argument made in this subchapter can be found in Schneider (2005).

or XCOMP (the latter for control) dependent in f-structure; accordingly their recursion (expressed by the Kleene star) is COMP* or XCOMP*.

According to Tree-Adjoining Grammar (TAG), the only context-sensitive operation that is needed to express natural language is Adjoining, from which LFG functional uncertainty has been shown to follow as a corollary (Joshi and Vijay-Shanker, 1989). Functional uncertainty, which is expressed on the level of f-structure, would then be the only extension needed to an otherwise context-free processing of natural language.

6.5.2 A chunks and F-structure version of LFG

We therefore suggest that, since f-structures can then be derived context-freely, full-fledged c-structures are not strictly needed in LFG, and that chunks and dependencies may be sufficient for a formal grammar theory. The chunks & dependencies model has been suggested by Abney (1995). Frank (2003) presents a (albeit non-probabilistic) chunks & dependencies model for LFG. Chunks can be freely combined, subject to adjacency and projectivity constraints, which leads to a context-free parsing algorithm. Except for the added book-keeping functional annotations, her parsing algorithm is akin to CYK, which we use.

A major motivation for C-structure has been its context-freeness. We have shown that the majority of long-distance dependencies can be expressed in a context-free way by extending locality to the clause level, and can thus be expressed by a local dependency. Functional theories (LFG and DG alike), if they use mild-context sensitivity in the form of Adjoining or functional uncertainty or another form of recursion over functional or clausal structures can then obviate all other forms of long-distance dependencies. We can then parse for f-structure in a context-free way.

Combining (1) Frank (2004)'s revelations on restricting grammatical complexity in TAG, (2) LFG's invention of functional uncertainty on f-structures, and (3) Joshi and Vijay-Shanker (1989)'s suggestion that structures modelled by LFG functional uncertainty and TAG mild context-sensitivity are equivalent, C-structures can be obviated for syntactic analysis.

6.6 Conclusions

We have discussed how we extract local and non-local lexical information from the Penn Treebank. We have shown that the vast majority of long-distance depen-

6.6. Conclusions

dencies can be modelled locally in a functional representation (such as Functional DG) by extending locality to the clause level. DG locality naturally extends to the clause level. Out of the remaining, trans-clausal, long-distance dependencies most can be treated recursively (A-movement, such as control-structure dependencies), they can safely be treated by post-processing, parsing can then stay context-free. Furthermore, WH-question pronouns (the only $\bar{A}$-movement across clause boundaries) can be treated by extending context-free parsing to mild context-sensitivity known from TAG. Mild context-sensitivity is a form of recursion over syntactic structures in TAG or equivalently recursion over f-structure in LFG.

Following these considerations, the LFG suggestion by Frank (2003), as well as our broad-coverage evidence (Schneider, Dowdall, and Rinaldi, 2004; Rinaldi et al., 2004a; Rinaldi et al., 2004; Weeds et al., 2005), we suggest that C-structures or other configurational "surface" representations can be obviated for the robust broad-coverage syntactic analysis of natural language. By reducing grammar complexity (Frank, 2002; Frank, 2004), by reducing parsing complexity to mostly context-free parsing and finite-state based chunking (Schneider, 2003; Schneider, 2004), and by bridging the gap between language engineering and Formal Grammar (Kaplan et al., 2004a). We conclude that chunks and dependencies (Abney, 1995; Frank, 2003) are sufficient for robust broad-coverage parsing of natural language.

We have sketched a version of TAG Adjoining in DG and discussed our implementation. We do not provide any formal proof of equivalence between TAG Adjoining and our pre-parsing approach, we cannot be certain that we treat all English long-distance dependencies, but we have shown by quantitative and qualitative evidence that our local approach successfully treats the vast majority of English long-distance dependencies, both on a token-based as well as on a type-based count. We believe that a formal proof, or difficult claims about total coverage of long-distance dependencies, are neither necessary nor beneficial for a robust system optimising on precision and recall. We have extensively evaluated our approach, including long-distance dependencies, and present detailed results in chapter 7.

Traditional wisdom has it that a grammar formalism is either deep-syntactic or context-free. We have shown that functional DG is mostly context-free, but at the same time deep-syntactic, i.e. expressing all major long-distance dependencies. Only non-argument position ($\bar{A}$) relations across clause-boundaries, i.e. complex WH-movements, need context-sensitivity. Mild context-sensitivity, which is well studied, is sufficient (Frank, 2004; Kuhlmann and Nivre, 2006). Mild context-sensitivity extends locality beyond the clause under clearly defined conditions. We have discussed our implementation of mild context-sensitivity and presented how we disambiguate attachment ambiguities of the WH-pronoun, based on a corpus study.

Chapter 7

Evaluation and Discussion

7.1 Introduction

In this chapter we evaluate the performance of the Pro3Gres parser. First we discuss different evaluation metrics and present the evaluation method that we use. In section 7.2 we evaluate on GREVAL, a standard 500 sentence test corpus (Carroll, Minnen, and Briscoe, 2003) and compare to the related works of Carroll and Briscoe (2002), Lin (1998) and Collins (1999). In section 7.4 we evaluate on a random subset from the GENIA corpus of biomedical texts (Kim et al., 2003a). In section 7.5 we present and evaluate methods exploring the trade-off between precision and recall. In section 7.6 we compare against the baseline and explore the contribution of the statistical models for lexical disambiguation and distance.

7.1.1 Traditional Syntactic Evaluation: Labelled Bracketing

Evaluations compare automatically annotated data, the so-called candidates, to manually, carefully annotated data, the so-called gold standard. The gold standard is assumed to be error-free. A candidate is assumed to be correct if its annotation coincides with the one in the gold standard. Errors are partitioned into recall errors and precision errors. Recall measures how much of the data in the gold standard is recovered in the candidate, and precision measures how much noise is in the candidate data returned by the automatic procedure. For a more detailed introduction to the topic of evaluation in CL and syntactic parsers, readers are referred to Jurafsky and Martin (2000, p. 464).

A widely-used evaluation method is PARSEVAL (Black et al., 1991), which measures the accuracy of syntax trees delivered by a constituency based parser as follows.

labelled recall: $\frac{\#\text{of correct constituents in candidate}}{\#\text{of correct constituents in gold standard}}$

labeled precision: $\frac{\#\text{of correct constituents in candidate}}{\#\text{of all constituents in candidate}}$

cross-brackets: # of brackets crossing between candidate and gold standard

While the PARSEVAL evaluation measure has been used widely, it cannot be directly applied for a dependency based parser. Also, PARSEVAL has come under serious criticism, raising doubts about how reliable its results are, as we discuss in the following.

7.1.2 Dependency-Based Evaluation: Lin 1995

Lin (1995) suggests evaluating on the intuitive level of dependencies rather than on the constituency level. He points out that PARSEVAL suffers from the following serious problems.

PARSEVAL may count a single error multiple times Given the following gold standard annotation

(109) [I [saw [[a man][with [[a dog] and [a cat]]]][in [the park]]]]

and the two following incorrect parser analyses

(110) [I [saw [[a man][with [[a dog] and [[a cat][in [the park]]]]]]]]

(111) [I [saw [a man] with [a dog] and [a cat][in [the park]]]]

PARSEVAL yields a counter-intuitive assessment of the quality of the analyses.

In (109) we have only one error, and it involves a difficult construction: a PP-attachment error. The PP *in the park* has been attached to *cat* instead of to *saw*,

According to PARSEVAL, this constitutes 3 crossing brackets:

1. [a dog and a cat] vs. [a cat in the park]

2. [with a dog and a cat] vs. [a dog and a cat in the park]

3. [a man with a dog and a cat] vs. [with a dog and a cat in the park]

7.1. Introduction

This analysis scores a recall of 6/10 and precision of 7/11.

(110), on the other hand, is a very shallow, insufficient analysis. As it has no crossing brackets, however, it scores a higher recall of 7/10 and a higher precision of 7/7.

Lin (1995) mentions the following, additional PARSEVAL problems.

Constituency based approaches often have low agreement between parsing schemes for some constructions This criticism has partly been answered by PARSEVAL by removing certain bracketing information from consideration; for example negation, auxiliaries, punctuation, or traces, since Lin (1995).

No distinction between different processing levels For cascading systems, different levels, which are often marked by differing degrees of difficulty, cannot be distinguished. For Pro3Gres, for example, chunking vs. parsing performance could not be distinguished. Also, the fact that base-NP internal syntax is left underspecified means that standard PARSEVAL cannot be applied.

7.1.3 Desiderata

A maximally flexible and informative evaluation should respect the following criteria.

Selective evaluation to support error analysis: Results should be classifiable by different syntactic phenomena, for example to identify more and less difficult phenomena, to identify which parser is particularly suitable for which construction, or to distinguish between semantically more and less serious errors. Grammatical relations provide such a division into meaningful classes naturally.

Ability to ignore inconsequential differences: It should be possible to ignore differences that are inconsequential, either for a certain task or because of semantic closeness. A task-specific example is the biomedical application of Pro3Gres, which focuses on the discovery of potential relations between proteins, where truth-value and modality modifications (typically expressed by adverbs and sentence-subordination) are of secondary importance. An example of semantic closeness is the distinction between full clauses and small clauses: it can be argued that a parsing schenme that does not distinguish between the two should not be punished.

7.1. Introduction

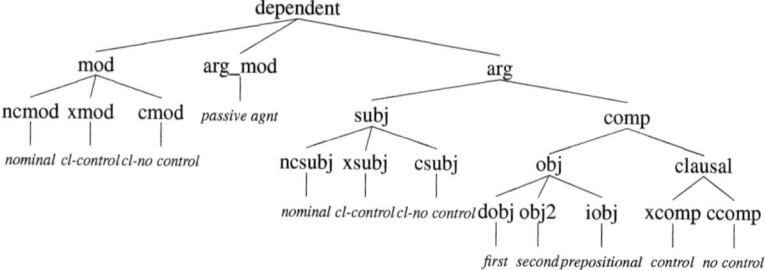

Figure 7.1: The hierarchy of grammatical relations suggested in GREVAL

Facilitate error diagnostics: it would be helpful if an evaluation specified what actually goes wrong and helped the developer pinpoint the error source. In the above example (109), it is helpful to know that a PP-attachment error occurred. An analysis that uses perspicuous and intuitive grammar concepts and annotation schemes further supports developers or users in this task.

Following Lin's criticisms and suggestions as well as the above desiderata, an evaluation based on grammatical relations instead of mapping to constituency and evaluation with PARSEVAL seemed appropriate for evaluating the performance of Pro3Gres. For dependency parsers, it has become customary to use grammatical relations for evaluation, for instance in Buchholz and Marsi (2006).

7.1.4 An Annotation Scheme for Evaluation: Carroll et al. 1999, 2003

Carroll, Minnen, and Briscoe (1999) and Carroll, Minnen, and Briscoe (2003) present a dependency-based evaluation scheme, GREVAL (GR stands for grammatical relations), and offer a dependency-based manual annotation of 500 random sentences from the Susanne corpus to the linguistic community. Their test corpus and a version of their evaluation scheme have been used in the following.

They suggest a hierarchy of relations that on the one hand allow us to do the selective evaluations demanded by (Lin, 1995), on the other hand total figures can also be given. Since relations inside base NPs remain underspecified in Pro3Gres at parse-time, we needed a mapping effort and post-processing to deliver such total figures. In section 7.2 we conduct extensive selective evaluations.

The hierarchy of relations (Carroll, Minnen, and Briscoe, 2003, 303) is illus-

ncmod(_, flag, red).	% a red flag
ncmod(on, flag, roof).	% flag on the roof
xmod(without, eat, ask).	% he ate the cake without asking
cmod(because, eat, be).	% he ate the cake because he was hungry
arg_mod(by, kill, 'Brutus').	% killed by Brutus
ncsubj(she, eat, _).	% she was eating
xsubj(win, require, _).	% to win the America's Cup requires heaps of cash
csubj(leave, mean, _).	% that Nellie left meant she was angry
dobj(read, book,_).	% read books
dobj(mail, 'Mary', iobj).	% mail Mary the contract (3rd arg is initial_gr)
iobj(in, arrive, 'Spain').	% arrive in Spain
obj2(give,present,_).	% give Mary a present
xcomp(to, intend, leave).	% Paul intends to leave
xcomp(_, be, easy).	% Swimming is easy
xcomp(in, be, 'Paris').	% Mary is in Paris
ccomp(that, say, leave).	% I said that he left

Table 7.1: Examples of grammatical relations in the GREVAL scheme

trated in figure 7.1 (the $subj\_or\_dobj$ relation is left out as it is at least extremely rare in English). As a rule of thumb, relations are distinguished among modification, adjunct (*mod* versus argument (complement) *arg*; clausal (*c*) versus non-clausal (e.g. nominal, *nc*); control (*x*) versus no control. For example *He$_1$ wants [t$_1$ to leave]* (control) vs. *He says [that she left]* (no control). Examples are illustrated in table 7.1.

7.2 GREVAL: A standard 500 sentence test corpus

The 500 sentence evaluation corpus GREVAL has been introduced above. Its format is similar to the Pro3Gres parser output, but not identical. Therefore, a mapping function is necessary. Crouch et al. (2002) warn that mapping is a true challenge, and that due to mapping results can only be indicative. A small selection of examples that lead to spurious errors is discussed in appendix B.

7.2.1 Bidirectional Mapping of Pro3Gres to GREVAL

As a starting point, one could assume a naive direct mapping, where c-subscript (short for Carroll et. al.) indicate GREVAL relations: $subj$ corresponds to $ncsubj_c$; obj corresponds to $dobj_c$; $pobj$ corresponds to $iobj_c$; $modpp$ corresponds to $ncmod_c$; etc.

Such a mapping only partly works, because it misses a number of differences between the Pro3Gres output and the GREVAL format, for example: Pro3Gres makes no adjunct/complement distinction for PPs; Pro3Gres' use of Tesnière translations complicates the picture; often, different grammatical assumptions are made. For example, GREVAL does not consider relative pronoun antecedents to be subjects or objects. The mapping thus becomes more involved, as will be explained in the following. While the mapping that we introduce addresses many of the differences, a considerable number of differences remain unmapped and can lead to spurious errors, as is discussed in the appendix and in the detailed analysis of errors. A graphical summary of the mapping is presented in figure 7.2.

Subjects

The subjects of reduced relative clauses, which are expressed in the Pro3Gres $modpart$ relation, are subjects in GREVAL ($ncsubj_c$). Each $subj$ and each $modpart$ relations is thus mapped to an $ncsubj_c$ relation.

The antecedent of a relative pronoun is not assumed to be a subject in GREVAL. A long-distance $subj$ relation expressing a relative pronoun antecedent corresponds to a $cmod_c$ relation with a relative pronoun in the gold standard. $cmod_c$ is also used for other types of clausal modification, but checking for a relative pronoun in the correct argument position ensures that only $cmod_c$ relations expressing the resolution of relative pronouns are mapped.

Object

No distinction between primary obj and secondary $obj2$ object is made at this stage. The mapping is straightforward, as table 7.2 shows.

7.2. GREVAL: A standard 500 sentence test corpus

Subject $\left\{\begin{array}{l} subj \text{ OR } modpart \leftrightarrow ncsubj_c \text{ OR } cmod_c(\text{with relative pronoun}) \\ \underline{\hspace{1cm}} \\ Legend: \\ ncsubj_c = \text{non-clausal subject} \\ cmod_c = \text{clausal modification, used e.g. for relative clauses} \end{array}\right.$

Object $\left\{\begin{array}{l} obj \text{ OR } obj2 \leftrightarrow dobj_c \text{ OR } obj2_c \\ \underline{\hspace{1cm}} \\ Legend: \\ dobj_c = \text{first object} \\ obj2_c = \text{second object} \end{array}\right.$

PP-Attachment $\left\{\begin{array}{l} modpp \text{ OR } pobj \leftrightarrow \begin{array}{l} ncmod_c(\text{with prep}) \text{ OR} \\ iobj_c(\text{with prep}) \text{ OR} \\ arg\_mod_c \text{ OR} \\ xcomp_c(\text{with prep}) \end{array} \\ \underline{\hspace{1cm}} \\ Legend: \\ ncmod_c = \text{non-clausal modification} \\ iobj_c = \text{prepositional object} \\ arg\_mod_c = \text{passive agent} \\ xcomp_c \text{ for PP-attachment to copular verbs} \end{array}\right.$

Clausal $\left\{\begin{array}{l} \begin{array}{l} sentobj \text{ OR} \\ modrel \text{ OR} \\ modpart \text{ OR} \\ obj(\text{with copular verb}) \text{ OR} \\ pobj(\text{with copular verb}) \text{ OR} \\ predadj \end{array} \leftrightarrow \begin{array}{l} xcomp_c \text{ OR } xmod_c \text{ OR} \\ ccomp_c \text{ OR } cmod_c \end{array} \\ \underline{\hspace{1cm}} \\ Legend: \\ xcomp_c = \text{clausal complement, control} \\ xmod_c = \text{clausal modifier, control} \\ ccomp_c = \text{clausal complement, overt subordinate subject} \\ cmod_c = \text{clausal modifier, overt subordinate subject} \end{array}\right.$

Figure 7.2: Bidirectional Mapping the Pro3Gres output to the GREVAL format. GREVAL relations bear a c-subscript

PP-attachment

The PP-attachment relations, *modpp* for verbal attachment and *pobj* for nominal attachment, typically correspond to the following GREVAL relations: $ncmod_c$, non-clausal modification, which expresses adjunct dependencies; $iobj_c$, indirect object, which expresses prepositional arguments; and arg_mod_c, which expresses the *by* agent of a passive verb. Such a mapping is not satisfactory, however. The PP-attachment mapping would miss cases in which the PP-internal noun is a verb that has undergone Tesnière translation to a noun, for example in *the dangers of swimming_VBG*. Therefore, a PP-attachment relation that has a clausal modification counterpart $xmod_c$ should also be counted as correct. $xmod_c$ typically expresses clausal modification. It is important to restrict the mapping to a PP-attachment relation to cases where $xmod_c$ contains a preposition in order to get a bidirectional mapping.

Clausal Relations

The mapping needed for clausal relations is quite complex, as illustrated in figure 7.2. Clausal relations in Pro3Gres are $sentobj$ for subordinated sentences, which typically corresponds to $xcomp_c$ or $ccomp_c$, and *modrel* for relative clauses. But also the reduced relative clause *modpart* relation expresses a clausal dependency. Both relative clauses and reduced relative clauses are typically expressed by $cmod_c$ in GREVAL. Complements of copular verbs, which we express by an *obj* relation if the complement is nominal, *predadj* if the complement is an adjective, or *pobj* if the complement is a PP, are also clausal relations.

Since we do not distinguish between clausal adjuncts and arguments, *sentobj* in a control situation corresponds to either $xcomp$ or $xmod$, and either to $ccomp$ or $cmod$ if the subordinate clause has an overt subject.

Results

The currently best results using this mapping are given in table 7.2. We have used Ratnaparkhi's Maximum Entropy tagger for this result. The mapping that we have used is not perfect. For example, the assumption is made that each *modpart* relation corresponds to an $ncsubj_c$ relation. This is not true if the *modpart* relation has a present participle governor, for example in *a case involving/VBG seven persons*, where it should correspond to an object. If we exclude these *modpart* relations from the subject evaluation, precision would increase to 92.7%. Since the

	Subject	Object	PP-attachment	clausal
Prec.	92.3% (865/937)	85.3% (353/414)	76.9% (702/913)	74.3% (451/607)
Recall	78.0% (865/1095)	82.5% (353/428)	68.6% (702/1023)	61.7% (451/731)

Table 7.2: Currently best results on evaluating Pro3Gres on GREVAL test corpus on subject, object and PP-attachment relations

GREVAL annotation does not contain part-of-speech tag information, it is not possible to exclude these *modpart* relations from the calculation of recall, otherwise the mapping is not bidirectional. We thus had to accept the spurious error that the bidirectional mapping introduces. Results are therefore a lower bound.

We get slightly above 90% subject precision, object precision is at about 80%. Subject and object recall are about 80 %. PP-attachment precision is about 75%, recall about 70%. For clausal relations, we get almost 75% precision, but only about 60% recall.

Detailed Analysis of Subject Precision Errors

In order to get an impression of the error characteristics, the subject precision errors from the entire GREVAL corpus have equally been classified in table 7.3. Chunking and tagging errors are the primary source of error for subject precision. Parsing errors, which includes attachment errors, are less frequent.

7.2.2 Unidirectional Mapping of Pro3Gres to GREVAL

The mapping which we just presented has a few shortcomings. First, the PP-attachment evaluation is too coarse as it does not allow us to fully examine verbal and nominal attachment selectively. Secondly, it only evaluates some relations. In this subsection we explore possible answers to the first shortcoming, in the following subsections we explore possible answers to the second shortcoming.

The mapping we have discussed in figure 7.2 lumps all PP-attachments together, which is unsatisfactory as it does not allow us to distinguish between the performance on verbal and nominal PP-attachment. When observing the data a separation into verbal and nominal attachment seems straightforward. Precision values are obtained by simply splitting the evaluation into *modpp* part for nominal attachment and a separate *pobj* part for verbal attachment.

The calculation of recall values, where a mapping from the GREVAL relations

Spurious Error	Chunking or Tagging	Control	Parsing Error	Rel. Pronoun Resolution	Grammar Mistake or incompl. Parse	Grammar Assumption
7	21	9	15	4	8	8

Table 7.3: Error Classification of Subject Precision errors of all GREVAL corpus sentences

7.2. GREVAL: A standard 500 sentence test corpus 186

to our scheme is needed turns out to be more problematic. Since the GREVAL annotation does not provide part-of-speech tags there is no certain way to know if the governor in a PP-attachment relation is a verb or a noun, the attachment verbal or nominal. Nevertheless, strong tendencies exist: arg_mod_c is always verbal attachment, $ncmod_c$ frequently nominal, and $iobj_c$ mostly verbal. This allows us to get indicative recall values.

Strictly speaking, such a mapping is not mathematically well-defined, because unidirectional mappings that do not completely overlap in both directions are used. The mapping still preserves the characteristics of recall, expressing how many of the expected relations are returned by the parser. The performance values they allow us to deliver are more fine-grained and informative. We report them in table 7.4, with a word of warning. We will also the unidirectional mapping for PP-attachment in subchapters 7.5 to 7.8, where we will not compare to other parsers, but to other versions of Pro3res, such as a baseline system. A graphical summary of the mapping is presented in figure 7.3.

Nominal PP-attachment

Nominal PP-attachment recall calculates how many of the nominal (non-argument) relations expected in the gold standard, (expressed by the $ncmod_c$ relation, if it has a preposition), are reported by Pro3Gres. Since the GREVAL format does not contain part-of-speech tags, there is no certain way of knowing whether the $ncmod_c$ head is a noun or a verb. Typically, the head of an $ncmod_c$ relation is a noun, the relation thus corresponds to a *modpp* relation in Pro3Gres. But for verbal adjuncts, an $ncmod_c$ relation corresponds to a *pobj* Pro3Gres relation (i.e. verbal adjunct PP-attachment relation). This means that verbal adjunct PP-attachment recall counts are counted as nominal PP-attachment.

Verbal PP-attachment

$iobj_c$ expresses the PP-attachment of an argument, it is typically verbal attachment. arg_mod_c expresses the attachment of a *by* agent to a passive verb, it is always verbal.

Nominal argument PPs, for example in ... *Mr. Buckley holds the key to the Democratic organization's acceptance* ... are also expressed by an $iobj_c$ relation, which mostly expresses the attachment of verbal arguments. Again, since the GREVAL format does not contain part-of-speech tags, there is no certain way of knowing whether the $iobj_c$ head is a noun or a verb. These $iobj_c$ relations, like

7.2. GREVAL: A standard 500 sentence test corpus

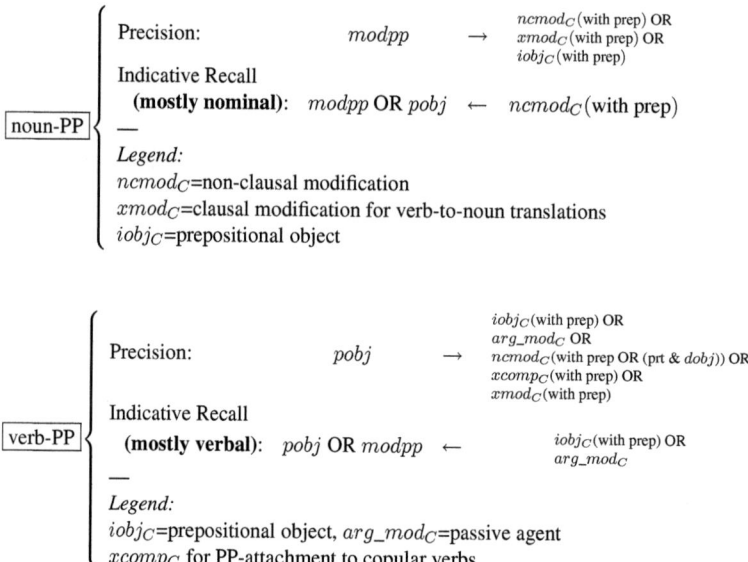

Figure 7.3: Mapping the Pro3Gres output to the GREVAL format for precision, and the reverse mapping for recall

	Nominal PP-attachment	Verbal PP-attachment
Precision	78.7% (354/450)	74.9% (347/463)
Indicative Recall	66.0% (529/801)	86.9% (173/199)

Table 7.4: Evaluating Pro3Gres on the GREVAL corpus on PP-attachment relations

all other $iobj_c$ relations, also appear as verbal PP-attachment, although they are nominal.

As for verbal PP-attachment recall, the PP-adjunct cases are treated by $ncmod_c$ recall and thus appear as nominal PP-attachment recall. The main verb-PP argument attachment relation is $iobj_c$, the verb-passive agent attachment relation is arg_mod_c. Recall of $iobj_c$ and arg_mod_c is either reported separately, or micro-averaged, then labelled as verbal PP-attachment recall, but we should bear in mind that it only covers arguments, while verbal PP-adjuncts form part of $ncmod_c$ recall, and that it also includes nominal PP-attachments in which the PP is a noun argument.

Since Pro3Gres leaves the distinction between preposition and verbal particle underspecified, a verbal particle plus a corresponding $dobj_c$ are also correct. Like for nominal attachment, a verbal PP-attachment relation that has an $xmod_c$ counterpart in the gold standard is a correct case involving a PP-internal noun that has undergone translation from gerund to noun. PP-attachment to copular verbs is expressed by $xcomp_c$ in GREVAL.

Results

Results using this unidirectional mapping are given in table 7.4. The verbal PP-attachment recall appears considerably higher than nominal PP-attachment. This is partly due the following two reasons. First, as the mapping describes, verb-PP recall largely describes the attachment of arguments, while noun-PP recall largely describes the attachment of adjuncts. For arguments, lexicalisation is considerably more beneficial than for adjuncts. Second, in our putative context (see chapter 2) a noun and a verb are in competition. If several nouns compete, then their attachment probabilities are only compared indirectly via the likelihood of competing verbal attachment.

Although better results have been reported for PP-attachment disambiguation in isolation, the same results cannot be expected to be found in the context of real parsing. On the one hand, some PP-attachments are unambiguous, which should lead to better results. On the other hand, some PP-attachments are multiply ambiguous (they have more than two possible attachment sites) or occur fronted in a sentence-initial position, or a participant in the PP-relation is mistagged or mischunked. Mistagging and mischunking is involved in about 20-25 % of the PP-attachment precision errors.

Detailed Analysis of PP-Attachment Errors

Detailed error analyses have been conducted by manually comparing the errors of Pro3Gres and tracking down error sources. The errors of the first 100 GREVAL sentences have been manually compared and broken down into error classes in table 7.5. The analysis reveals that in addition to the expected attachment errors (51%), mistagging and mischunking are important sources of error (24%), but also that differing grammar assumptions are a problem for our hand-written grammar approach (12%), introducing spurious errors. The fact that the grammar is either incomplete, a wrong rule leads to the most likely parse or that the parse does not span the whole sentence is responsible for 13 % of the errors.

PP Complements and PP Adjuncts

It is especially rewarding to compare the difference in recall between PP complements (which have the $iobj_c$ label) and PP adjuncts (which have the $ncmod_c$ label). Due to the strong lexical preference, performance on complements is considerably higher (87% (173 / 199)) than on adjuncts (66% (529 / 801)), where lexical preferences are often absent: an adjunct can attach anywhere. The fact that adjuncts can attach anywhere has been used to detect adjuncts by means of a entropy measure. If the entropy for possible lexical heads is very high, this is a strong indicator for adjuncthood (Merlo and Esteve Ferrer, 2006).

The fact that recall on complements is high entails that bilexical parsers, while not very successful on adjuncts because they are based on an incorrect assumption, are useful tools for lexicology and the discovery of argument structure. A manual categorisation of the 21 $iobj_c$ recall errors on GREVAL has been conducted. The first 10 errors are given for illustration in table 7.6. Only 3 of the 21 errors are attachment errors, which is considerably lower than for PP attachment generally, where about half of the errors are attachment errors (see table 7.5). Only one of these 3 errors, the error in sentence 229, is not corrected in the second highest ranked reading. This means that complement recall can be increased to a very high level using high recall approaches as described in section 7.5.1. It also means that

Relation	Attachment Error	Head Extraction Error	Chunking or Tagging	compl/prep Error	Grammar Mistake or incompl. Parse	Grammar Assumption
Noun-PP Precision	22	1	8	0	3	3
Noun-PP Recall	25	1	14	0	12	5
Verb-PP Precision	12	1	5	1	1	2
Verb-PP Recall	2	0	1	0	0	0
Totals	61	3	28	1	16	10
Proportions	51 %	3 %	24 %	1 %	13 %	8 %

Table 7.5: Detailed Analysis of the PP-attachment errors in the first 100 GREVAL sentences

7.2. GREVAL: A standard 500 sentence test corpus

Gold Standard	Parser Output	Error Category	Explanation	Different tagger/chunker?	2nd-ranked reading?
iobj(go,thru,draft)	ncmod1(several,thru,_)	Chunking	36: ... I would say it's got to go thru several more drafts. [thru several drafts]	yes	
iobj(say,about,mate)	obj(run,mate,_)	Chunking	87: ... I will have something definite to say about running mates. running [mates]		
iobj(call,for,overhaul)	modpp(call,for,overhaul)	Morphology	114: The contract called for overhauling of 120 joints. spurious error		
iobj(subject,to,provocation)	–	Conjunction	222: ... Northerners have been subjected to embarrassment or provocation. Conjunction not resolved		
iobj(owe,to,nation)	modpp(nation,to,nation)	Attachment	229: ... duty was owed by his nation to other nations.		
iobj(limit,to,nations)	–	Conjunction	231: ... a concept not limited to the United Sates or even to the Western nations. Conjunction not resolved		
iobj(adherence,to,principle)	pobj(imply,to,principle)	Attachment	232: ... implies adherence to principles of ideological supranationalism.		yes
iobj(put,to,ground)	adjtrans(mouth,put,_)	NP Constr.	267: He bent down, a black cranelike figure, and put his mouth to the ground.		yes
iobj(hop,to,branch)	sentobj(hop,branch,they)	Tagging	269: They lay, with the birds hopping from branch to branch above them, ... from_IN branch_NN to_TO branch_VB above_IN them_PRP		
iobj(expose,to,what)	–	Grammar	300: I consider it to be my job to expose to the public what is being written.		

Table 7.6: Manual categorisation of the first 10 $iobj_c$ recall errors on GREVAL

for IR tasks, where argument relations are typically more important than adjunct relations, the parser may be more useful than it seems *prima facie*.

7.2.3 Long-Distance Dependencies

The reported results generally include both local and long-distance dependencies. About 10% of the subjects in the GREVAL corpus are non-local, i.e. they involve a long-distance dependency. The best subject precision data in table 7.2 yields 93.9% precision for local subjects and 87.7% for non-local dependency subjects. The annotation in the GREVAL corpus does not always indicate if a relation is local or not. We identify a subject relation as non-local if Pro3Gres reports it as a control subject, an anaphor of a relative clause, or a WH-word. This allows us to report precision values. But since the GREVAL corpus does, for example, not indicate control relations as such, we cannot report reliable recall values for all relations, since it is not always possible to attain a bidirectional mapping. For the example of subject control recall, one can approximate the denominator by constraining the subordinate clause relation $xcomp_c$ to sentences where the subordinate clause is introduced by the infinitive marker *to*, and where there are two $ncsubj_c$ relations with an identical subject, one containing the matrix verb, the other containing the subordinate verb. This constraint delivers 48 cases, out of which the parser returns 33. At the first sight, this corresponds to a recall of 69%, but the fact that we get a lower numerator than for precision indicates that the constraint applied to the gold standard does not deliver all cases, our calculation of the recall would only be incomplete.

Table 7.7 shows a long-distance dependency evaluation, as far as the GREVAL annotations permit. Since some of the counts are low, absolute numbers are included. Generally, the performance on long-distance dependencies is only slightly below the performance on local relations, which indicates that our approach to treating long-distance dependencies is successful. We discuss this approach in detail in chapter 6.

While the general parsing results can be compared to other approaches (see following subsections), it is difficult to compare our results on long-distance dependencies, for two reasons. First, most of the published results are on parts of the Penn Treebank. Second, due to the GREVAL annotation we can only give selective figures, and not always both precision and recall. Only some authors give selective evaluations, for example Dienes and Dubey (2003). We juxtapose our results to their antecedent recovery based on the output of a lexicalised parser (Collins, 1999). We would like to stress that this can at best lead to an indicative compari-

Relation	Counts Correct	Precision	Recall	in Penn Treebank
WH-Subject	60	93.8%	73.2%	WHNP-NP (row 3)
WH-Object	7	53.8%	100.0%	WHNP-NP (row 3)
Anaphora of rel. clause subject	43	91.5%	68.3%	–
Passive subject	128	88.9%	80.0%	NP-NP (row 1)
Subject-control	45	84.9%	n/a	NP-NP (row 1)
Object-control	5	100.0%	50.0%	NP-NP (row 1)
modpart relation	32	74.4%	n/a	NP PRO (row 2)
Topicalized verb-attached PPs	26	70.3%	n/a	S-S (row 6)

Table 7.7: Evaluation of Long-Distance Dependencies

	Antecedent	POS	Label	Count	Description/Example
1	NP	NP	*	22,734	NP trace *Sam* was seen *
2		NP	*	12,172	NP PRO * to sleep is nice
3	WHNP	NP	*T*	10,659	WH trace the woman *who* you saw *T*
(4)			*U*	9,202	Empty units $ 25 *U*
(5)			0	7,057	Empty complementizers Sam said 0 Sasha snores
(6)	S	S	*T*	5,035	Moved constituents *Sam had to go*, Sasha said *T*
7	WHADVP	ADVP	*T*	3,181	WH-trace Sam explained *how* to leave *T*
(8)		SBAR		2,513	Empty clauses *Sam had to go*, said Sasha (SBAR)
(9)		WHNP	0	2,139	Empty relative pronouns the woman 0 we saw
(10)		WHADVP	0	726	Empty relative pronouns the reason 0 to leave

Table 7.8: The distribution of the 10 most frequent types of empty nodes and their antecedents in the Penn Treebank (adapted from Johnson 2002). Row numbers in parentheses indicate cases that are inherently local in our functional DG

son. An overview of the most frequent Penn Treebank empty node and trace types (chapter 6, table 6.2), is repeated as table 7.8 for reference.

For NP-NP traces (row 1 in table 7.8) Dienes and Dubey (2003) report 74% precision and 67% recall. Passive subject and control contribute the majority of NP-NP traces. We report 88% precision and 76% recall for constructing the dependency (which requires both recognising the trace and finding the antecedent). These values are encouraging, but we omit the difficult task of indexed gerund recovery, and we use the incomplete subject control recall calculation discussed above – as a consequence, recall can be expected to be considerably lower on the identical task. For WHNP-NP traces (row 3 in table 7.8) Dienes and Dubey (2003) report 91% precision and 75% precision. We have evaluated WH-subjects and WH-objects, which completely or almost completely cover WHNP-NP traces. We report 87% precision and 75% recall. While these numbers cannot be directly compared, we are confident that they show that the performance of our approach is

	Pro3Gres		
	Subject	Object	PP-Attachment
Precision	92%	85%	77%
Recall	78%	82%	69%
	Lin 1998 (on the whole Susanne corpus)		
	Subject	Object	PP-attachment
Precision	89%	88%	78%
Recall	78%	72%	72%

Table 7.9: Comparison of Pro3Gres to Lin's MINIPAR

good.

7.2.4 Comparison to Lin's MINIPAR

The results of the parsing evaluation that we have made can be compared to Lin (1998), although Lin gives results for the whole Susanne corpus. The comparison is shown in table 7.9. Results for subject and object are slightly better, results for PP-attachment slightly worse when using Pro3Gres.

7.2.5 Comparison to Carroll and Briscoe's RASP

Carroll and Briscoe have evaluated their own parser, RASP, with their own GREVAL evaluation scheme in Carroll and Briscoe (2002) and Carroll, Minnen, and Briscoe (2003) (see figure 7.1). Carroll, Minnen, and Briscoe (2003) reports the numbers shown in table 7.10. The plus symbols indicate the level in the hierarchy.

The relations in bold are the relations that we have evaluated: the terminals in the GREVAL hierarchy, except the relations that we do not express ($xmod_c$, $xsubj_c$, and $csubj_c$), and except for $xcomp$ and $ccomp$, where we have evaluated on the pre-terminal $clausal_c$ relation, since we do not make a distinction between clausal relations with or without explicit subject.

In order to compare to this evaluation, we partly used the mapping presented in 7.2.1, and we partly needed additional pre- and post-processing, as we explain in the following.

For $subj$, the mapping discussed in subsection 7.2.1 (see figure 7.2) is used. Mapping for obj is almost one to one, the one difference being that we had to assign

7.2. GREVAL: A standard 500 sentence test corpus

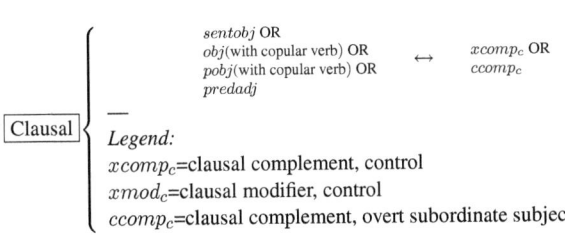

Legend:
$xcomp_c$=clausal complement, control
$xmod_c$=clausal modifier, control
$ccomp_c$=clausal complement, overt subordinate subject

Figure 7.4: Mapping for the preterminal $clausal_c$ relation

	RASP		Pro3Gres			
Relation	P	R	Precision		Recall	
	%	%	%	Counts	%	Counts
dependent incl. detmod & aux	–	–	84.5	4473/5292	71.9	4473/6221
dependent	75	75	81.1	3113/3840	66.0	3113/4716
+mod	74	70	84.3	1486/1763	57.2	1486/2599
++ncmod	78	73	84.4	1434/1699	60.0	1434/2391
++xmod	70	52	–	–	–	–
++cmod	67	48	81.3	52/64	25.0	52/208
+arg_mod	84	41	79.1	19/24	47.5	19/40
+arg	77	84	78.3	1608/2053	77.4	1608/2077
++subj	84	88	88.9	865/973	79.0	865/1095
+++ncsubj	85	88	88.9	865/973	79.0	865/1095
+++xsubj	100	40	–	–	–	–
+++csubj	14	100	–	–	–	–
++comp	70	79	68.8	743/1080	75.7	743/982
+++obj	68	79	75.8	454/599	78.0	454/582
++++dobj	86	84	84.0	340/405	83.1	340/409
++++obj2	39	84	90.0	9/10	56.3	9/16
++++iobj	42	65	57.1	105/184	66.9	105/157
+++clausal	73	78	60.1	289/481	72.3	289/400
detmod	–	–	93.5	1018/1089	90.6	1018/1124
aux	–	–	94.2	342/363	89.8	342/381

Table 7.10: RASP evaluation results compared to Pro3Gres

copular verb complements to $xcomp_c$ (see chapter 5). Mapping for $obj2$ is one to one. The arg_mod_c relation can be approximated by filtering all passive verbs that are introduced by the preposition *by*. Such a simple approach overgenerates, including local and temporal *by*-phrases, which leads to the expected low precision, while recall outperforms RASP.

The mapping that we use for the pre-terminal $clausal_c$ relation is given in figure 7.4. For $cmod_c$ we use a very coarse approximation. A large subset of $cmod_c$ are relative clauses, which can be clearly identified. Since relative clauses are only a subset, we get very poor recall. The many $cmod_c$ that are expressed by a *sentobj* relation cannot be easily recognised. They affect the precision of the $clausal_c$ relation, to which the majority of *sentobj* relations correspond. The relations that we do not express have low frequency (5 $xsubj_c$, 5 $csubj_c$, 128 $xmod_c$). For the top node in the GREVAL hierarchy, *dependent*, we give two numbers. The first one does not include $detmod_c$ and aux_c, for which Carroll, Minnen, and Briscoe (2003) does not report values. The second number includes $detmod_c$ and aux_c.

There are two prominent reasons why some relations are difficult to map: first, we do not express relations that occur inside chunks. Second, we do not make a distinction between PP arguments and adjuncts. We describe our pre- and post-processing implementation to approximate these relations in the following.

Relations inside Chunks The following GREVAL relations often occur inside chunks:

1. $detmod_c$ (modification by determiner) typically occurs inside a noun chunk
2. $ncmod_c$ (non-clausal modification): many types of non-clausal modification, specifically adjectives and non-head nouns, occur inside noun chunks.
3. aux_c (auxiliary) typically occurs inside verb chunks

We have implemented a pre-processing module into Pro3Gres that recovers relations inside chunks. This module is called between tagging and parsing. The module is rule-based, but has a statistical component. It is based on the following assumptions.

1. Generally, all non-head words in a chunk modify the head. There are four exceptions to this rule:
    - In verb chunks, every verb modifies the succeeding verb (example: *would have been going*).

Relation	P%	R%	Counts Correct
detmod	93.5	90.6	1018
ncmod	83.1	67.9	1080
aux	94.2	89.8	342

Table 7.11: Percentage and absolute values for chunk-internal relations

- If a noun chunk contains an adjective and more than one noun, the adjective modifies the succeeding non-head noun if it is seen more often before the non-head noun lemma than the head noun lemma in the British National Corpus (example: *conventional forces strengthening*).
- If a noun chunk contains more than two nouns, the frontmost noun modifies the succeeding non-head noun if it is seen more often before the non-head noun lemma than the head noun lemma in the British National Corpus (example: *Eisenhower administration effort*).
- If a noun chunk contains more than two proper names, every proper name modifies the succeeding proper name (example: *Fulton County Grand Jury*).

2. Generally, the modification type deterministically follows from the part-of-speech tag of the head and the modifier. There is one exception.

- Words that can be determiners or adjectives, for example *several, many, few, one* are assigned a *detmod* relation to the head noun if they occur as the frontmost word in the chunk, and a *ncmod* relation otherwise.

Using the Ratnaparkhi tagger, we get the performance shown in figure 7.11. *ncmod* performs relatively poorly. There are several important sources of errors. First, the statistical component often makes errors due to sparse data. For example, in *automobile title law*, the counts are too low. Second, adverbs are included in the verb chunk, although adverbs in copular verb chunks typically modify the verb complement. For example *generally* in *[was generally] favourable* is prevented from modifying the predicative adjective *favourable*. Third, very long base NPs contain very many *ncmod* relations, but are also at highest risk of being chunked incorrectly. The *ncmod* relation is thus much more affected by chunking errors than the *detmod* relation.

PP arguments and adjuncts disjunction   Merlo (2003) and Merlo and Esteve Ferrer (2006) have shown that there is a small correlation between attachment and ar-

Relation	P%	R%	Counts Correct
iobj	57.1	66.9	105
ncmod	78.7	44.2	354

Table 7.12: Percentage and absolute values for the PP-attachment argument/adjunct distinction

gumenthood. In a 4-way distinction peformance is up to 3 percent higher than if the attachment ambiguity is resolved first, and the argument/adjunct ambiguity afterwards. We miss out on this generalisation by using a post-processing approach that classifies attached PPs as arguments ($iobj_c$) or as adjuncts ($ncmod_c$). The task is problematic because inter-annotator agreement is low, and because the Penn Treebank does not provide reliable training data. We use the conservative approach of counting verbal PP-attachments with the functional label *CLR* as arguments, all others as adjuncts. We get the results in table 7.12. $ncmod$ recall is most seriously affected by the bidirectional mapping, which in this case marks all verbal adjunct PP-attachments as incorrect.

We can conclude that we perform slightly better on chunk-external relations except clausal relations, and slightly worse on chunk-internal relations than RASP. We can also conclude that we have higher precision than RASP, but lower recall. The clausal relation is seriously affected by the very coarse post-processing that we used. Especially recall is affected by the fact that Pro3Gres does not express some of the distinctions made, and very coarse approximations have to be used. On a more subjective level, we would like to conclude that the fact that our performance at the underspecified subordinate clause level in table 7.2 is much higher than our and Carroll's performance for highly specified relations indicates that current technology is not mature yet to express this fine-grained level of specificity, that our robust, underspecifying approach may be appropriate for many NLP tasks.

7.2.6 Comparison to Buchholz, Charniak, and Collins, according to Preiss

Preiss (2003) is a comprehensive evaluation of statistical parsers according to the GREVAL evaluation scheme. The tested parsers are Collins (1999), Charniak (2000), Buchholz (2002), and Briscoe and Carroll (1993). The latter is a version of RASP (Carroll, Minnen, and Briscoe, 2003). In her evaluation of RASP, Preiss (2003) partly reports lower values than Carroll, Minnen, and Briscoe (2003). This

	Buchholz		Charniak		Collins 1		Collins 2		Pro3Gres	
Relation	P %	R%	P%	R%	P%	R%	P%	R%	P%	R%
detmod	92.4	90.9	90.2	87.5	92.1	89.1	92.1	88.8	93.2	90.3
ncmod	66.7	51.6	79.8	46.3	81.5	47.4	81.1	47.3	84.4	60.0
aux	93.7	89.8	89.8	83.4	87.0	86.1	89.9	86.6	94.2	89.8
arg_mod	75.7	68.3	78.1	60.1	82.9	70.7	82.9	70.7	79.1	47.5
ncsubj	85.8	72.9	81.8	70.1	79.2	66.0	81.3	69.5	88.9	79.0
dobj	88.4	76.5	84.4	75.5	86.2	74.6	84.9	75.3	84.0	83.1
obj2	46.1	31.6	61.5	42.1	81.8	47.4	61.5	42.1	90.0	56.3
iobj	57.8	51.9	27.5	67.1	27.1	69.6	27.0	70.3	57.1	66.9

Table 7.13: Preiss's precision (P) and recall (R) evaluation results of Buchholz, Charniak, and Collins, compared to Pro3Gres

raises doubts about Preiss's mapping function. Unfortunately, not much is said about the mapping function, except that her evaluation software produces some different results, such as not expanding conjunctions. Further clarifications would be needed. The comparison of her results to Pro3Gres is shown in table 7.13.

Although these results are very encouraging, with Pro3Gres performing best on all relations except arg_mod, it is not clear how reliable they are, due to the shortcomings of Preiss's presentation.

7.2.7 Comparison to Collins's Model 1

As a consequence of our doubts about Preiss (2003), we have performed our own evaluation of Collins's Model 1 (Collins, 1999) on the GREVAL 500 sentence corpus and compared the results to Pro3Gres. We have used the Ratnaparkhi tagger (Ratnaparkhi, 1996) for preprocessing, with the same parameters as for Pro3Gres. Parsing with Collins's Model 1 is an order of magnitude slower than with Pro3Gres.

We have applied the Treebank patterns described in chapter 6 to the output of Collins's Model 1 parser. Some of the patterns needed to be adapted, so that they do not depend on functional labels or long-distance dependencies, which are not expressed in Collins's parser output. An example of such a relation is the $subj$ relation, where this shortcoming entails that, for example, control relations are necessarily lost. In other relations, the original extraction patterns could be kept, for example in the PP-attachment relations. In this case, long-distance relations such as fronted PPs are equally lost for our Pro3Gres training and in the Collins parser output. But since fronted PPs are annotated in the GREVAL corpus and often parsed correctly by Pro3Gres, a decrease in recall can also be expected, especially for verb-PP attachment, because fronted PPs normally modify the verb. An additional modification was necessitated by the fact that Collins attaches punctuation to arbitrary constituents.

Evaluation results are given in table 7.14. We use the mapping scheme presented in subsection 7.2.1 and illustrated in figure 7.2. While the precision values are similar, recall values are considerably lower for the Collins Parser. This is partly due to the following two reasons. First, Collins does not express long-distance dependencies: out of the 892 subjects reported by Pro3Gres on the GREVAL corpus, 58 are control subjects and 44 are resolved relative pronouns. More than 10% of all subject relations are thus long-distance dependencies and necessarily left unexpressed in Collins. This explains over two thirds of the recall loss for the subject relation in comparison to Pro3Gres. Still, Pro3Gres outperforms Collins Model 1 also on the local subjects. Other relations are also affected by the lack of long-distance dependencies, though to a lesser degree. For example, 34 of the reported 494 verb-PP attachment relations are fronted PPs. Second, there are parsing errors across the subtrees: Whenever a subtree involved in a dependency relation contains an error, the risk that the extraction patterns cannot find the dependency is extremely high, as Johnson (2002) stresses. Relations across more subtrees are more seriously affected, which explains that difference is bigger in the PP-attachment relations than in the subject or object relation. We would like to point out that there is the potential problem that there is no way to guarantee that the patterns we have devised have full recall. Although we have checked the output carefully, some correct parses may escape unmapped. We can be confident that its effect is far smaller than the reported recall performance difference between Collins Model 1 and Pro3Gres.

The conversion from trees to syntactic dependencies is complex and delivers worse results when based on Collins Model 1 than when using Pro3Gres directly. Functional dependencies are closer to predicate-argument structures and shallow semantic structures and thus a more suitable level for applications that need such structures, such as text mining, answer extraction, information retrieval, and knowledge management generally. Pro3Gres directly delivers functional dependencies, in an order of magnitude less time then Collins.

	Collins 1			Pro3Gres		
Relation	P%	R%	Counts Correct	P%	R%	Counts Correct
Subject	90.7%	60.4%	661	92.3%	87.0%	865
Object	89.7%	73.4%	314	85.3%	82.5%	353
PP-Attachment	77.8%	60.0%	614	76.9%	68.6%	702

Table 7.14: Comparison of parsing performance between Collins Model 1 and Pro3Gres

Dependency Type	Description
AMOD	Modifier of adjective or adverb (phrase adverbial)
DEP	Other dependent (default label)
NMOD	Modifier of noun (including complement)%
OBJ	Object
P	Punctuation
PMOD	Modifier of preposition (including complement)
PRD	Predicative complement
ROOT	Dependent of special root node
SBAR	Head verb of subordinate clause dependent on complementizer
SBJ	Subject
VC	Verb chain
VMOD	Modifier of verb

Table 7.15: Nivre (2006) Dependency Types

7.3 Tentative Comparison to Nivre's MaltParse

The set of dependencies used only contains 12 dependency types, so that it appears slightly less fine-grained than ours, and considerably less fine-grained than GREVAL (Carroll, Minnen, and Briscoe, 2003).

7.3.1 Comparison Across Different Corpora

Nivre (2006b) also reports selective evaluations on each dependency type. Nivre (2006b) gives a detailed evaluation of his parser. A comparison can only be indicative, because he uses a different evaluation corpus, Penn Treebank section 23. The set of dependency types, according to Nivre (2006b), is shown in table 7.15.

The dependency types are derived form the Penn Treebank as follows. Collins (1999)'s complex labels <mother (M), head (H), daughter (D), direction> are used as input and converted into a single label r. In order of descending priority, the rules are as follows.

1. if D is a punctuation category, $r = P$.

2. if D contains the function tag SBJ, $r = $ SBJ.

3. if D contains the function tag PRD, $r = $ PRD.

4. if $M = VP$, H is a part-of-speech tag and $D = NP$ (without any function tag), $r = OBJ$.

5. if $M = VP$, H is a part-of-speech tag and $D = VP$, $r = VC$.

6. if $M = SBAR$ and $D = S$, $r = SBAR$.

7. if $M = VP, S, SQ, SINV$ or $SBAR$, $r = VMOD$.

8. if $M = NP, NAC, NX$ or $WHNP$, $r = NMOD$.

9. if $M = ADJP, ADVP, QP, WHADJP$ or $WHADVP$, $r = AMOD$.

10. if $M = PP$ or $WHPP$, $r = PMOD$.

11. Otherwise, $r = DEP$.

This mapping is arguably simplistic (see, e.g. Samuelsson (2007)) and less elaborate then ours, which is listed in the appendix. More research addressing mapping questions is needed.

We give a few examples of the linguistic errors and inconsistencies that such a mapping introduces. This list is not meant to be complete or representative, but reflects a few cases that are obvious when browsing the gold standard corpus provided in the CoNLL-XI shared task (Nivre et al., 2007).

- Adjuncts as Objects: Nouns with adjunct function are very often erroneously attached as objects. In *But while the New York Stock Exchange did n't fall apart Friday as the Dow Jones Industrial Average plunged 190.58 points* the adjuncts *Friday* and *points* are both labelled *OBJ*. Adjuncts are not consistently mislabelled, however. In *Shares of UAL, the parent of United Airlines, were extremely active all day Friday*, the adjunct *Friday* is correctly labelled as *VMOD* (verbal modification)

- Indirect Objects The label *IOBJ* exhibits the same error. In *Big Board Chairman John J. Phelan said yesterday the circuit breaker " worked well mechanically. ... yesterday* is labelled as *IOBJ*. The majority of noun labelled *IOBJ* are direct objects, only few are really indirect objects. In *... he has had trouble finding stocks he likes.* the object *trouble* is labelled *IOBJ*. This error is potentially triggered by the error that *finding* is attached to the verb *had* instead of the expected noun *trouble*. For the *IOBJ* label, the mapping generally introduces more errors than correct results.

7.3. Tentative Comparison to Nivre's MaltParse

Dependency Type	Occurrence	Precision	Recall
AMOD	2072	80.7 %	76.7 %
DEP	259	56.5 %	30.1 %
NMOD	21002	91.1 %	90.8 %
OBJ	1960	86.5 %	76.7 %
PMOD	5593	87.7 %	89.5 %
PRD	832	75.9 %	71.8 %
ROOT	2401	78.8 %	86.4 %
SBAR	1195	87.1 %	85.1 %
SBJ	4108	90.6 %	88.1 %
VC	1771	93.4 %	96.6 %
VMOD	8175	76.5 %	77.1 %
Total	49368	86.3 %	86.3 %

Table 7.16: Nivre (2006) Evaluation Results

- Parentheticals The status of parentheticals is unclear

- Internal structure of noun chunk

- Status of infinitive clauses

- Attachment of punctuation The attachment of punctuation is partly arbitrary.

- verb-chain attachment

Mapping is an error-prone task in principle and usually not possible in a loss-free fashion. Our answer to the problem of mapping the Penn Treebank to dependency is to use an involved, linguistically motivated mapping that has very high precision but slightly incomplete recall, and that does not map all structural configurations. This leads to a mapping that delivers reliable relations but not fully connected trees.

The reported labelled attachment results are shown in table 7.16. If we assume that subject and object dependency types are comparable, we get similar results, although Nivre (2006b) is better at subject recall, and we are better at object recall. Nivre's $NMOD$ relation comprises our noun-PP attachment $modpp$, and additionally our chunk-internal $detmod$ and $ncmod$ relations. At first sight, with a precision of 88.2% on this set of relations we seem to perform worse. There is an important difference in the annotation of chunk-internal modifiers, however.

7.3. Tentative Comparison to Nivre's MaltParse

a.

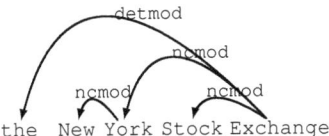

b.

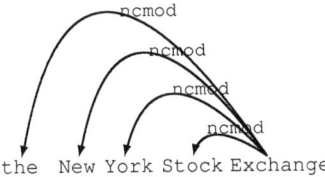

Figure 7.5: Semantic and syntactic dependency annotation of *New York Stock Exchange*

While GREVAL (Carroll, Minnen, and Briscoe, 2003) uses a semantic annotation in which *New York Stock Exchange* is annnotated as in figure 7.5 a) – as we have discussed in subsection 7.2.5 – Nivre derives and uses the cascading annotation shown in 7.5 b) that always leaves the semantic dependencies underspecified. Nivre's $VMOD$ relation corresponds to our *pobj* and clausal relations. We achieve similar precision (74.6 %), while recall is difficult to establish due to the GREVAL annotation scheme, although on PP attachment and clausal relations we generally get a slightly lower recall. Nivre's $PMOD$ relation corresponds to our *prep* relation, where we achieve similar precision (89.6%) and slightly lower recall (82.3%). Nivre's VC relation corresponds to our *aux* relation, where we achieve similar precision (94.2%) and slightly lower recall (89.8%). We can conclude that, as a tendency, we seem to get similar precision at slightly lower recall. A major reason for lower recall is that we do not always get a full parse.

7.3.2 Comparing with the same Corpus: Participation in CoNLL-XI Shared Task

An opportunity to compare Pro3Gres to MaltParse and many other dependency parsers was provided by the recent CoNLL 2007 shared task on on dependency parser domain adaptation (Nivre et al., 2007) in which we participated (Schneider et al., 2007). We have achieved average results in the CoNLL domain adaptation track open submission (Marcus, Santorini, and Marcinkiewicz, 1993a; Johansson and Nugues, 2007; Kulick et al., 2004; MacWhinney, 2000; Brown, 1973). Two domains were used for adaptation: chemical texts (Kulick et al., 2004) and child language (MacWhinney, 2000; Brown, 1973). The performance of the parser is seriously affected by mapping problems to the particular dependency representation used in the shared task, which is a representation that is identical or very close to the one used in (Nivre, 2006b).

Domain Adaptation Based on our experience with parsing texts form the biomedical domain, we have used the following two adaptations to the domain of chemistry.

(Hindle and Rooth, 1993) exploit the fact that in sentence-initial *NP PP* sequences the PP unambiguously attaches to the noun. We have observed that in sentence-initial *NP PP PP* sequences, also the second PP frequently attaches to the noun, the noun itself often being a relational noun. We have thus used such sequences to learn relational nouns from the unlabelled domain texts.

Multi-word terms, adjective-preposition constructions and similar domain-specific expressions have strong collocational force. We have thus used the collocation extraction tool XTRACT (Smadja, 2003) to discover collocations from large domain corpora. Since the tagging quality of the Chemistry testset is high, the impact of multi-word term recognition was lower than the biomedical domain when using a standard tagger, as we have shown in (Rinaldi et al., 2007).

For the CHILDES domain, we have not used any adaptation. The hand-written grammar fares quite well on most types of questions, which are very frequent in this domain. In the spirit of the shared task, we have not attempted to correct tagging errors, which were frequent in the CHILDES domain. We have restricted the use of external resources to the hand-written, domain-independent grammar, and to WordNet. Due to serious problems in mapping our LFG f-structure based dependencies to the CoNLL representation, much less time than expected was available for the domain adaptation.

7.3. Tentative Comparison to Nivre's MaltParse 208

deprel	gold	correct	system	recall (%)	prec. (%)
ADV	366	212	302	57.92	70.20
AMOD	87	8	87	9.20	9.20
CC	11	0	0	0.00	NaN
COORD	402	233	342	57.96	68.13
DEP	9	0	0	0.00	NaN
EXP	2	0	0	0.00	NaN
GAP	14	0	0	0.00	NaN
IOBJ	3	0	0	0.00	NaN
LGS	37	0	0	0.00	NaN
NMOD	1813	1576	1763	86.93	89.39
OBJ	185	146	208	78.92	70.19
P	587	524	525	89.27	99.81
PMOD	681	533	648	78.27	82.25
PRN	34	13	68	38.24	19.12
ROOT	195	138	190	70.77	72.63
SBJ	279	217	296	77.78	73.31
VC	129	116	136	89.92	85.29
VMOD	167	116	149	69.46	77.85
unknown	0	0	287	NaN	0.00

Table 7.17: Prec.&recall of DEPREL

Our results: We have reported the following results: Labeled attachment score: 3151 / 5001 * 100 = 63.01, unlabeled attachment score: 3327 / 5001 * 100 = 66.53, label accuracy score: 3832 / 5001 * 100 = 76.62. These results are about 10 % below what we typically obtain when using our own dependency representation or GREVAL (Carroll, Minnen, and Briscoe, 2003), a deep-syntactic annotation scheme that is close to ours. Our mapping was quite poor, especially when conjunctions are involved. Also punctuation is attached poorly. 5.7 % of all dependencies remained unmapped (*unknown* in the figure). We give an overview of the the relation-dependent results in figures 7.17 and 7.18. Relations between heads of chunks, which are central for predicate-argument structures which Pro3Gres aims to recover, such as *SBJ, NMOD, ROOT*, perform better than those for which Pro3Gres was not originally designed, particularly *ADV, AMOD, PRN, P*. Performance on *COORD* was particularly disappointing.

We have obtained results slightly above average on the CHILDES domain, although we did not not adapt the parser to this domain in any way (unlabeled attachment score: 3013 / 4999 * 100 = 60.27 %). The hand-written grammar, which includes rules for most types of questions, fares relatively well on this domain since questions are rare in the Penn Treebank (see (Hermjakob, 2001)).

We have learnt from our participation that mapping to different representations is an often underestimated task (see e.g. Crouch et al. (2002)) and that a discussion of different representations possibly leading to a standardisation is vital. We believe that mapping problems between different representations would be smaller

deprel	gold	correct	system	recall (%)	prec. (%)
ADV	366	161	302	43.99	53.31
AMOD	87	5	87	5.75	5.75
CC	11	0	0	0.00	NaN
COORD	402	170	342	42.29	49.71
DEP	9	0	0	0.00	NaN
EXP	2	0	0	0.00	NaN
GAP	14	0	0	0.00	NaN
IOBJ	3	0	0	0.00	NaN
LGS	37	0	0	0.00	NaN
NMOD	1813	1392	1763	76.78	78.96
OBJ	185	140	208	75.68	67.31
P	587	221	525	37.65	42.10
PMOD	681	521	648	76.51	80.40
PRN	34	12	68	35.29	17.65
ROOT	195	138	190	70.77	72.63
SBJ	279	190	296	68.10	64.19
VC	129	116	136	89.92	85.29
VMOD	167	85	149	50.90	57.05
unknown	0	0	287	NaN	0.00

Table 7.18: Prec.&recall of DEPREL+ATTACHMENT

if one used a dependency representation that maximally abstracts away from form to function, such as (Carroll, Minnen, and Briscoe, 2003). Our performance on the CHILDES task, where we did not adapt the parser at all, indicates that hand-written, carefully engineered *competence* grammars may be relatively domain-independent while *performance* disambiguation is more domain-dependent.

7.4 Evaluation on Biomedical Term-Annotated Corpora

In order to test Pro3Gres in one of its application areas, we have evaluated it on texts from the biomedical domain. We have evaluated Pro3Gres on texts form the biomedical domain with 3 questions in mind. First, biomedical texts are an important field of application for Pro3Gres (see e.g. Rinaldi et al. (2006) or Weeds et al. (2005)), so that its usefulness depends on the performance. Second, we wanted to test how the Pro3Gres parser performs over domains markedly different from the training corpus. Third, we wanted to test whether terminology is the key to a successful parsing system, and to assess the impact of tagging and chunking errors.

7.4.1 Evaluation on 100 Random Sentences from the GENIA Corpus

The parser has been applied to the GENIA corpus (Kim et al., 2003b), 2000 MEDLINE abstracts of more than 400,000 words describing the results of biomedical research. GENIA is annotated for multi-word terms. This includes information on where a multi-terms starts and where it ends. Multi-word term boundaries can be understood as base NP boundaries, thus delivering near-perfect chunking for domain terms.

GENIA presents very technical and complex language: average sentence length is 26.5 words, opposed to 21.2 for the Penn Treebank. The most striking characteristic of this domain is the frequency of multi-word terms which are known to cause serious problems for NLP systems (Sag et al., 2002; Dowdall et al., 2003). The token to chunk ratio (NPs = 2.3 , VPs = 1.3, number of tokens divided by the number of chunks) is unusually high. Also the complexity of PPs is a striking characteristic of this domain. Figure 7.6 provides an example of a typical domain sentence, showing the tagged parser input and a predicate-argument version of the parser output for the top-ranked reading.

The GENIA corpus does not include any syntactic annotation (making standard evaluation more difficult) but approximately 100,000 multi-word terms are annotated and assigned a semantic type from the GENIA ontology. We wanted to determine how parsing performance interacts with multi-word term recognition as well as the applicability and possible improvements to the probabilistic model over this domain.

100 random sentences from the GENIA corpus have been manually annotated and compared to the parser output (Rinaldi et al., 2004b). The results are given in table 7.19[1]. When the terminology information contained in the GENIA corpus is used ("clean"), parsing results are comparable to, or even better than those on general text.

This slightly better performance on Genia is partly due to the fact we have annotated our test corpus with the Pro3Gres scheme (there are no mapping errors), and partly due to the fact that the near-perfect tagging and multi-word term information is better than automatic chunker output. But it also indicates that the grammar and even the lexicalization is not very domain-specific. Without knowledge on terminology ("dirty") parser performance drops considerably due to mistagging and mischunking on unknown medical domain words.

---

[1]This is a small set. Average sentence length is 17.9 chunks, compared to 17.0 in the whole GENIA, so we can assume that it is fairly representative

```
Interaction_NN of_IN nuclear_JJ extracts_NNS from_IN
various_JJ cell_NN lines_NNS and_CC tissue_NN
with_IN the_DT MNP_NN site_NN leads_VBZ to_TO
the_DT formation_NN of_IN fast-migrating_JJ
protein-DNA_JJ complexes_NNS with_IN similar_JJ
but_CC distinct_JJ electrophoretic_JJ mobilities_NNS

prep('extract#3', 'of#2', _, '(<-)').
prep('line#5', 'from#4', _, '(<-)').e
conj('tissue#7', 'and#6', _, '(<-)').
conj('line#5', 'tissue#7', 'and#6', '(->)').
prep('site#9', 'with#8', _, '(<-)').
 modpp('line#5', 'site#9', 'with#8', '(->)').
modpp('extract#3', 'line#5', 'from#4', '(->)').
modpp('interaction#1', 'extract#3', 'of#2', '(->)').
subj('lead#10', 'interaction#1', _, '(<-)').
prep('formation#12', 'to#11', _, '(<-)').
prep('complex#14', 'of#13', _, '(<-)').
modpp('formation#12', 'complex#14', 'of#13', '(->)').
pobj('lead#10', 'formation#12', 'to#11', '(->)').
prep('mobility#16', 'with#15', _, '(<-)').
pobj('lead#10', 'mobility#16', 'with#15', '(->)').
```

Figure 7.6: A sample sentence illustrating the complexity of noun-modifying PPs, with its top-ranked grammatical relation annotation

	GENIA "dirty"		GENIA "clean"	
Relation	P%	R%	P%	R%
Subject	83	74	90	86
Object	70	77	94	95
noun-PP	68	64	83	82
verb-PP	67	68	82	84
subord. clause	63	60	71	75

Table 7.19: Evaluation comparing LTChunk chunking ("dirty") and near-perfect multi-word knowledge ("clean") on GENIA corpus

This indicates that base phrase parsing is more domain-specific than parsing between these base phrases. This entails that taggers and chunkers or base-phrase rules for parsers need to be adapted more to a given domain than the rules for parsing between base phrases, that parsing between base phrases as Pro3Gres does is quite domain-independent and robust.

We have added one domain-specific extension for parsing texts from the biomedical domain. Pro3Gres failed to attach more than one PP to relational nouns from the domain, such as *phosphorilation*, *triggering* or *down-regulation*. Based on the fact that sentence-initial <NP PP*> sequences are typically unambiguous (Hindle and Rooth, 1993), we have added an unsupervised module that learns which nouns are typically allowed to be modified by several PPs. This extension explains the high noun-PP attachment recall.

7.4.2 Evaluation with the Stanford Dependency Scheme on 900 BioInfer sentences

Haverinen et al. (2008) have mapped the output of Pro3Gres to the Stanford dependency scheme and evaluated the parser's performance. The Stanford scheme (de Marneffe, MacCartney, and Manning, 2006) is a recent extension of Carroll, Minnen, and Briscoe (2003) and is a widely used dependency representation. Haverinen et al. (2008) have evaluated the output of Pro3Gres after the automatic conversion to the Stanford scheme. They report a total F-score of 74.3% on the 900 sentence BioInfer corpus (Pyysalo et al., 2007). They conclude that Pro3Gres has state-of-the-art performance.

7.4.3 Task-Oriented, Practical Evaluation of Pro3Gres relation extraction

The interest of an application of Pro3Gres to the biomedical domain lies in the discovery of domain specific relations, such as "Protein *activates* Gene". Most of the NLP techniques applied to the domain of molecular biology focus on the discovery of entities, such as genes and proteins, (see for instance Ananiadou and Tsujii (2003)). However there are also interesting applications aiming at detecting syntactic and semantic relations among those entities. Examples of systems aiming at detecting relations are the following.

Craven and Kumlien (1999) identifies possible drug-interaction relations between proteins and chemicals using a "bag of words" approach applied to the sentence level. Ono et al. (2001) reports on extraction of protein-protein interactions based on a combination of syntactic patterns. Friedman et al. (2001) describes a system (GENIES) which extracts and structures information about cellular pathways from the biological literature. Pustejovsky et al. (2002) processes titles and abstracts of MEDLINE articles focusing on relation identification (in particular the *inhibit* relation). Gaizauskas et al. (2003) uses a template-based Information Extraction approach, focusing on the roles of specific amino-acid residues in protein molecules.

In order to discover domain specific relations we believe that an accurate detection of predicate-argument relations is essential. We have asked domain experts to evaluate the quality of the extracted relations, so far focusing on triples of the form (predicate - subject - object).[2] The analysis of the whole GENIA corpus resulted in 10072 such triples (records). For the evaluation of biological relevance we selected only the records containing the following predicates: *activate, bind* and *block*. This resulted in 487 records. The extraction algorithm aims at maximally expanding the arguments of the predicate, following all their dependencies. Each argument is then assigned a type (a concept of the GENIA Ontology), based on its head. The type assignment depends on the manual annotation performed by the GENIA annotators, so we have taken it as reliable and have not further evaluated it. We then removed all records where a type had not been assigned to either subject or object: this left 169 fully qualified records.[3] This remaining set was inspected by a domain expert.

---

[2] This evaluation has been performed in collaboration with Biovista (http://www.biovista.com/)

[3] This step is meant to remove records where one of the arguments cannot be clearly assigned a type. This is generally caused by pronouns, which explains why in the error evaluation (see table 7.21) the number of pronouns appears so low.

7.4. Evaluation on Biomedical Term-Annotated Corpora 214

A first evaluation was based on assigning a simple key code to each record: 'P' for positive (biologically relevant and correct, 53 cases), 'Y' for acceptable (biologically relevant but not completely correct, 102 cases) and 'N' (not biologically relevant or seriously wrong, 14 cases). This result was considered encouraging as it showed 91.7% of relevant records.

We then asked the expert to evaluate in detail. In this second evaluation the expert had to evaluate each argument separately and mark it according to the following codes:

- [Y] the argument is correct and informative
- [N] the argument is completely wrong
- [Pr] the argument is correct, but it is a pronoun, and it would need to be resolved to be significant (e.g. "This protein").
- [A+] the argument is "too large" (which implies that a prepositional phrase has been erroneously attached to it)
- [A-] the argument is "too small" (which implies that an attachment has been omitted)

In table 7.20 we show as an example the evaluation of the following sentences:

178. *Interleukin-2 (IL-2) rapidly activated Stat5 in fresh PBL, and Stat3 and Stat5 in preactivated PBL.*

807. *Thus, we demonstrated that IL-5 activated the Jak 2 -STAT 1 signaling pathway in eosinophils.*

5212. *Spi-B binds DNA sequences containing a core 5-GGAA-3 and activates transcription through this motif.*

16919. *The higher affinity sites bind CVZ with 20- to 50-fold greater affinity, consistent with CVZ's enhanced biological effects.*

The values of this evaluation are shown in table 7.21. They indicate that the performance of Pro3Gres is sufficient for the application to this task. The biggest source of error is over-expansion of the object, plus there was a small but significant problem in the detection of the subject which we have corrected in the meantime. Overexpansion (A+) is only a minor problem for an expert searching for interaction between entities, since the reported subject or object does contain the entity (followed by additional, irrelevant information, typically PPs). Underexpansion (A-) means that an expert needs to scan the documents along a few words (usually to the right) to find all the relevant information.

No	relation	subj	subj type	subj eval	obj	obj type	obj eval
178	activate	Interleukin-2 (IL-2)	G#amino_acid	Y	Stat5 in fresh PBL, and Stat3 and Stat5 in preactivated PBL	G#amino_acid	A+
807	activate	IL-5	G#amino_acid	Y	the Jak 2 -STAT 1 signaling pathway	G#other_name	Y
5212	bind	Spi-B	G#amino_acid	Y	DNA sequences	G#nucleic_acid	A-
16919	bind	The higher affinity sites	G#other_name	Pr	CVZ with 20-	G#other-_organic-_compound	N

Table 7.20: Some example sentences of the task-oriented evaluation on biomedical texts

	Y	N	Pr	A+	A-
Subject	146	11	4	6	2
Object	99	1	4	59	6

Table 7.21: Distribution of GENIA parsing errors in the application-oriented evaluation

Despite parsing errors the results can be considered satisfactory, as they show 86.4% and 58.6% correct results in the detection of subjects and objects (respectively). If all overexpanded and underexpanded cases are considered as positive (excluding only the 'N' cases), these results increase to 93.5% and 99.4% (respectively).

7.5 Exploring Precision and Recall Trade-Offs

Although the performance of Pro3Gres is competitive, its output is far from perfect. This section addresses the question of how much manual interaction is necessary to obtain perfect analyses, of how much precision can be optimised at the expense of recall, or vice versa. A scenario where recall can be maximised at the cost of precision is building up a corpus, where it is much less labour-intense for an annotator to choose the correct analysis among a relatively short, ordered list than to annotate from scratch. For an application building up a knowledge base, we rather want to be almost certain that a given relation is correct. Natural language redundancy often compensates for recall errors, but precision errors leading to the assertion of wrong facts to a knowledge base is a more serious problem. This constitutes a scenario where precision can be maximised at the cost of recall.

The percentages reported for the reference model in subsections 7.5 to 7.8 differ slightly from those in section 7.2. The reasons are that we have used a slightly older version of Pro3Gres, that we have used the unidirectional mapping described in subsection 7.2.2 for PP-attachment, that we have not included *modpart* in the evaluation of subjects, and that we have excluded $obj2$ from the evaluation of objects. Since the evaluations shown in subsections 7.5 to 7.8 do not compare to other parsers, but each experiment compares to a version of the parser that is identical except for the parameters discussed in the experiment, these small differences are not relevant for the discussion.

7.5. Exploring Precision and Recall Trade-Offs

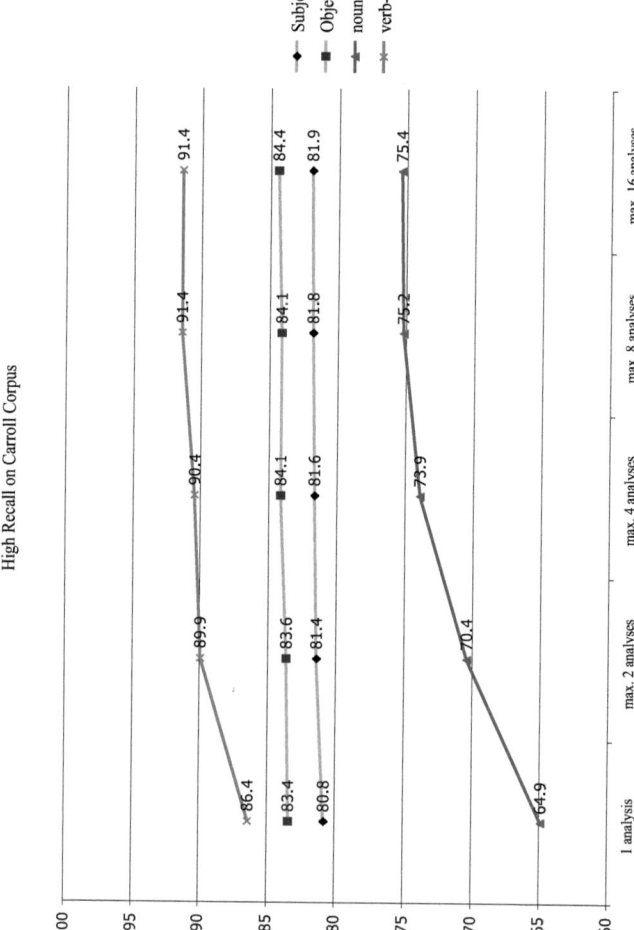

Figure 7.7: Graph of percentage results of recall among first N-ranked analyses on the GREVAL corpus

7.5. Exploring Precision and Recall Trade-Offs

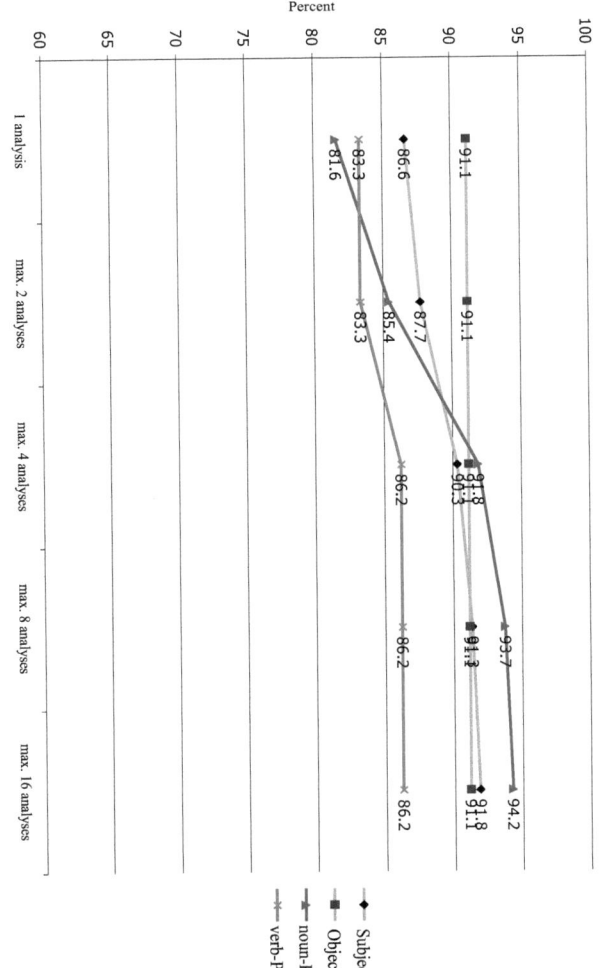

Figure 7.8: Graph of percentage results of recall among first N-ranked analyses on GENIA

7.5.1 High Recall Parsing

An annotation task is greatly facilitated if the annotator, instead of being asked to annotate every sentence manually, can choose from a (relatively short) ranked list of analyses. Brants and Plaehn (2000) have shown that parser-assisted annotation (in their case an interactive scenario with a shallow parser (Brants, 1999)) greatly increases annotation speed. Also for classical corpus linguistics tasks, optimising on recall is desired. While it is important to retrieve most instances of the investigated phenomenon, a modest amount of manual filtering of results is seen as acceptable and often unavoidable.

Figures 7.7 and 7.8 show the increase in recall in relation to the length of the list of analyses. Lists longer than 16 readings of a sentence (which convey 4 2-way ambiguous relations) were assumed to be prohibitively long for manual scanning.

The $subj$, obj and the two PP-relations together average above 90% recall in GENIA, which means that less than one in ten of these relations would need to be added manually by an annotator.

7.5.2 High Precision Parsing

In order to keep the necessity for intervention of a human annotator during corpus annotation to a minimum, it is desirable to recognise a maximum number of unproblematic relations. In an annotation scenario one can report the highest ranked parse and point out to the human annotator the few difficult and highly ambiguous relations in a given analysis. Parsing methods that optimise precision while reducing recall up to an acceptable point are required. A related study on this subject is Carroll and Briscoe (2002). High-precsion parsing is also important for building up knowledge databases automatically, where recall deficiencies are often compensated by natural language redundancy, but asserting wrong knowledge arising from low precision poses a serious problem. The following experiments have been conducted to improve precision.

Experiment 1: Tagger Agreement Different taggers often make different mistakes. We have used two alternative taggers for preprocessing, LTPos (Mikheev, 1997) and Ratnaparkhi's Maximum Entropy tagger (Ratnaparkhi, 1996). In a simple experiment, only sentences where both taggers deliver identical tags are used. Precision increases, but the large cost of decrease in recall is unacceptable, as shown in table 7.22.

7.5. Exploring Precision and Recall Trade-Offs

Experiment 1	Subject	Object	noun-PP	verb-PP
Precision	92.2	95.4	85.6	71.6
Recall	31.5	30.7	23.2	27.8

Table 7.22: Percentage results of Experiment 1: keeping only sentences with identical tags from two taggers, on the GREVAL corpus on subject, object and PP-attachment relations

Experiment 2	Subject	Object	noun-PP	verb-PP
Precision	94.1	93.0	73.3	75.4
Recall	76.4	78.8	60.5	80.3

Table 7.23: Percentage results of Experiment2: keeping only agreeing relations arising from parsing with two taggers, on the GREVAL corpus on subject, object and PP-attachment relations

Experiment 2: Grammatical Relations Agreement when using different Taggers In order to minimise the loss in recall in the previous experiment, the output of each tagger is used as input to the LTChunk chunker and the Pro3Gres parser. Only grammatical relations that are different due to the tagging differences are discarded. The increase in precision is similar to experiment 1 (noun PP-attachment is slightly worse) while the decrease in recall is much more moderate, as table 7.23 shows.

Experiment 3: Parsing Alternatives Agreement In this experiment, the relation intersection between the two top ranked analyses is kept. This amounts to discarding only the most ambiguous relation of any given sentence. The decrease in recall (table 7.24) is higher than in experiment 2. Mainly the PP-attachment relations profit, which are often the most ambiguous relations, and which are more affected by attachment ambiguities than other relations.

Experiment 4: Trust Short Distances Relation spanning short distances are intuitively thought to be easier for the parser to find. Experiment 4 discards all relations that are longer than a certain threshold. Length is measured in chunks. The experiment has been conducted at several distances for the GREVAL corpus (figures 7.9 and 7.10) and for the 100 manually annotated GENIA sentences (figures 7.11 and 7.12).

The results reveal interesting differences between different relation types. For $subj$, longer distances are almost as reliable. obj relations are almost exclusively

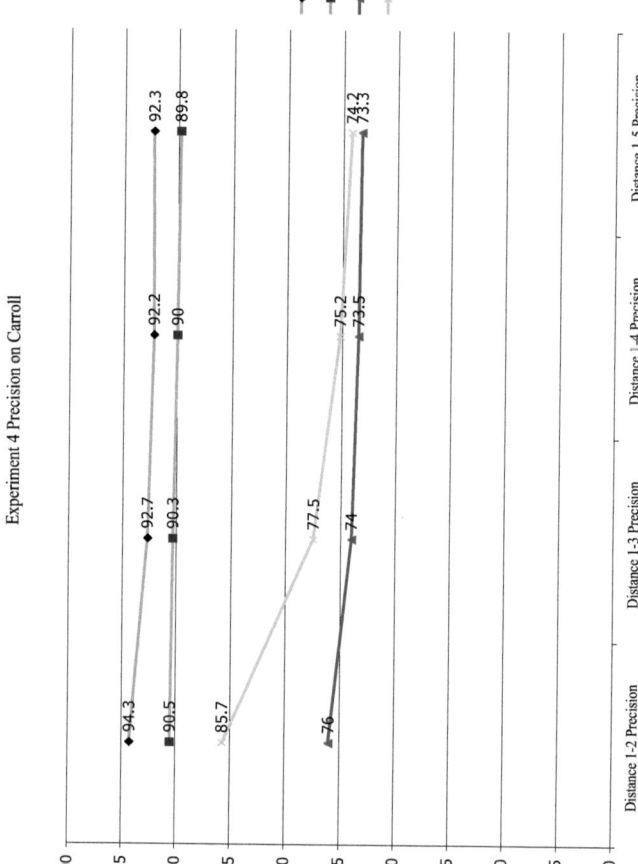

Figure 7.9: Graph of Precision of Experiment 4 on GREVAL

7.5. Exploring Precision and Recall Trade-Offs

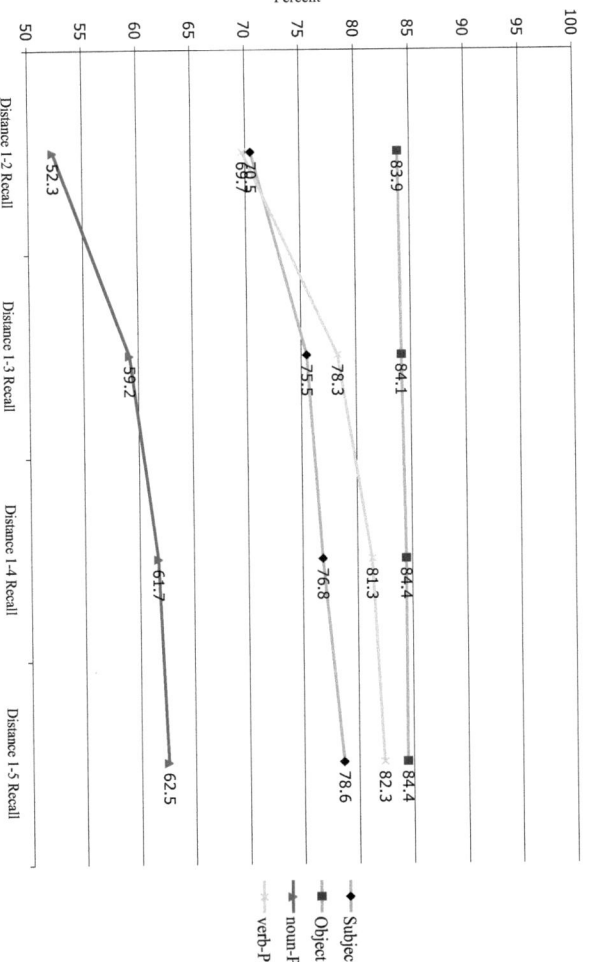

Figure 7.10: Graph of Recall of Experiment 4 on GREVAL.

7.5. Exploring Precision and Recall Trade-Offs

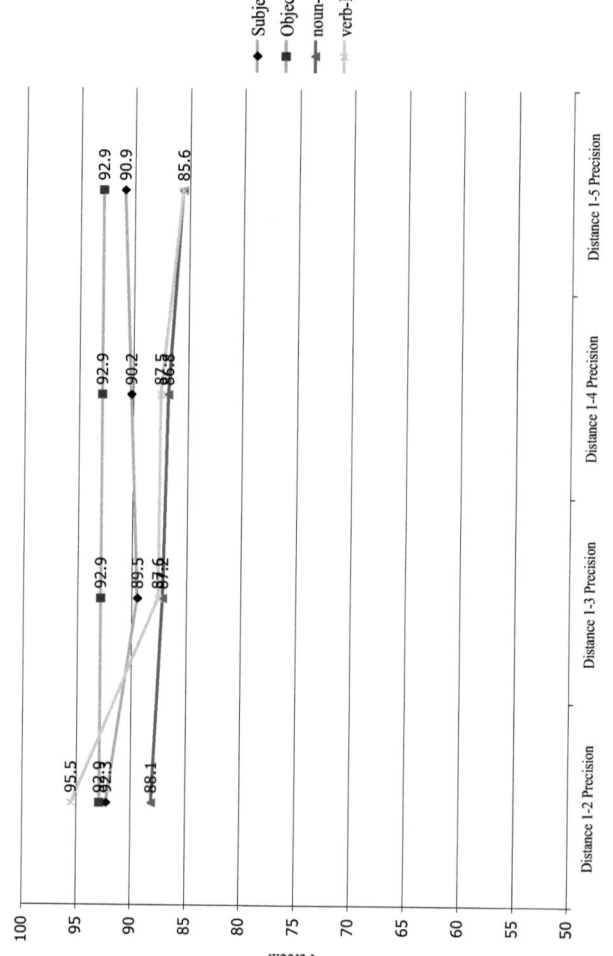

Figure 7.11: Graph of Precision of Experiment 4 on GENIA

7.5. Exploring Precision and Recall Trade-Offs   224

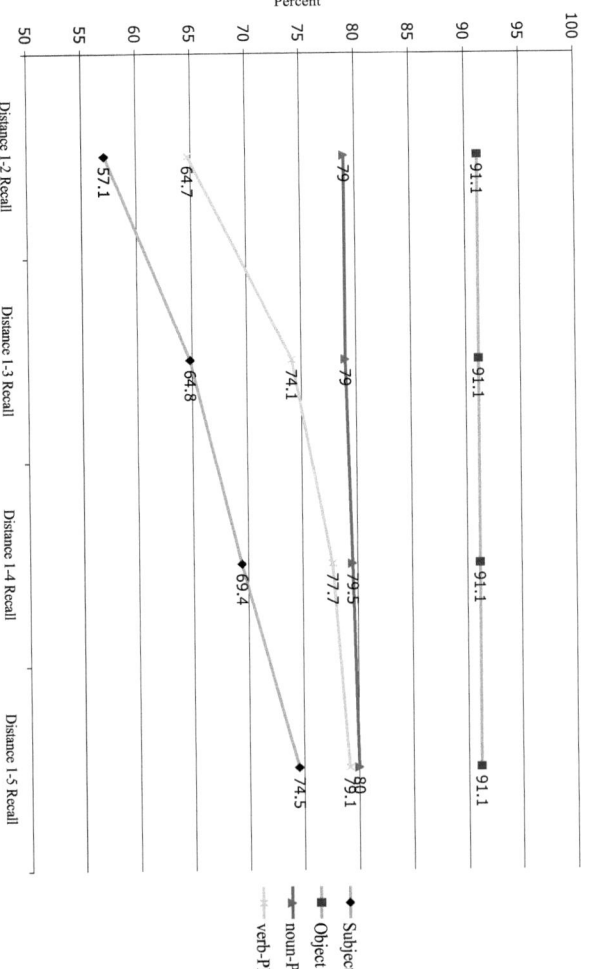

Figure 7.12: Graph of Recall of Experiment 4 on GENIA

	Experiment 3	Subject	Object	noun-PP	verb-PP	subord. S
GREVAL	Precision	92.6	90.1	76.6	76.7	68.2
	Recall	76.8	63.6	53.7	67.2	n/a
GENIA	Precision	91.1	93.4	87.0	84.2	65.2
	Recall	78.1	65.8	68.0	70.5	60.4

Table 7.24: Percentage results of Experiment 3: discarding the most ambiguous relation in each sentence, for subject, object, PP-attachment and subordinate sentence relations

very short. Subordinate clause relations are difficult and mostly very long, about 20% spanning at least 5 chunks. For envisaged applications, e.g. protein interaction relations, sentence subordination is less important. PP-attachment relations very strongly depend on distance. This is largely due to the fact that many PP-attachments across longer distances[4] are in competition with intervening other PPs and thus exponentially lower the baseline[5].

When comparing the two evaluation corpora and genres a major difference is constituted by PP-attachments. The complexity of medical language partly stems from very complex nouns with embedded PPs (see e.g. fig. 7.6). The noun-PP-attachment per sentence ratio is 2.1 in our GENIA 100 test corpus and 1.6 in GREVAL. The fact that the performance on GENIA is better than on GREVAL can largely be explained by our remarks in section 7.5.1.

Experiment 5: Cut low probability parsing decisions In a first attempt, experiments with an increased probability cut-off at parse time were conducted. However, they had the effect of greatly increasing the amount of partial parses, thus returning many local analyses that the syntactic parsing context would have disambiguated. Precision remained comparable, while recall dropped. In a second approach, the parsing algorithm remains unchanged, but only relations whose probability is above a certain threshold are reported. Pro3Gres probabilities express decision probabilities at each given ambiguous point. Experiment 5 have been made on the highly ambiguous PP-attachment relations. The results are shown in figures 7.13 and 7.14 for the GREVAL corpus, and in figures 7.15 and 7.16 for the GENIA corpus.

---

[4]Observe that "longer distances" does not entail a long-distance dependency traditionally expressed by coindexing or movement, although a considerable portion of the "longer distances" here are long-distance dependencies, for example fronted PPs attaching to the verb

[5](Church and Patil, 1982) describe for PP attachment that a sequence <verb-NP-PP*> with n PPs has C_{n+1} analyses, where C_{n+1} is the $(n+1)$'th Catalan number. The Catalan number C_n is defined as $\frac{1}{n+1}\binom{2n}{n}$

7.5. Exploring Precision and Recall Trade-Offs 226

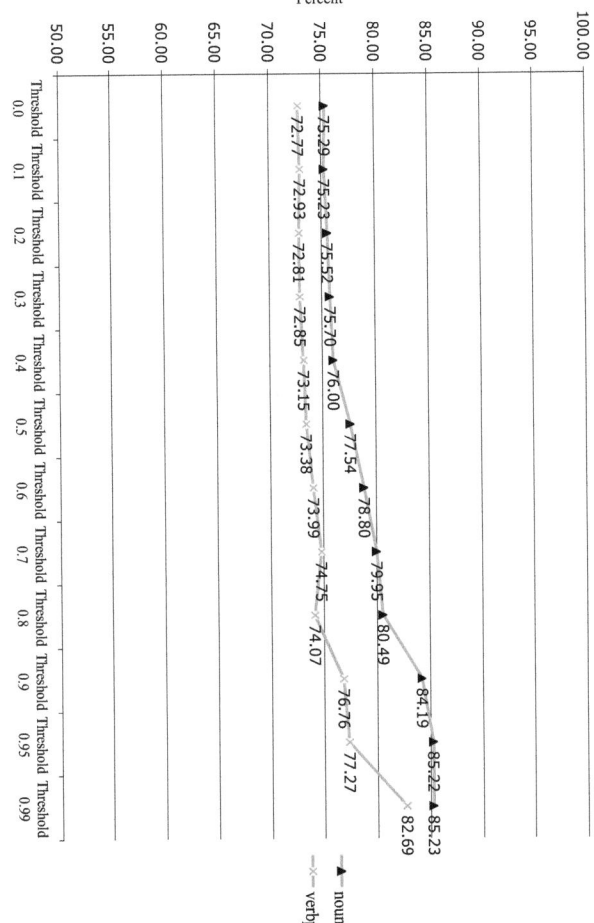

Figure 7.13: Graph of Precision of Experiment 5 on GREVAL

7.5. Exploring Precision and Recall Trade-Offs

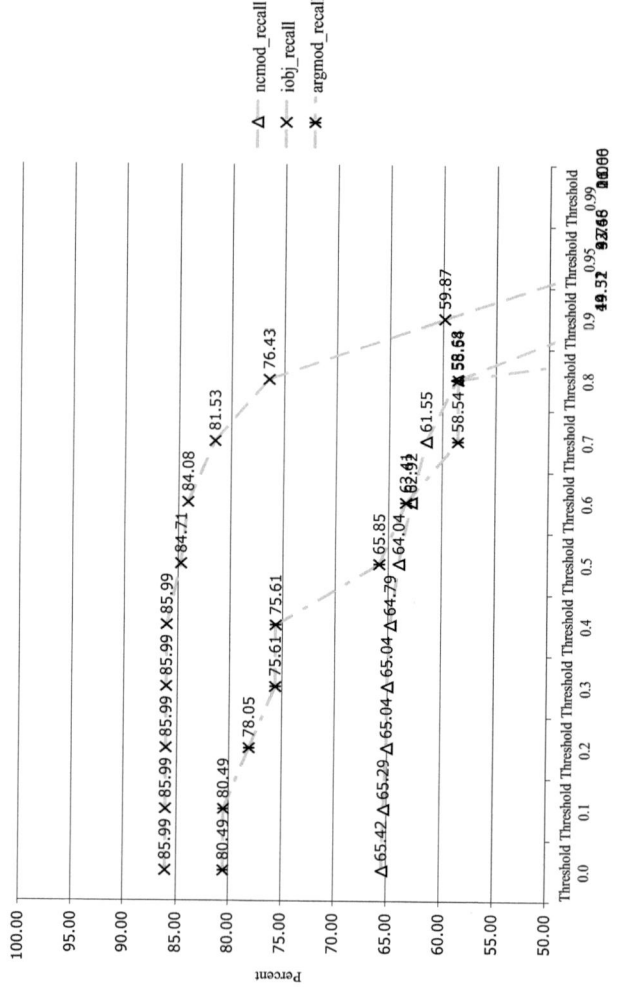

Figure 7.14: Graph of Recall of Experiment 5 on GREVAL.

7.5. Exploring Precision and Recall Trade-Offs

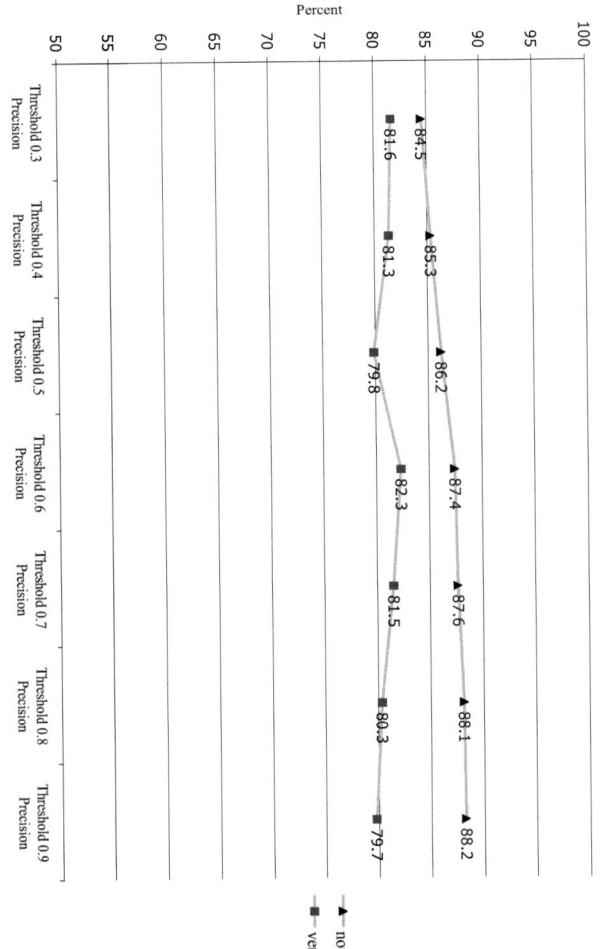

Figure 7.15: Graph of Precision of Experiment 5 on GENIA

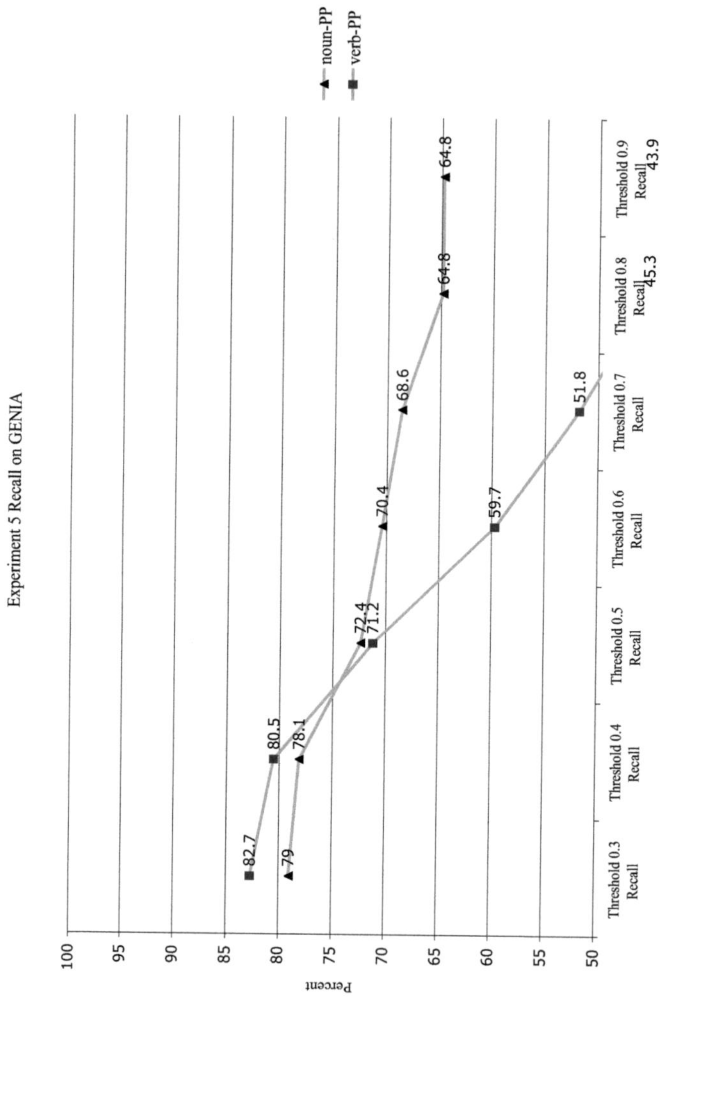

7.5. Exploring Precision and Recall Trade-Offs

Figure 7.16: Graph of Recall of Experiment 5 on GENIA

7.5. Exploring Precision and Recall Trade-Offs

Backoff Levels	
0	full: head & prep & description noun
1	head & prep & description noun class
2	head & prep
3 / 3.1	head class & prep & description noun
4 / 4.1	head class & prep & description noun class
5	prep & description noun
6	prep
7	NONE

Table 7.25: PP-attachment backoff level legend

MaxEnt-tagged Parsing	Subject	Object	noun-PP	verb-PP
Keeping all				
Precision	92.6	89.6	76.6	74.4
Recall	81.1	83.9	67.4	89.2
Discarding levels 5 and 6 for non-*by*-PP-attachment				
Precision	92.6	89.6	78.4	74.8
Recall	81.1	83.9	65.3	85.6

Table 7.26: Evaluation of the currently best parser output on the GREVAL corpus on subject, object and PP-attachment relations, discarding backoff levels 5 and 6 for non-*by*-PP-attachment

Below threshold values of about 0.5 there is a reasonable trade-off in gained precision for lost recall. With higher thresholds, precision stagnates while recall drops off. While there is a clear correlation between noun attachment probability and correctness, verb attachment less clearly exhibits the expected correlation.

Experiment 6: Informedness and Backoff Levels Better informed decisions, i.e. decisions that can be made earlier in the back-off process, are expected to be better. Experiment 6 reveals that this is indeed the case, the difference in precision is considerably larger than in any of the other experiments. This is a strong indication that lexicalization is pivotal for disambiguation Experiment 6 has only been done on GREVAL, and only using the Ratnaparkhi tagger.

After a first inspection of the results it was noticed that verb-PP attachment with the preposition *by* still performs very well at late backoff stages. This is due to the fact that active sentence subjects and passive sentence by-agent counts are

231   7.5. Exploring Precision and Recall Trade-Offs

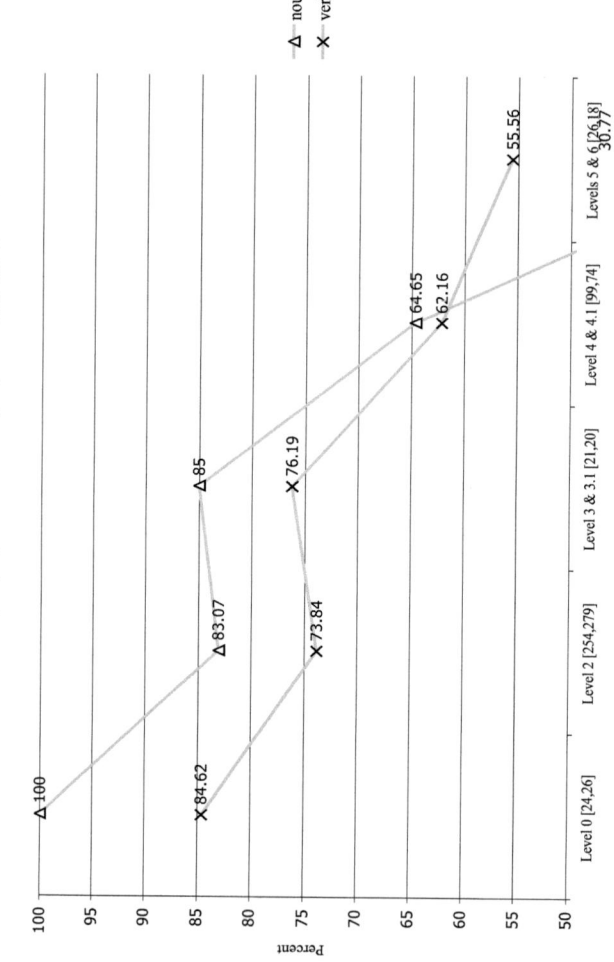

Figure 7.17: Graph of Precision of Experiment 6 on GREVAL

Experiments	GREVAL				GENIA			
3,4,5 combined	ubject	Object	noun-PP	verb-PP	Subject	Object	noun-PP	verb-PP
Precision	92.6	90.1	78.9	80.5	92.4	93.5	87.9	88.1
Recall	75.0	63.4	51.2	67.2	67.3	67.0	66.7	65.5

Table 7.27: Percentage results of Experiments 3, 4 and 5 combined at threshold 0.4 and distances 1 to 5

not mapped to each other, so that because of the general rarity of passives, counts are very sparse. But the attachment is not very ambiguous – a passive verb is never followed by an object – performance is thus quite good. We have therefore re-run the experiment excluding the preposition *by*. The result on GREVAL is shown in graph 7.17. Counts reported by the parser are in square brackets. A description of the PP backoff levels is in table 7.25.

PP-attachment backoff bevels 5 and 6, where the governor candidate's head is dropped, are low-count and performance drops off completely. It may therefore be beneficial to generally discard them. Applying a filter that discards all level 5 and level 6 PP-attachment relations except for *by*-PPs to the currently best model (shown in table 7.2, repeated here) results in the high-precision performance figure in table 7.26.

Combinations Most of the above high-precision experiments can be combined in various ways. E.g. combinations of experiment 3, 4 and 5 are reported in tables 7.27 with threshold 0.4 and distances 1 to 5. This sample combination on the GENIA annotation task allows us to reach about 9 out of 10 precision at 2 out of 3 recall for all reported relations.

7.6 Baseline, Distance Measure, Lexicalisation

In order to assess the difficulty of the task for the statistical disambiguation model, we have built a baseline system. Then we show how much the two factors in the model, the distance measure and the lexicalisation, contribute to improving the performance of the parser. Finally, we discuss questions related to lexicalisation.

7.6.1 The Baseline System

In the baseline system, dependencies can span unlimited distances, subject to the fact that dependencies are not allowed to cross each other, and lexical information

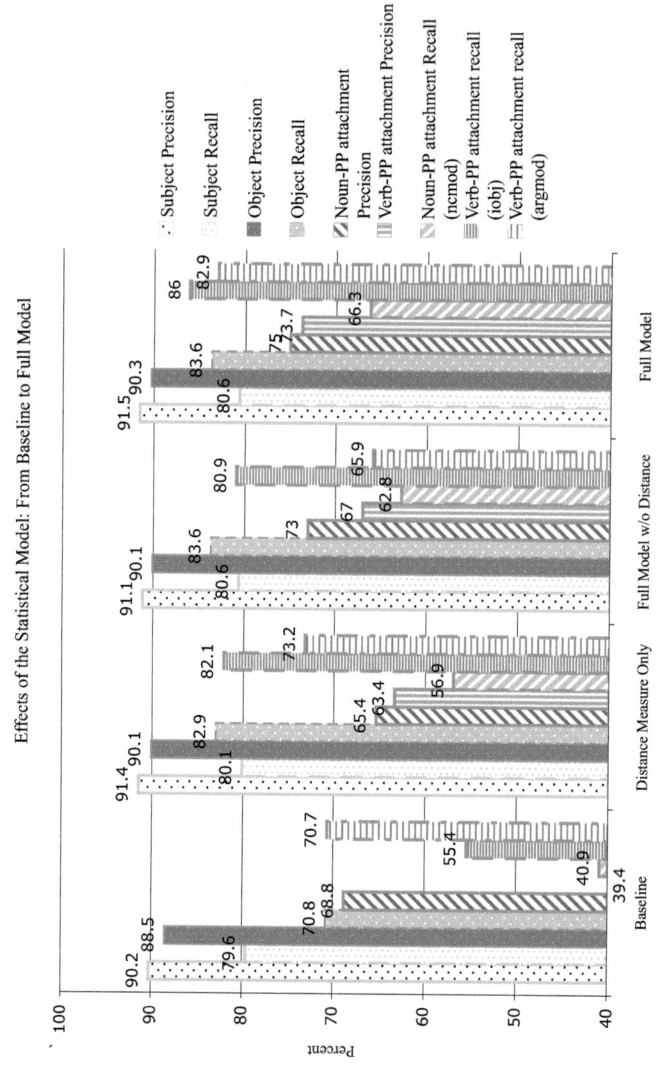

7.6. Baseline, Distance Measure, Lexicalisation

Figure 7.18: Comparison between Baseline, Distance Measure Only, Full Model without Distance Measure, and Full Model

is not taken into account. The most left-hand quarter of figure 7.18 shows the performance, which is, as expected, rather poor. The values for verb-PP-attachment are especially low because ambiguous attachments get equal weight, which means that whether a verb- or noun-PP-attachment is ranked as the first parse depends on chance factors: The CYK algorithm finds the closer noun attachment first, but the module that finds the best path through a sentence is stack-driven, starting with the last found analyses and preferring them if all analyses have equal weight, which leads to a strong preference for verb-PP-attachment.

It would theoretically be possible to extend the grammar to include distance and lexicalisation information. Wide-coverage lexical information, and especially distance information are very cumbersome to include in a grammar. The use of empirical measures is desirable.

7.6.2 The Distance Measure

The distance between a head and a dependent is a limiting factor for the probability of a dependency between them. Not all relations have the same typical distances, however. While objects are most frequently immediately following the verb, a PP attached to the verb may easily follow only at the second or third position, after the object and other PPs etc. A relation-specific simple MLE estimation is thus employed to prefer typical distances. Distance is measured in chunks.

Formula 7.1 shows our MLE calculation (see chapter 2): the probability of a certain $Distance$ across which to span, given the relation R, corresponds to the corpus count of the instances of relation R that span this distance divided by the count of all instances of relation R.

$$P(Distance|R) = \frac{\#(R \wedge Distance)}{\#R} \qquad (7.1)$$

The distance measure leads to a large increase in performance, as shown in the second leftmost quarter of figure 7.18, which confirms our intuitions. To a lesser degree, the algorithm's preference for verb-PP attachment is still apparent. We give separate values for the two verb-PP relations. Verb-PP arguments profit very much from distance information, while the *by*/agent of passive phrases, expressed by the arg_mod_c relation, already shows quite good performance in the baseline model, and hardly improves.

The full model with distance only is the full model without lexicalisation. In the following we now investigate the lexicalisation model, which is the full model

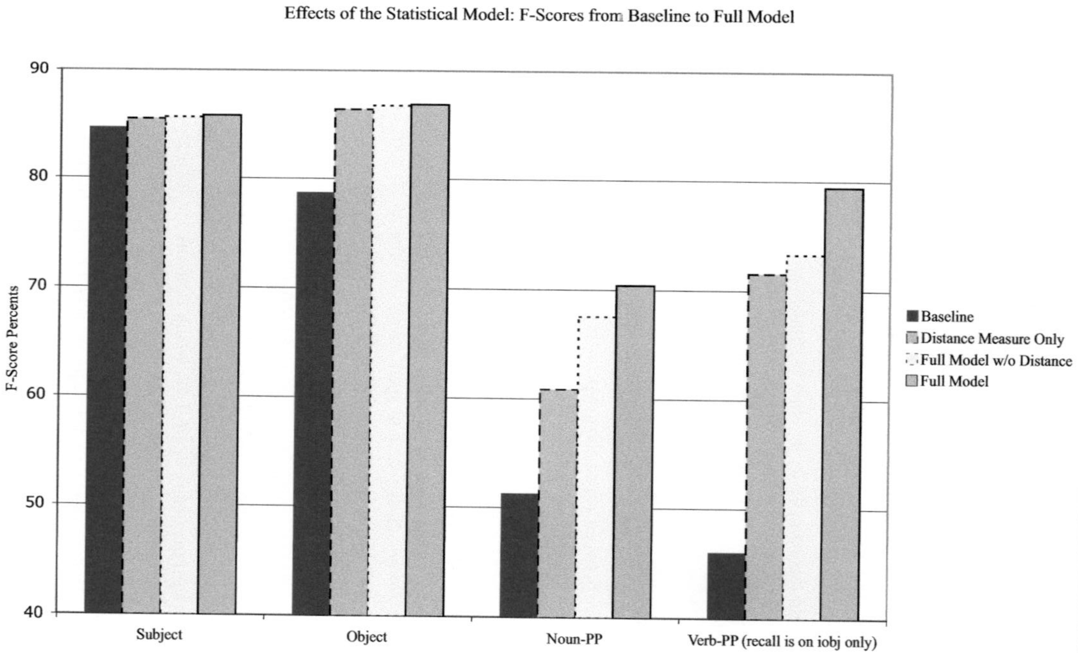

Figure 7.19: F-Score Comparison between Baseline, Distance Measure Only, Full Model without Distance Measure, and Full Model

without distance measure.

7.6.3 Lexicalisation

The contribution of the distance measure system can be illustrated by comparing the distance measure system to the full system, and to the full system without the distance measure (the purely lexicalized system). All these systems are compared in figure 7.18. Used in combination, a significant increase can be observed in the full system. This confirms our intuition that the types of information provided by distance and by lexicalisation are not redundant. The subject relation already performs well without the statistical model, the object relation profits slightly, the PP-attachment relations increase very much.

The results are presented in a different arrangement in figure 7.19. The effects of the interdependence between precision and recall have been eliminated by showing f-scores only. The groups are arranged by model, so that the increase and the changes in the increase from model to model become apparent. One can see that the increase in performance from lexicalisation is bigger than the one form distance.

The arg_mod_c recall has not been included, since it is least affected by distance and lexicalisation. This change has the effect that Verb-PP recall is now dominated by arguments, and the noun-PP recall is dominated by adjuncts. Since noun-PP attachments are far more often adjuncts than verb-PP attachments are, noun-PP precision is also quite strongly dominated by adjuncts. Arguments show strong selectional restrictions, while adjuncts occur in a wide distribution over different governors. As a consequence, one would expect lexicalisation to work considerably better on PP-argument than on PP-adjuncts. On the one hand, this is confirmed by the bigger increase that verb-PP attachment shows over the baseline, and the generally better performance on verb-PP attachment. On the other hand, the difference between the distance model and the lexicalised model is bigger in noun-PP attachment. This, however, does not indicate that lexicalisation works particularly well for noun-PP attachment, for two reasons. First, noun-PP performance is still below verb-PP performance in the lexicalisation model; second, distance is simply a relatively bad model for noun-PP. Figures 7.9 and 7.11 show that short distances perform almost as poorly for noun-PP as long distances, in sharp contrast to verb-PP, where short distances perform very well. A noun does usually not attach across a verb, but a verb (or a different noun) very often attaches across a noun; a short distance is therefore no good indication for attachment.

Lexicalisation and Backing Off

The probability model is backed off across more levels than in Collins and Brooks (1995), following Merlo and Esteve Ferrer (2006). Before discarding lexical participants, semantic classes are also used in all the modelled relations, for verbs the Levin classes (Levin, 1993) and/or the top Wordnet class of the most frequent sense, for nouns the top Wordnet class (Fellbaum, 1998), also of the most frequent sense.

Where Decisions are Taken The backoff decision points for the GREVAL corpus are shown in table 7.28. It reveals that full count decisions, especially in the case of PP-attachment, are relatively rare. This is due to sparse data, most pronouncedly in noun-PP-attachment, where a Zipfian head noun as well as a Zipfian description noun (the noun inside the PP) is involved.

The values at level 6 and 7 of verb-PP-attachment are very high because there are prepositions that are very rarely verb-attaching (e.g. *of*) and because the Penn Treebank preposition tag (*IN*) is also used for complementizers. In these cases, very low MLE probabilities occur at the preposition-backoff level 6 or 7, in which case a low non-zero probability is assigned. If aggressive pruning is used, these values at level 6 and 7 are much lower.

How Important is Lexicalization? We have seen in experiment 6 of section 7.5.1 (figure 7.17) that full lexicalization seems to be pivotal. Decisions taken at early stages in the back-off chain are far better. Results by (Klein and Manning, 2003) and by (Gildea, 2001) suggest the opposite: partial lexicalisation is as good as full lexicalisation, suggesting that the earliest levels in the back-off chain are redundant. (Gildea, 2001) compares a bilexical parser (conditioned on the head word and the dependent word) parser that follows Collins Model 1 (Collins, 1996) to an equivalent model that is only monolexicalized (conditioned only on the dependent word). He reports that performance is only half a percent higher for the bilexicalized parser. Tested on a domain that differs from the training corpus ((Gildea, 2001) trains on the Treebank and tests on Brown) performance is largely equivalent. Also in experiments that we conducted with Pro3Gres, full lexicalisation hardly increases performance. More research is needed to answer this question.

Relation		Degree of Lexicalisation	Counts
subj	0	full	377
	1	verbclass & nounclass	530
	2	verb	384
	3	noun	41
	4	NONE	15
obj	0	full	437
	1	verb & nounclass	939
	2	verbclass & noun	32
	3	verbclass & nounclass	145
	4	verb	92
	5	noun	40
	6	NONE	12
pobj	0	full	124
	1	verb & prep & nounclass	2624
	2	verb & prep	2631
	3	verbclass & prep & noun	337
	4	verbclass & prep & nounclass	5004
	5	prep & noun	995
	6	prep	4762
	7	NONE	4747
modpp	0	full	30
	1	noun & prep & descnounclass	197
	2	nounclass & prep & descnoun	100
	3	noun & prep	208
	4	nounclass & prep	696
	5	prep & descnoun	73
	6	prep	227
	7	NONE	281
modpart	0	full	0
	1	nounclass & verbclass	144
	2	verb	45
	3	noun	7
	4	NONE	11

Table 7.28: Backoff decision points for the Fully Lexicalized, Backed-Off System on the GREVAL corpus

7.6. Baseline, Distance Measure, Lexicalisation

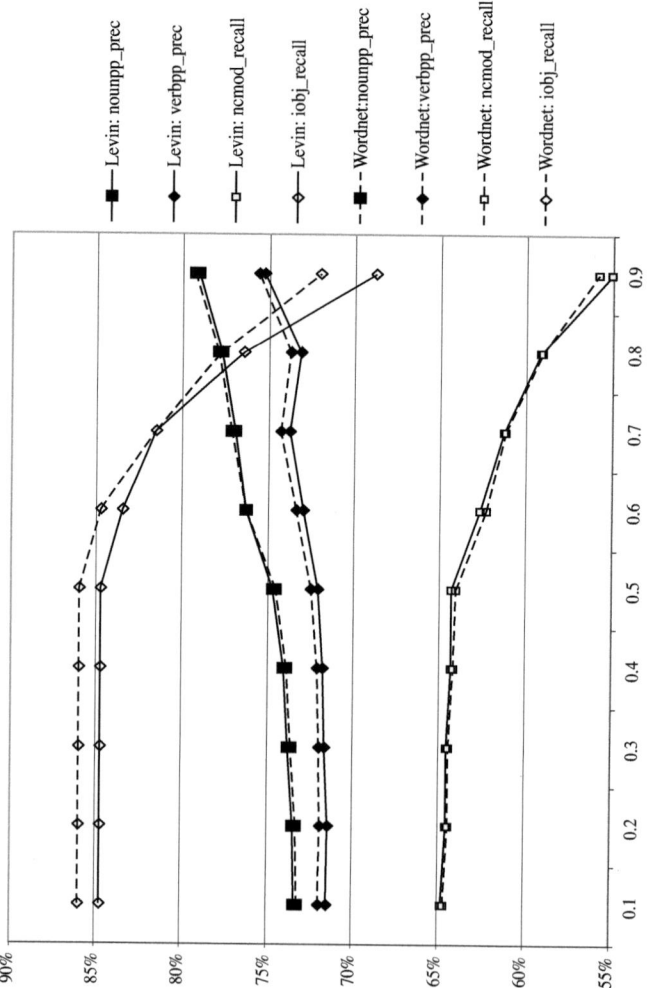

Figure 7.20: Comparison of Levin or Wordnet verb classes for backing off

Different Semantic Classifications for Backing Off

Originally, Pro3Gres uses Wordnet for nouns and Levin classes for verbs. We have decided to use Levin Classes because they are situated at the interface level between syntax and semantics. As an alternative, Wordnet can also be used for verbs. We have re-run experiment experiment 5 from section 7.5.2, this time comparing the use of Wordnet or Levin at the corresponding backoff-level. The results on PP-attachment are shown in figure 7.20. As expected, mainly the verb-PP attachment relation's performance changes (there is also an indirect influence on noun-PP attachment, with which verb-PP attachment is typically in competition). Both verb-PP precision and $iobj$-recall (which measures verb argument recall) is higher when using Wordnet. Only the rare $argmod$ relation, which has not been included in the graph, has lower recall: e.g. 33 out of 41 at 0.1 threshold with Levin compared to 31 out of 41 with Wordnet. Due to the low count this result is not reliable. We can see that Wordnet verb classes perform better for PP-attachment than Levin classes. Since Levin classes have considerably lower coverage than Wordnet classes, no theoretical conclusions should be drawn from this practical result.

7.7 Disambiguation from the Parsing Context

We have illustrated the extent to which the distance model and the lexicalisation model disambiguate the sentences during parsing, and we have evaluated their performance. There is an additional factor that disambiguates parses in a parsing approach: parsing itself. In this section we investigate the impact that parsing has on the performance of discovering syntactic relations.

7.7.1 Parsing Speed, Pruning, and Local Maxima

Parsing speed is an important factor for the practical applicability of parser, and hence an aspect of its evaluation. Parsing speed largely depends on the pruning parameters used. In complex real-world sentences, constructing all possible chart entries can become very time-consuming. It has been shown (see e.g. Brants and Crocker (2000)) that discarding locally very improbable partial analyses hardly affects a parser's performance, because the chance that locally very improbable analyses become parts of the most probable analysis later is very small.

We have conducted similar experiments. In the experiment that we report here, we have limited the number of alternatives per span, using a fixed beam search.

7.7. Disambiguation from the Parsing Context

# Span Alternatives	1	2	3	4	5	10
Execution time (secs.)	53	71	82	92	105	149
Subject Precision	92.33	92.77	93.18	93.18	93.18	93.18
Subject Recall	81.27	81.79	81.79	81.79	81.79	81.79
Object Precision	85.49	85.44	85.71	85.71	85.71	85.71
Object Recall	84.65	85.42	85.67	85.67	85.67	85.67
Noun-PP Precision	78.78	78.47	78.22	78.44	78.44	78.49
Noun-PP Recall	65.29	65.66	65.79	65.91	65.91	66.04
Verb-PP Precision	74.89	74.30	74.56	74.56	74.56	74.73
Verb-PP Recall	87.37	87.37	87.37	87.37	87.37	87.37
Subord. Clause Precision	69.15	72.18	73.11	73.11	73.11	73.11
Subord. Clause Recall	66.86	66.86	66.86	66.86	66.86	66.86

Table 7.29: Beam size effects on parsing speed and performance

Even if only one alternative is used, which means that local maxima are deterministically assumed to be global maxima, the performance does not suffer very much, while parsing speed increases considerably. We have parsed the 500 sentence GREVAL corpus. Execution times are for the whole corpus, in seconds. The results are summarised in table 7.29. At a maximum of about 5 alternatives, the improvement flattens out completely.

The subordinate clause relation (*sentobj*) precision improves 4 percent from a beam of size 1 to size 10. There are relatively many situations affecting this relation, especially in relation with zero relative clauses (*modpart*), a configuration that can sometimes give rise to a garden path reading. A simple example is the following sentence (number 303 in the GREVAL corpus).

(112) You want a *job guaranteed* when you return, I continued my attack.

Locally, the probability that *job* is the subject of *guarantee* is higher than the correct reading in which *job* is relativised by the participle *guaranteed*. When using a beam of size 1, the correct reading is pruned, and a global analysis constructed. This global analysis expresses the meaning of *You want that a job guaranteed something when you return* .... When using a bigger beam, the correct, locally less likely *modpart* reading is kept and later becomes part of the globally most probable reading. The parsing context corrects the local paring error. Also the subject and object relations improve up to a percent between a beam of 1 and 10. An example of improvement for the subject relation is also sentence 111, where *job* becomes subject of *guarantee*. Table 7.29 also illustrates that PP-attachment is largely unaffected by the parsing context. We mainly get small, random fluctuations for the PP-attachment relations. This indicates that disambiguation algorithms like Collins and Brooks (1995) or Merlo and Esteve Ferrer (2006) can also profitably be applied to the output of a parser or chunker in a post-processing phase.

The parsing times reported in table 7.29 can be further reduced by setting other pruning parameters, which have been unused for this experiment in order to exclude interactions. The different parameters have been introduced in chapter 2. Parsing speed for a sentence is a fraction of a second on average. The entire British National Corpus (BNC) parses in just over 24 hours on the latest fast multi-core Apple Macintosh server.

The fact that local maxima do not always lead to global maxima are one of the reasons why Briscoe and Carroll (2002) are sceptical whether shallow parsing can reach the levels of accuracy of full parsing.

7.7.2 Local Readings Constrain Each Other

We have just illustrated in subsection 7.7.1 that the parsing context corrects situations in which a locally most likely reading is not globally most likely. There is a second method by which parsing approaches disambiguate, again by refuting locally probable readings. Many locally possible readings are ruled out because they cannot be accommodated with the surrounding readings into a possible global reading. Let us consider the following example sentence.

(113) Experts fear the virus will spread.

The locally possible object relation with *fear* as governor and *virus* as dependent is ruled out because the rest of the sentence cannot be attached, while the reading in which *virus* is the subject of a subordinate clause allows the parser to construct a span covering the entire sentence.

It is difficult to assess this effect of the parsing context exactly, but some indications can be given. If we restrict the CYK parsing levels (see chapter 2) to only sentence fragments, structures of a certain maximal length only can be constructed, thus enforcing a restricted parsing context. The locally most likely readings for the partial structures of this maximal length are collected by the parse collector and returned. We have again parsed the 500 sentence GREVAL corpus. Execution times are for the whole corpus, in seconds. The results of this experiment are shown in table 7.30. Parsing less than 3 CYK levels is not very interesting, since

# CYK levels	3	5	7	10	15
Execution time (secs.)	21	41	54	70	74
Subject Precision	88.24	91.39	92.75	92.96	93.91
Subject Recall	71.65	80.75	81.79	81.58	81.79
Object Precision	89.09	85.31	85.44	85.71	85.71
Object Recall	76.47	83.12	85.42	85.67	85.67
Noun-PP Precision	72.39	74.92	78.29	78.82	78.44
Noun-PP Recall	30.21	52.93	62.04	65.66	65.91
Verb-PP Precision	46.63	56.53	68.27	73.77	74.56
Verb-PP Recall	62.12	69.69	80.80	86.86	87.37
Subord. Clause Precision	71.21	67.14	70.67	72.50	73.11
Subord. Clause Recall	35.54	61.44	66.26	66.26	66.86

Table 7.30: Disambiguation from the Context. Maximal span size effects on parsing speed and performance

no PP-attachment has been made. After 15 levels, the improvement has flattened out completely.

Recall is low when the CYK levels are restricted, for the obvious reason that structures which are longer than the maximum length cannot be found. But precision is also considerably lower (except for the object relation), although we have seen in section 7.5.2 that relations across short distances are generally more reliable. This increase in precision gives us an indication of the degree to which parsing improves the discovery of syntactic relations[6]. The increase in precision from 2 CYK levels to 15 levels varies: 2 % for the subordinate clause relation, 5 % for the subject relation (see example 113), 6 % for noun-PP attachment, almost 30 % for the verb-PP attachment relation. We can see that the parsing contexts considerably constrain each other. This is a significant advantage of parsing approaches. The effect on performance is bigger then the correction of local maxima that wee have discussed in subsection 7.7.1.

---

[6]Non-parsing approaches that use a sophisticated context model, for example Buchholz (2002), model these parsing context restrictions up to a point

with standard grammar	Subject	Object	noun-PP	verb-PP	subord. clause
Precision	93.2	86.1	78.4	74.7	73.1
Recall	81.6	85.2	65.9	87.4	66.7
grammar without constraints	Subject	Object	noun-PP	verb-PP	subord. clause
Precision	72.3	58.8	67.4	68.5	47.8
Recall	60.1	76.7	58.1	84.3	57.8

Table 7.31: Currently best system on the GREVAL corpus with the standard grammar and the grammar without restrictions compared

7.8 Linguistic constraints

Linguistic knowledge has allowed us to place strong restrictions on the co-occurrence of different relation types. Verbs that have attached adjuncts cannot attach complements, since this would violate X-bar constraints. Verbs that have no object cannot attach a secondary object. The application of dependency rules can often be lexically restricted: for example, only temporal expressions occur as NP adjuncts. We have formulated constraints based on a long tradition of grammar writing. We have explained these constraints in detail in chapter 5. Dependency rules specify a head tag, a dependent tag, sometimes also a head word and or head tag, and the said linguistic constraints. We have created a version of the grammar in which all rules – except for conjunction, comma, and $nchunk$ rules, which overgenerated massively – have no linguistic constraints. We have again parsed the 500 sentence GREVAL corpus. Parsing speed was two orders of magnitude slower due to the search space explosion. This means that the linguistic constraints have even a bigger impact than pruning. The performance results are shown in table 7.31, but they should be interpreted with caution.

One important reason why the performance is so low is that due to inflated search spaces when restrictions are absent, many sentences created so many chart entries that they ran into aggressive pruning mode (normally only a small fraction of sentences do). We had to use default pruning settings in this experiment, otherwise the parser exited with memory overflow. Aggressive pruning leads to a strong fragmentation into partial parses, like in the experiment in subsection 7.7.2 above. A second important reason is that Pro3Gres was not written to be used without linguistic constraints. Minor relations, for example a subject relation to the right, or *strandprep*, relations which are normally constrained to very specific tasks, overgenerate and lead to absurd results.

Still, we can conclude that linguistic constraints make an important contribution to the parser's speed and robustness, and that at least on practical grounds, the parser owes much of its performance to linguistic constraints.

7.9 Conclusions

We have evaluated Pro3Gres and shown that its performance is very good. We have shown a detailed comparison of Pro3Gres to RASP (Carroll, Minnen, and Briscoe, 2003). We have shown that we outperform Collins Model 1 (Collins, 1999). We have reported a tentative comparison to (Nivre, 2006b). We have reported the results of a task-based practical application evaluation of using Pro3Gres on texts from the biomedical domain. We have shown that if high-quality recognition of multi-word domain terms is provided, the parser performs as well on the biomedical domain as on general text.

We have shown how the parser can be used for applications that need to optimise on precision or on recall. We have compared our full model to a baseline and shown how the two main factors in our probability estimation, distance and lexicalisation, contribute to the performance. We have raised a crucial question that is still open: how important is lexicalisation?

Concerning the practical applicability of Pro3Gres we have illustrated the speed of the parser, and how pruning affects parsing speed and performance. We have given quantitative indications of how much the use of a parsing approach improves the discovery of syntactic relations, and we have shown the tremendous impact that linguistic constraints have.

Chapter 8

Conclusions

We have presented a parsing architecture that is fast, robust and efficient enough to allow users to do broad-coverage parsing of unrestricted texts from different domains. We have discussed its implementation, Pro3Gres, and shown that its performance is very good.

8.1 The Cornerstones of Pro3Gres

We have presented five elements that combine to make Pro3Gres a fast, robust, and high-performance parser. Each of the five elements, which are summarised in the following, is essential to achieve this goal.

Hand-written Grammar with Linguistic Constraints We have discussed the hand-written grammar in detail in chapter 5. We have shown that the expense needed to write a broad-coverage grammar for English is manageable. A hand-written grammar allows one to model structures that are rare in the training corpus, for example questions. A hand-written grammar also allows one to place powerful constraints on the application of rules, for example by restricting the co-occurrence of dependency types, thereby implementing linguistic principles like subcategorisation, X-bar theory, lexical semantics and other non-local restrictions. We have shown in the evaluation in chapter 7 that the grammar covers the majority of the structures found in English. We have also shown (in section 7.8) that the powerful linguistic constraints boost performance and the parsing speed. Parsing speed increases by two orders of magnitude thanks to the linguistic constraints. The linguistic constraints are probably the element that increases parsing speed most. We have discussed in section 4.6.3 that such linguistic constraints are related to supertagging.

Lexicalisation We have presented the statistical performance model as an extension of PP-attachment research (Collins and Brooks, 1995) to all syntactic relations in chapters 2 and 4. We have compared our model to Collins (1999) in chapter 4. Pro3Gres is different from Collins (1999) because it exploits the possibilities that Dependency Grammar offers (see chapter 3), for example using dependency labels to process subcategorisation or representing entire subtrees corresponding to long-distance dependencies in a single dependency. We have presented a sophisticated back-off model which is partly based on Merlo and Esteve Ferrer (2006), including semantic classes in the back-off. We have shown in the evaluation in section 7.6.3 that lexicalisation leads to a tremendous increase in performance over the non-lexicalised base model. Lexicalisation is the one of its seven elements that increases performance most.

Distance Measure We use a distance measure that differs from Collins (1999) (see chapter 4). Instead of a vector of features, we measure the real distance in chunks. We have shown in section 7.6.2 how the distance measure improves on the baseline model. We have shown that the lexicalisation model and the distance model are not redundant.

Tagging, Lemmatising and Chunking Preprocessing We have shown that the parser Pro3Gres uses a task-specific division of labour, delegating tasks that can be solved with sufficient accuracy by methods that use less resources than parsing. They are finite-state based lemmatising, part-of-speech tagging, and base-phrase chunking. Kaplan et al. (2004b) describe the integration of finite-state morphology and part-of-speech tagging as an essential step for the development of truly broadcoverage grammar and robust parser such as Riezler et al. (2002). Prins (2005) shows that tagging preprocessing systems are up to an order of magnitude faster, and that the accuracy increases slightly if reasonable filtering parameters are used. Abney (1996) suggests a parsing architecture for DG that only parses between heads of chunks. We have followed this suggestion. DG is especially suitable for such an architecture because of endocentricity, and because it partly eliminates the need for dependencies that have no valency interpretation. Prins (2005) shows that chunking preprocessing in parsing generally leads to a moderate increase in speed[1].

Treatment of Long-Distance Dependencies We have shown that inherently complex linguistic problems can be broken down and approximated sufficiently well by less complex methods. This applies in particular to long-distance dependencies. We have shown in chapter 6 that the majority of them can be approximated by using a labeled DG that extends locality to the clause level, by context-free finite-state based patterns, and by post-processing. The few remaining long-distance dependencies, complex WH-questions, only need mild context-sensitivity. We have shown that a slightly extended DG allows us to use mildly context-sensitive operations known from Tree-Adjoining Grammar (TAG).

Besides these five elements, Pro3Gres relies on a number of standard techniques, such as pruning and full parsing. While pruning does not improve the accuracy of the parser, it increases parsing speed by one or several orders of magnitude (Brants and Crocker, 2000). We have presented the pruner and its parameters in chapter 2. We have shown in an evaluation in section 7.7.1 that the accuracy of the parser is hardly affected until extremely aggressive pruning parameters are set. We have parsed the entire 100 million word British National Corpus (BNC) with the default pruning settings that we have used for the standard evaluations reported in this thesis. Pro3Gres parses the BNC in just over 24 hours on the latest fast multi-core Apple Macintosh server. We have shown that the parsing context improves the performance if a full parsing approach is used. First, structures mutually constrain each other. Second, local maxima do not always lead to global maxima. We give indications of the impact of these effects in evaluations in sections 7.7.2 and 7.7.1.

8.2 A Hybrid Architecture

We have discussed that Pro3Gres is a hybrid approach at several levels. First, it is hybrid because it uses a hand-written linguistic *competence* grammar (see chapter 5) combined with a statistical *performance* disambiguation model (see chapter 2). Unlike formal grammars to which post-hoc statistical disambiguators are added in a later stage, Pro3Gres has been designed to be hybrid, carefully distinguishing between tasks that can best be solved by finite-state methods, rule-based methods and statistical methods. While grammar writing is easy for a linguist, the scope

---
[1] There is no doubt that speed increases with chunking preprocessing, but accuracy potentially decreases slightly, see e.g. Haverinen et al. (2008)

of application and the amount of ambiguity a rule creates is considerable and best handled by a statistical system.

Second, it is hybrid because it uses a task-based division of labour: a finite-state based approach for lemmatising, tagging and the base phrase level, context-free parsing for the surface syntactic level, and graph rewriting and mild context-sensitivity for the deep syntactic processing. The designing philosophy for Pro3Gres has been to stay as shallow as possible to obtain reliable results for each task necessary to transform raw text into a functionally annotated structure. Long-distance dependencies are expressed in a context-free fashion as far as it is possible (see chapter 6) . The full expressiveness of context-sensitivity is never called for. In the very few sentences where context-sensitivity is needed for English, in complex WH-questions, we use a simple mildly context-sensitive extension based on Tree-Adjoining Grammar (see chapter 6). Recent research in DG suggests that mild context-sensitivity as expressed in TAG is precisely the extension to context-freeness that is needed to cover naturally occurring text (Kuhlmann and Nivre, 2006).

Third, it is hybrid because it is a DG approach trained on a constituency treebank. On the one hand, the use of our own functional concept of DG has allowed us to treat long-distance dependencies in a simple and elegant way, as discussed in chapter 6. It has also allowed us to parse directly for a simple LFG f-structre without needing c-structure as an intermediate step. On the other hand, our approach exhibits a number of mapping challenges (see chapters 6 and 7), which have especially made the evaluation difficult. Since we do not have a gold standard expressed in our formalism, our current evaluation of long-distance dependencies is not complete.

Fourth, it is hybrid between a statistical parser and a formal grammar-based parser. Kaplan et al. (2004a) compare speed and accuracy of a successful probabilistic context-free parser (Collins, 1999) to a robust LFG system based on Riezler et al. (2002). They show that the gap between probabilistic context-free parsing and deep-linguistic full LFG parsing can be closed.

A conclusion that can be drawn from previous and our own research is that simplifying, restricting and limiting formal grammar expressiveness is bridging the gap between probabilistic parsing and formal grammar-based parsing, and between shallow parsing and full parsing. We argue that our parser covers the middle ground between statistical parsing and formal grammar-based parsing. The parser has competitive performance (see chapter 7) and has been applied widely. We have also presented a practical, user-based evaluation on an application domain.

A further conclusion that can be drawn from our research on parsing texts from the biomedical domain is that base phrase parsing is more domain-specific than parsing between these base phrases. This entails that taggers and chunkers or base-phrase rules for parsers need to be adapted more to a given domain than the rules for parsing between base phrases, and that parsing between base phrases by Pro3Gres is quite domain-independent, robust and efficient enough for large-scale application.

8.3 Applications

Pro3Gres has been employed in a number of applications. To conclude, we list some of the applications and relevant publications.

- Information Retrieval: Burger and Bayer (2005).

- Question Answering: Rinaldi et al. (2004a).

- Parsing and Text Mining in Biomedicine: Rinaldi et al. (2004), Rinaldi et al. (2006), Rinaldi et al. (2007), Haverinen et al. (2008), Rinaldi et al. (2008).

- Terminology and Ontology Detection: Weeds et al. (2005).

- Corpus Linguistics: We have given a presentation and led the workshop at the International Corpus Archive of Modern and Medieval English Conference (ICAME) 2008. Our proceedings article has been accepted for publication.

- Psycholinguistics: Schneider et al. (2005).

References

Abney, Steven. 1991. Parsing by chunks. In *Principle-Based Parsing*. Kluwer Academic Publishers, Dordrecht.

Abney, Steven. 1994. Dependency grammars and context-free grammars. Unpublished manuscript, Linguistics Department, University of Tübingen.

Abney, Steven. 1995. Chunks and dependencies: Bringing processing evidence to bear on syntax. In Jennifer Cole, Georgia Green, and Jerry Morgan, editors, *Computational Linguistics and the Foundations of Linguistic Theory*, pages 145–164. CSLI.

Abney, Steven. 1996. Partial parsing via finite-state cascades. In John Carroll, editor, *Proc. of the Workshop on Robust Parsing at the 8th Summer School on Logic, Language and Information*, number 435 in CSRP, pages 8–15. University of Sussex, Brighton.

Abney, Steven. 1997. Stochastic attribute-value gammars. *Computational Linguistics*, 23(4):597–618.

Aliod, Diego Mollà, Gerold Schneider, Rolf Schwitter, and Michael Hess. 2000. Answer Extraction Using a Dependency Grammar in ExtrAns. *Traitement Automatique de Langues (T.A.L.), Special Issue on Dependency Grammar*.

Ananiadou, Sophia and Jun'ichi Tsujii, editors. 2003. *Proceedings of the ACL 2003 Workshop on Natural Language Processing in Biomedicine*.

Appelt, D., J. Hobbs, J. Bear, D. Israel, M. Kameyama, A. Kehler, D. Martin, K. Myers, and M. Tyson. 1995. The SRI FASTUS system, MUC-6 test results and analysis. In *Proceedings of the 6th Message Understanding Conference*, pages 237–248. Morgan Kaufmann, San Mateo, CA.

Aston, Guy and Lou Burnard. 1998. *The BNC Handbook. Exploring the British National Corpus with SARA*. Edinburgh University Press, Edinburgh.

Bangalore, Srinivas and Aravind K. Joshi. 1999. Supertagging: An approach to almost parsing. *Computational Linguistics*, 25(2):237–265.

Barton, G. Edward. 1985. The computational difficulty of ID/LP parsing. In *Meeting of the Association for Computational Linguistics*, pages 76–81.

Basili, Roberto, Maria Teresa Pazienza, and Fabio Massimo Zanzotto. 1998. Evaluating a robust parser for Italian language. In *Proceedings of Evaluations of Parsing Systems Workshop, held jointly with 1st LREC*, Granada,Spain.

Basili, Roberto and Fabio Massimo Zanzotto. 2002. Parsing engineering and empirical robustness. *Journal of Natural Language Engineering*, 8/2-3.

Baumgärtner, Klaus. 1970. Konstituenz und Dependenz. Zur Integration der beiden grammatischen Prinzipien. In H. Steger, editor, *Vorschläge für eine strukturale Grammatik des Deutschen*. Wissenschaftliche Buchgesellschaft, Darmstadt, pages 52–77.

Bies, Ann, Mark Ferguson, Karen Katz, and Robert MacIntyre. 1995. Bracketing guidelines for Treebank II style Penn Treebank project. Technical report, University of Pennsylvania.

Bikel, Daniel. 2004. *On the Parameter Space of Lexicalized Statistical Parsing Models*. Ph.D. thesis, Department of Computer and Information Science.

Black, E., S. Abney, D. Flickinger, C. Gdaniec, R. Grishman, P. Harrison, D. Hindle, R. Ingria, F. Jelinek, J. Klavans, M. Liberman, M. Marcus, S. Roukos, B. Santorini, and T. Strzalkowski. 1991. A procedure for quantitatively comparing the syntactic coverage of english grammars. In *Proceedings of the DARPA Speech and Natural Language Workshop*, Pacific Grove, CA.

Black, Ezra, Fred Jelinek, John Lafferty, David M. Magerman, Robert Mercer, and Salim Roukos. 1993. Towards history-based grammars: Using richer models for probabilistic parsing. In *Proceedings of ACL'93*, pages 31–37, Columbus, OH.

Blaheta, Don. 2004. *Function Tagging*. Ph.D. thesis, Department of Computer Science.

Bod, Rens. 1992. A computational model of language performance: Data oriented parsing. In *Proceedings COLING'92*, Nantes, France.

Bod, Rens. 2001. What is the minimal set of fragments that achieves maximal parse accuracy? In *Proceedings ACL-2001*, Toulouse, France.

Bod, Rens, Remko Scha, and Khalil Sima'an, editors. 2003. *Data-Oriented Parsing*. Center for the Study of Language and Information, Studies in Computational Linguistics (CSLI-SCL). Chicago University Press.

Bouma, Gosse, Gertjan van Noord, and Robert Malouf. 2001. Alpino: Wide-coverage computational analysis of dutch. In *Computational Linguistics in The Netherlands 2000*.

Brants, Thorsten. 1999. Cascaded markov models. In *Proceedings of the Ninth Conference of the European Chapter of the Association for Computational Linguistics (EACL'99)*, pages 118–125, Bergen, Norway. University of Bergen.

Brants, Thorsten and Matthew Crocker. 2000. Probabilistic parsing and psychological plausibility. In *Proceedings of 18th International Conference on Computational Linguistics COLING-2000*, Saarbrücken/Luxembourg/Nancy.

Brants, Thorsten, Roland Hendriks, Sabine Kramp, Brigitte Krenn, Cordula Preis, Wojciech Skut, and Hans Uszkoreit. 1997. Das NEGRA-Annotationsschema. Technical Report NEGRA Project Report, Computational Linguistics Department, Saarland University, Saarbrücken, Germany.

Brants, Thorsten and Oliver Plaehn. 2000. Interactive corpus annotation. In *Proceedings of the Second International Conference on Language Resources and Evaluation (LREC-2000)*, Athens, Greece.

Bresnan, Joan, editor. 1982. *The Mental Representation of Grammatical Relations*. The MIT Press, Cambridge, Massachusetts.

Bresnan, Joan. 2001. *Lexical-Functional Syntax*. Blackwell, Oxford.

Briscoe, Ted and John Carroll. 1993. Generalised probabilistic LR parsing of natural language (corpora) with unification-based grammars. *Computational Linguistics*, 19(1):25 – 60.

Briscoe, Ted and John Carroll. 2002. Robust accurate statistical annotation of general text. In *Proceedings of the 3rd International Conference on Language Resources and Evaluation*, pages 1499–1504, Las Palmas, Gran Canaria.

Briscoe, Ted, Claire Grover, Bran Boguraev, and John Carroll. 1987. A formalism and environment for the development of a large grammar of English. In *Proceedings of the 10th International Joint Conference on Artificial Intelligence*, Milan,Italy.

Bröker, Norbert, Udo Hahn, and Susanne Schacht. 1994. Concurrent lexicalized dependency parsing: The ParseTalk model. In *Coling 94*, pages 379–385.

Brown, R. 1973. *A First Language: The Early Stages*. Harvard University Press.

References

Buchholz, Sabine. 2002. *Memory-Based Grammatical Relation Finding*. Ph.D. thesis, University of Tilburg, Tilburg, Netherlands.

Buchholz, Sabine and Erwin Marsi. 2006. Conll-x shared task on multilingual dependency parsing. In *Proceedings of the Tenth Conference on Computational Natural Language Learning (CoNLL-X)*, pages 149–164, New York City, June. Association for Computational Linguistics.

Burger, John D. and Sam Bayer. 2005. MITRE's Qanda at TREC-14. In E. M. Voorhees and Lori P. Buckland, editors, *The Fourteenth Text REtrieval Conference (TREC 2005) Notebook*.

Burke, M., A. Cahill, R. O'Donovan, J. van Genabith, and A. Way. 2004. Treebank-based acquisistion of wide-coverage, probabilistic LFG resources: Project overview, results and evaluation. In *The First International Joint Conference on Natural Language Processing (IJCNLP-04), Workshop "Beyond shallow analyses - Formalisms and statistical modeling for deep analyses"*, Sanya City, Hainan Island, China.

Cahill, Aoife, Michael Burke, Ruth O'Donovan, Josef van Genabith, and Andy Way. 2004. Long-distance dependency resolution in automatically acquired wide-coverage PCFG-based LFG approximations. In *Proceedings of ACL-2004*, Barcelona, Spain.

Cahill, Aoife, Mairead McCarthy, Josef van Genabith, and Andy Way. 2002. Parsing with PCFGs and automatic F-structure annotation. In *Proceedings of the 7th International Lexical-Functional Grammar Conference, LFG'02*, Athens, Greece.

Campbell, Richard. 2004. Using linguistic principles to cover empty categories. In *Proceedings of ACL-2004*, pages 646–653, Barcelona, Spain.

Carroll, John and Ted Briscoe. 2002. High precision extraction of grammatical relations. In *Proceedings of the 19th International Conference on Computational Linguistics (COLING)*, Taipei, Taiwan.

Carroll, John, Guido Minnen, and Edward Briscoe. 2003. Parser evaluation: using a grammatical relation annotation scheme. In Anne Abeillé, editor, *Treebanks: Building and Using Parsed Corpora*. Kluwer, Dordrecht, pages 299–316.

Carroll, John, Guido Minnen, and Ted Briscoe. 1999. Corpus annotation for parser evaluation. In *Proceedings of the EACL-99 Post-Conference Workshop on Linguistically Interpreted Corpora*, Bergen, Norway.

Carroll, John, Nicolas Nicolov, Olga Shaumyan, Martine Smets, and David Weir. 1999. Parsing with an extended domain of locality. In *Proceedings of the Ninth Conference of the European Chapter of the Association for Computational Linguistics (EACL)*.

Charniak, Eugene. 1996. Tree-bank grammar. Technical Report Technical Report CS-96-02, Department of Computer Science, Brown University.

Charniak, Eugene. 2000. A maximum-entropy-inspired parser. In *Proceedings of the North American Chapter of the ACL*, pages 132–139.

Chomsky, Noam. 1955. *The logical structure of linguistic theory*. Distributed by University of Indiana Linguistics Club.

Chomsky, Noam. 1957. *Syntactic Structures*. Mouton, The Hague.

Chomsky, Noam. 1965. *Aspects of the Theory of Syntax*. MIT Press, Cambridge, MA.

Chomsky, Noam. 1970. Remarks on nominalization. In R. Jacobs and P. Rosenbaum, editors, *Readings in Transformational Grammar*. Ginn and Co., Boston, pages 184–221.

Chomsky, Noam. 1981. *Lectures on Government and Binding*. Foris Publications, Foris Publications.

Chomsky, Noam. 1986. *Barriers*. The MIT Press, Cambridge, MA.

Chomsky, Noam. 1995. *The Minimalist Program*. The MIT Press, Cambridge, Massachusetts.

Chung, Hoojung and Hae-Chang Rim. 2003. A new probabilistic dependency parsing model for head-final, free word order languages. *IEICE Transaction on Information & System*, E86-D, No. 11:2490–2493.

Church, K. and R. Patil. 1982. Coping with synactic ambiguits or how to put the block in the box on the table. *American Journal of Computational Linguistics*, 8(3-4):139–149.

Cinque, Guglielmo. 1990. *Types of $\bar{A}$-dependencies*. MIT press, Cambridge, MA.

Clark, Stephen and James R. Curran. 2004. Parsing the WSJ using CCG and log-linear models. In *Proceedings of COLING 04*, pages 103–110, Geneva, Switzerland.

Collins, Michael. 1996. A new statistical parser based on bigram lexical dependencies. In *Proceedings of the Thirty-Fourth Annual Meeting of the Association for Computational Linguistics*, pages 184–191, Philadelphia.

Collins, Michael. 1997. Three generative, lexicalised models for statistical parsing. In *Proc. of the 35th Annual Meeting of the ACL*, pages 16–23, Madrid, Spain.

Collins, Michael. 1999. *Head-Driven Statistical Models for Natural Language Parsing*. Ph.D. thesis, University of Pennsylvania, Philadelphia, PA.

Collins, Michael. 2003. Head-driven statistical models for natural language parsing. *Computational Linguistics*, 29:589 – 637.

Collins, Michael and James Brooks. 1995. Prepositional attachment through a backed-off model. In *Proceedings of the Third Workshop on Very Large Corpora*, Cambridge, MA.

Cook, Vivian and Mark Newson. 1996. *Chomsky's Universal Grammar, 2nd. Ed.* Blackwell, Oxford.

Copestake, Ann and Dan Flickinger. 2000. An open-source grammar development environment and broad-coverage English grammar using HPSG. In *Proceedings of the Second Conference on Language Resources and Evaluation (LREC-2000)*, Athens, Greece.

Covington, Michael A. 1992. GB theory as Dependency Grammar. Technical Report AI1992-03, University of Georgia, Athens, Georgia.

Covington, Michael A. 1994. An empirically motivated reinterpretation of Dependency Grammar. Technical Report AI1994-01, University of Georgia, Athens, Georgia.

Craven, M. and J. Kumlien. 1999. Constructing biological knowledge bases by extracting information from text sources. *Proceedings of the 8th International Conference on Intelligent Systems for Molecular Biology (ISMB-99)*.

Crouch, Richard, Ronald M. Kaplan, Tracy H. King, and Stefan Riezler. 2002. A comparison of evaluation metrics for broad-coverage stochastic parsers. In *Beyond PARSEVAL workshop at 3rd Int. Conference on Language Resources an Evaluation (LREC'02)*, Las Palmas.

Curran, James R. and Stephen Clark. 2004. The importance of supertagging for wide-coverage ccg parsing. In *Proceedings of COLING 04*, pages 282–288, Geneva, Switzerland.

Daelemans, Walter. 1999. Memory-based language processing. introduction to the special issue. *Journal of Experimental and Theoretical Artificial Intelligence*, 11:287–292.

Daelemans, Walter, Sabine Buchholz, and Jorn Veenstra. 1999. Memory-based shallow parsing. In *Proceedings of the third Computational Natural Language Learning workshop (CoNLL)*, Bergen, Norway.

de Marneffe, Marie-Catherine, Bill MacCartney, and Christopher D. Manning. 2006. Generating typed dependency parses from phrase structure parses. In *5th International Conference on Language Resources and Evaluation (LREC 2006)*, Genoa, Italy.

Debusmann, Ralph, Denys Duchier, Alexander Koller, Marco Kuhlmann, Gert Smolka, and Stefan Thater. 2004. A relational syntax-semantics interface based on Dependency Grammar. In *Proceedings of ACL 04*, Geneva, Switzerland.

Dienes, Peter and Amit Dubey. 2003. Antecedent recovery: Experiments with a trace tagger. In *Proceedings of the 2003 Conference on Empirical Methods in Natural Language Processing (EMNLP)*, Sapporo, Japan.

Dowdall, James, Fabio Rinaldi, Fidelia Ibekwe-Sanjuan, and Eric SanJuan. 2003. Complex structuring of term variants for Question Answering. In *Proceedings of the ACL workshop on MultiWord Expressions: Analysis, Acquisition and Treatment*, Sapporo, Japan, July.

Eisner, Jason. 1996. Three new probabilistic models for dependency parsing: An exploration. In *Proceedings of the 16th International Conference on Computational Linguistics (COLING-96)*, pages 340–345, Copenhagen, August.

Eisner, Jason. 2000. Bilexical grammars and their cubic-time parsing algorithms. In Harry Bunt and Anton Nijholt, editors, *Advances in Probabilistic and Other Parsing Technologies*. Kluwer.

Engel, Ulrich. 1994. *Syntax der deutschen Gegenwartssprache. 3. Auflage*. Schmidt, Berlin.

Evert, Stefan and Sebastian Hoffmann. 2006. BNCweb (CQP-edition). In *Proceedings of the the 27th conference of the International Computer Archive of Modern and Medieval English (ICAME)*.

Fellbaum, Christiane, editor. 1998. *WordNet: An Electronic Lexical Database*. MIT Press, Cambridge, MA.

References

Fillmore, Charles J. 1968. The case for case. In Emmon Bach and Robert Harms, editors, *Universals in Linguistic Theory*. Holt, Rinehart and Winston, New York, pages 1–88.

Fong, Sandiway. 1991. *Computational Properties of Principle-Based Grammar Theories*. Ph.D. thesis, MIT Artificial Intelligence Lab, Cambridge, MA.

Frank, Anette. 2003. Projecting F-structures from chunks. In Mriram Butt and Traci Holloway King, editors, *Proceedings of the LFG03 Conference*, Albany, NY. CSLI.

Frank, Robert. 2002. *Phrase Structure Composition and Syntactic Dependencies*. MIT Press, Cambridge, MA.

Frank, Robert. 2004. Restricting grammatical complexity. *Cognitive Science*, 28(5).

Friedman, C., P. Kra, H. Yu, M. Krauthammer, and A. Rzhetsky. 2001. GENIES: a natural-language processing system for the extraction of molecular pathways from journal articles. *Bioinformatics*, 17(1):S74–S82.

Friedman, J. B. 1989. Computational testing of linguistic models in syntax and semantics. In I. S. Batori, W. Lenders, and W. Putschke, editors, *Computational Linguistics - Computerlinguistik*. de Gruyter, Berlin, pages 252–259.

Gabbard, Ryan, Seth Kulick, and Mitchell Marcus. 2006. Fully parsing the penn treebank. In *Proceedings of the Human Language Technology Conference of the NAACL*, pages 184–191, New York City, USA, June. Association for Computational Linguistics.

Gaifman, Haim. 1965. Dependency systems and phrase-structure systems. *Information and Control*, 8:304–337.

Gaizauskas, R., G. Demetriou, P. J. Artymiuk, and Willett P. 2003. Protein Structures and Information Extraction from Biological Texts: The PASTA System. *Bioinformatics*, 19:135–143.

Gildea, Daniel. 2001. Corpus variation and parser performance. In *Proceedings of the 2001 Conference on Empirical Methods in Natural Language Processing (EMNLP)*, pages 167–202, Pittsburgh, PA.

Grefenstette, Gregory. 1996. Light parsing as finite-state-filtering. In Wolfgang Wahlster, editor, *Workshop on Extended Finite-state models of language, ECAI 96*, Budapest, Hungary. John Wiley and Sons.

Grimshaw, Jane. 1991. Extended projection. manuscript.

Group, XTAG Research. 2001. A lexicalized tree adjoining grammar for english. Technical Report IRCS-01-03, IRCS, University of Pennsylvania.

Hajič, Jan. 1998. Building a syntactically annotated corpus: The Prague Dependency Treebank. In Eva Hajičová, editor, *Issues of Valency and Meaning. Studies in Honor of Jarmila Panevová*. Karolinum, Charles University Press, Prague, pages 106–132.

Harris, Zellig. 1957. Co-occurrence and transformation in linguistic structure. *Language*, 33:283–340.

Haverinen, Katri, Filip Ginter, Sampo Pyysalo, and Tapio Salakoski. 2008. Accurate conversion of dependency parses: targeting the stanford scheme. In *Proceedings of Third International Symposium on Semantic Mining in Biomedicine (SMBM 2008)*, Turku, Finland.

Helbig, Gerhard. 1992. *Probleme der Valenz- und Kasustheorie*. Konzepte der Sprach- und Literaturwissenschaft. Niemeyer, Tübingen.

Henderson, James. 2003. Inducing history representations for broad coverage statistical parsing. In *Proceedings of HLT-NAACL 2003*, Edmonton, Canada.

Henderson, James, Paola Merlo, Ivan Petroff, and Gerold Schneider. 2002. Using syntactic analysis to increase efficiency in visualising text collections. In *Proceedings of the 19th International Conference on Computational Linguistics (COLING 2002)*, Taipei, Taiwan.

Hermjakob, Ulf. 2001. Parsing and question classification for question answering. In *Proceedings of the ACL 2001 Workshop on Open-Domain Question Answering*, Toulouse, France.

Hindle, Donald and Mats Rooth. 1993. Structural ambiguity and lexical relations. *Computational Linguistics*, 19:103–120.

Hockenmaier, Julia. 2003. *Data and Models for Statistical Parsing with Combinatory Categorial Grammar*. Ph.D. thesis, University of Edinburgh, Edinburgh.

Hockenmaier, Julia and Mark Steedman. 2002. Generative models for statistical parsing with combinatory categorial grammar. In *Proceedings of 40th Annual Meeting of the Association for Computational Linguistics*, Philadelphia.

Huang, C.T. 1982. *Logical Relations in Chinese and the Theory of Grammar*. Ph.D. thesis, Massachusetts Institute of Technology, Cambridge, MA.

Hudson, Richard. 1984. *Word Grammar*. Basil Blackwell, Oxford.

Hudson, Richard. 1987. Zwicky on heads. *Journal of Linguistics*, 23:109 – 132.

Hudson, Richard. 1990. *English Word Grammar*. Basil Blackwell, Oxford.

Jackendoff, Ray. 1977. *X' Syntax: A Study of Phrase Structure*. The MIT Press, Cambridge, Massachusetts.

Jijkoun, Valentin and Maarten de Rijke. 2004. Enriching the output of a parser using memory-based learning. In *Proceedings of the 42nd Meeting of the Association for Computational Linguistics (ACL'04)*, pages 311–318, Barcelona, Spain.

Johansson, R. and P. Nugues. 2007. Extended constituent-to-dependency conversion for English. In *Proc. of the 16th Nordic Conference on Computational Linguistics (NODALIDA)*.

Johnson, Mark. 1998. PCFG models of linguistic tree representations. *Computational Linguistics*, 24:613–632.

Johnson, Mark. 2001. Joint and conditional estimation of tagging and parsing models. In *Proceedings of the 39th Meeting of the ACL*, pages 314–321, Toulouse, France.

Johnson, Mark. 2002. A simple pattern-matching algorithm for recovering empty nodes and their antecedents. In *Proceedings of the 40th Meeting of the ACL*, University of Pennsylvania, Philadelphia.

Johnson, Mark, Stuart Geman, Stephen Canon, Zhiyi Chi, and Stefan Riezler. 1999. Estimators for stochastic unification-based grammars. In *Proceedings of the 37th Annual Meeting of the ACL*.

Joshi, Aravind. 1985. How much context-sensitivty is required to provide reasonable syntactic descriptions: Tree Adjoining Grammars. In David Dowty, Lauri Karttunen, and Arnold Zwicky, editors, *Natural Language Parsing: Psychological, computational, and theoretical perspectives*. CUP, Cambridge, pages 206–250.

Joshi, Aravind and Anthony Kroch. 1985. The linguistic relevance of Tree Adjoining Grammar. Technical Report MS-CS-85-16, Department of Computer and Information Sciences, University of Pennsylvania.

Joshi, Aravind K. and K. Vijay-Shanker. 1989. Treatment of long-distance dependencies in LFG and TAG: Functional uncertainty in LFG is a corollary in TAG. In *Proceedings of ACL '89*.

Jung, Wha-Young. 1995. *Syntaktische Relationen im Rahmen der Dependenzgrammatik*. Buske, Hamburg.

Jurafsky, Daniel and James H. Martin. 2000. *Speech and Language Processing: An Introduction to Natural Language Processing, Computational Linguistics, and Speech Recognition*. Prentice Hall, Englewood Cliffs, New Jersey.

Kahane, Sylvain, Alexis Nasr, and Owen Rambow. 1998. Pseudo-projectivity: A polynomially parsable non-projective dependency grammar. In *Proceedings of COLINGACL*, volume 1, pages 646–652, Montreal.

Kaplan, Ron, Stefan Riezler, Tracy H. King, John T. Maxwell III, Alex Vasserman, and Richard Crouch. 2004a. Speed and accuracy in shallow and deep stochastic parsing. In *Proceedings of HLT/NAACL 2004*, Boston, MA.

Kaplan, Ronald M., John T. Maxwell III, Tracy Holloway King, and Richard S. Crouch. 2004b. Integrating finite-state technology with deep lfg grammars. In *ESSLLI 2004 Workshop on Combining Shallow and Deep Processing for NLP (ComShaDeP 2004)*, Nancy, France.

Kaplan, Ronald M. and John T. Maxwell. 1996. LFG grammar writer's workbench. Technical report, Xerox PARC.

Karlsson, Fred, Atro Voutilainen, Juha Heikkilä, and editors Arto Anttila. 1995. *Constraint Grammar : a language-independent system for parsing unrestricted text*. Mouton de Gruyter, Berlin and New York.

Kim, J.D., T. Ohta, Y. Tateisi, and J. Tsujii. 2003a. GENIA corpus - a semantically annotated corpus for bio-textmining. *Bioinformatics*, 19(1):180–182.

Kim, J.D., T. Ohta, Y. Tateisi, and J. Tsujii. 2003b. GENIA corpus - a semantically annotated corpus for bio-textmining. *Bioinformatics*, 19(1):i180–i182.

Klein, Dan and Christopher D. Manning. 2003. Accurate unlexicalized parsing. In *Proceedings of the 41st Annual Meeting of the Association for Computational Linguistics*, pages 423–430, Sapporo, Japan.

Kromann, Matthias Trautner. 2003. The Danish Dependency Treebank and the DTAG treebank tool. In *Proceedings of Treebanks and Linguistic Theories (TLT) 2003*, pages 217–220, Växjö, Sweden.

References

Kübler, Sandra. 2006. How do treebank annotation schemes influence parsing results? or how not to compare apples and oranges. In N. Nicolov, K. Boncheva, G. Angelova, and R. Mitkov, editors, *Recent Advances in Natural Language Processing IV: Selected Papers from RANLP 2005*, Amsterdam. John Benjamins.

Kuhlmann, Marco and Joakim Nivre. 2006. Mildly non-projective dependency structures. In *Proceedings of the COLING/ACL 2006 Conference Poster Sessions*, pages 507–514, Sydney, Australia, July. Association for Computational Linguistics.

Kulick, S., A. Bies, M. Liberman, M. Mandel, R. McDonald, M. Palmer, A. Schein, and L. Ungar. 2004. Integrated annotation for biomedical information extraction. In *Proc. of the Human Language Technology Conference and the Annual Meeting of the North American Chapter of the Association for Computational Linguistics (HLT/NAACL)*.

Levin, Beth C. 1993. *English Verb Classes and Alternations: a Preliminary Investigation*. University of Chicago Press, Chicago, IL.

Levy, Roger. 2005. *Probabilistic models of word order and syntactic discontinuity*. Ph.D. thesis, Stanford University, Department of Linguistics.

Levy, Roger and Christopher Manning. 2004. Deep dependencies from context-free statistical parsers: Correcting the surface dependency approximation. In *Proceedings of the 42nd Meeting of the Association for Computational Linguistics (ACL'04), Main Volume*, pages 327–334, Barcelona, Spain.

Lin, Dekang. 1995. A dependency-based method for evaluating broad-coverage parsers. In *Proceedings of IJCAI-95*, Montreal.

Lin, Dekang. 1998. Dependency-based evaluation of MINIPAR. In *Workshop on the Evaluation of Parsing Systems*, Granada, Spain.

MacWhinney, B. 2000. *The CHILDES Project: Tools for Analyzing Talk*. Lawrence Erlbaum.

Magerman, David. 1995. Statistical decision-tree models for parsing. In *Proceedings of the 33rd Meeting of the Association for Computational Linguistics*, Boston, MA.

Marcus, M., B. Santorini, and M. Marcinkiewicz. 1993a. Building a large annotated corpus of English: the Penn Treebank. *Computational Linguistics*, 19(2):313–330.

Marcus, Mitch, Beatrice Santorini, and M.A. Marcinkiewicz. 1993b. Building a large annotated corpus of English: the Penn Treebank. *Computational Linguistics*, 19:313–330.

McDonald, Ryan, Fernando Pereira, Kirik Ribarov, and Jan Hajič. 2005. Non-projective dependency parsing using spanning tree algorithms. In *Proceedings of HLT-EMNLP*.

Mel'čuk, Igor. 1988. *Dependency Syntax: theory and practice*. State University of New York Press, New York.

Merlo, Paola. 2003. Generalised PP-attachment disambiguation using corpus-based linguistic diagnostics. In *Proceedings of EACL*, pages 251–258, Budapest, Hungary.

Merlo, Paola, Matthew Crocker, and Cathy Berthouzoz. 1997. Attaching multiple prepositional phrases: Generalized backed-off estimation. In *Proceedings of the Second Conference on Empirical Methods in Natural Language Processing*, Providence, RI.

Merlo, Paola and Eva Esteve Ferrer. 2006. The notion of argument in PP attachment. *Computational Linguistics*, 32(2):341 – 378.

Mikheev, Andrei. 1997. Automatic rule induction for unknown word guessing. *Computational Linguistics*, 23(3):405–423.

Miller, Philip H. 2000. *Strong Generative Capacity: the Semantics of Linguistic Formalism*. CSLI, Number 46 in Lecture Notes, Stanford, CA.

Minnen, Guido, John Carroll, and Darren Pearce. 2000. Applied morphological generation. In *Proceedings of the 1st International Natural Language Generation Conference (INLG)*, Mitzpe Ramon, Israel.

Miyao, Yusuke, Takashi Ninomiya, and Jun'ichi Tsujii. 2003. Probabilistic modeling of argument structures including non-local dependencies. In *the Proceedings of the Conference on Recent Advances in Natural Language Processing (RANLP) 2003*, pages 285–291.

Miyao, Yusuke, Takashi Ninomiya, and Jun'ichi Tsujii. 2005. Corpus-oriented grammar development for acquiring a Head-driven Phrase Structure Grammar from the Penn Treebank. In Keh-Yih Su, Jun'ichi Tsujii, Jong-Hyeok Lee, and Oi Yee Kwong, editors, *Natural Language Processing - IJCNLP 2004*, pages 684–693. Springer.

References

Miyao, Yusuke and Jun'ichi Tsujii. 2004. Deep linguistic analysis for the accurate identification of predicate-argument relations. In *Proceedings of Coling 2004*, pages 1392–1398, Geneva, Switzerland. COLING.

Mollá, Diego and Ben Hutchinson. 2003. Intrinsic versus extrinsic evaluations of parsing systems. In *Proceedings of EACL03 workshop on Evaluation Initiatives in Natural Language Processing*, pages 43–50, Budapest.

Müller, Stefan. 1996. The Babel-System–an HPSG Prolog implementation. In *Proceedings of the Fourth International Conference on the Practical Application of Prolog*, pages 263–277, London.

Musillo, Gabriele and Paola Merlo. 2005. Lexical and structural biases for function parsing. In *Proceedings of IWPT*, pages 83–93, Vancouver, Canada.

Nerbonne, John, Anja Belz, Nicola Cancedda, Alexander Clark, Herv'e D'ejean, James Hammerton, Rob Koeling, Stasinos Konstantopoulos, Miles Osborne, Franck Thollard, and Erik Tjong Kim Sang. 2001. Learning computational grammars. In *Proceedings of ACL Workshop CoNLL-2001*, pages 97–104, Toulouse, France. Association for Computational Linguistics.

Neuhaus, Peter and Norbert Bröker. 1997. The complexity of recognition of linguistically adequate dependency grammars. In *Proceedings of the 35th ACL and 8th EACL*, pages 337–343, Madrid, Spain.

Nivre, Joakim. 2003. An efficient algorithm for projective dependency parsing. In *Proceedings of the 8th International Workshop on Parsing Technologies (IWPT 03)*, Nancy.

Nivre, Joakim. 2004. Inductive dependency parsing. In *Proceedings of Promote IT*, Karlstad University.

Nivre, Joakim. 2006a. Constraints on non-projective dependency parsing. In *Proceedings of the European Chapter of the Association of Computational Linguistics (EACL) 2006*, pages 73 – 80, Trento, Italy. Association for Computational Linguistics.

Nivre, Joakim. 2006b. *InductiveDependency Parsing*. Text, Speech and Language Technology 34. Springer, Dordrecht, The Netherlands.

Nivre, Joakim, Johan Hall, Sandra Kübler, Ryan McDonald, Jens Nilsson, Sebastian Riedel, and Deniz Yuret. 2007. The CoNLL 2007 shared task on dependency parsing. In *Proceedings of the CoNLL Shared Task Session of EMNLP-CoNLL 2007*, pages 915–932.

Nivre, Joakim and Jens Nilsson. 2005. Pseudo-projective dependency parsing. In *Proceedings of the 43rd Annual Meeting of the Association for Computational Linguistics (ACL'05)*, pages 99–106, Ann Arbor, Michigan, June. Association for Computational Linguistics.

Nivre, Joakim and Mario Scholz. 2004. Deterministic dependency parsing of english text. In *Proceedings of Coling 2004*, pages 64–70, Geneva, Switzerland. COLING.

Ono, T., H. Hishigaki, A. Tanigami, and T. Takagi. 2001. Automated extraction of information on protein-protein interactions from the biological literature. *Bioinformatics*, 17(2):155–161.

Ouhalla, Jamal. 1999. *Transformational Grammar: from Principles and Parameters to Minimalism*. Arnold, New York.

Padó, Sebastian and Mirella Lapata. 2007. Dependency-based construction of semantic space models. *Computational Linguistics*, 33(2):161–199.

Perlmutter, David. 1983. *Studies in Relational Grammar I*. Chicago Unicersity Press, Chicago.

Pollard, Carl and Ivan Sag. 1994. *Head-Driven Phrase Structure Grammar*. Chicago University Press, Chicago, Illinois.

Preiss, Judita. 2003. Using grammatical relations to compare parsers. In *Proc. of EACL 03*, Budapest, Hungary.

Prins, Robbert. 2005. *Finite-State Pre-Processing for Natural Language Analysis*. Ph.D. thesis, Behavioral and Cognitive Neurosciences (BCN) research school, University of Groningen.

Pustejovsky, J., J. Castaño, J. Zhang, B. Cochran, and M. Kotecki. 2002. Robust relational parsing over biomedical literature: Extracting inhibit relations. In *Pacific Symposium on Biocomputing*.

Pyysalo, S., F. Ginter, J. Heimonen, J. Björne, J. Boberg, J. Järvinen, and T. Salakoski. 2007. Bioinfer: A corpus for information extraction in the biomedical domain. *BMC Bioinformatics, 8(50)*.

Quirk, Randolph, Sidney Greenbaum, Geoffrey Leech, and Jan Svartvik. 1985. *A Grammar of Contemporary English*. Longman, London.

References

Ratnaparkhi, Adwait. 1996. A Maximum Entropy Part-Of-Speech tagger. In *Proceedings of the Empirical Methods in Natural Language Processing Conference*, University of Pennsylvania.

Ratnaparkhi, Adwait. 1997. A linear observed time statistical parser based on maximum entropy models. In *Proceedings of the Second Conference on Empirical Methods in Natural Language Processing (EMNLP)*, Brown University, Providence, Rhode Island.

Ratnaparkhi, Adwait, Jeff Reynar, and Salim Roukos. 1994. A maximum entropy model for prepositional phrase attachment.

Riezler, Stefan, Tracy H. King, Ronald M. Kaplan, Richard Crouch, John T. Maxwell, and Mark Johnson. 2002. Parsing the Wall Street Journal using a Lexical-Functional Grammar and discriminative estimation techniques. In *Proc. of the 40th Annual Meeting of the Association for Computational Linguistics (ACL'02)*, Philadephia, PA.

Rinaldi, Fabio, James Dowdall, Gerold Schneider, and Andreas Persidis. 2004a. Answering Questions in the genomics domain. In *ACL-2004 workshop on Question Answering in restricted domains*, Barcelona, Spain.

Rinaldi, Fabio, James Dowdall, Gerold Schneider, and Andreas Persidis. 2004b. Answering Questions in the Genomics Domain. In *ACL 2004 Workshop on Question Answering in restricted domains*, Barcelona, Spain, 21–26 July.

Rinaldi, Fabio, Thomas Kappeler, Kaarel Kaljurand, Gerold Schneider, Manfred Klenner, Simon Clematide, Michael Hess, Jean-Marc von Allmen, Pierre Parisot, Martin Romacker, and Therese Vachon. 2008. OntoGene in BioCreative II. *Genome Biology*, 9:S13.

Rinaldi, Fabio, Gerold Schneider, James Dowdall, Christos Andronis, Andreas Persidis, and Ourania Konstanti. 2004. Mining relations in the GENIA corpus. In *Proceedings of the Second workshop on Data Mining and Text Mining for Bioinformatics*, Pisa, Italy.

Rinaldi, Fabio, Gerold Schneider, Kaarel Kaljurand, Michael Hess, Christos Andronis, Ourania Konstanti, and Andreas Persidis. 2007. Mining of functional relations between genes and proteins over biomedical scientific literature using a deep-linguistic approach. *Journal of Artificial Intelligence in Medicine*, 39:127 – 136.

Rinaldi, Fabio, Gerold Schneider, Kaarel Kaljurand, Michael Hess, and Martin Romacker. 2006. An environment for relation mining over richly annotated corpora: the case of GENIA. *BMC Bioinformatics*, 7(Suppl 3):S3.

Rizzi, Luigi. 1995. *Relativized Minimality*. The MIT Press, Cambridge, Massachusetts.

Ross, John R. 1967. *Constraints On Variables in Syntax*. Ph.d. thesis, MIT, Cambridge, Mass.

Sag, Ivan A., Timothy Baldwin, Francis Bond, Ann Copestake, and Dan Flickinger. 2002. Multiword Expressions: a Pain in the Neck for NLP. In *Proceedings of the Third International Conference, CICLing 2002*, pages 1–15, Mexico City, February.

Samuelsson, Christer. 2007. Book review: "Inductive Dependency Parsing" by Joakim Nivre. *Computational Linguistics*, 33(2):267–269.

Sarkar, Anoop and Aravind Joshi. 2003. Tree-Adjoining Grammars and its application to statistical parsing. In Rens Bod, Remko Scha, and Khalil Sima'an, editors, *Data-oriented parsing*. CSLI Publications, Stanford.

Sarkar, Anoop, Fei Xia, and Aravind Joshi. 2000. Some experiments on indicators of parsing complexity for lexicalized grammars. In *Proceedings of COLING '00*.

Schneider, Gerold. 1998. A linguistic comparison of constituency, dependency and Link Grammar. Master's thesis, Department of Informatics, University of Zurich.

Schneider, Gerold. 2003. Extracting and using trace-free Functional Dependencies from the Penn Treebank to reduce parsing complexity. In *Proceedings of Treebanks and Linguistic Theories (TLT) 2003*, Växjö, Sweden.

Schneider, Gerold. 2004. Combining shallow and deep processing for a robust, fast, deep-linguistic dependency parser. In *ESSLLI 2004 Workshop on Combining Shallow and Deep Processing for NLP (ComShaDeP 2004)*, Nancy, France.

Schneider, Gerold. 2005. A broad-coverage, representationally minimal LFG parser: chunks and F-structures are sufficient. In Mriram Butt and Traci Holloway King, editors, *The 10th international LFG Conference (LFG 2005)*, Bergen, Norway. CSLI.

Schneider, Gerold, James Dowdall, and Fabio Rinaldi. 2004. A robust and deep-linguistic theory applied to large-scale parsing. In *Coling 2004 Workshop on Robust Methods in the Analysis of Natural Language Data (ROMAND 2004)*, Geneva, Switzerland.

Schneider, Gerold, Kaarel Kaljurand, Fabio Rinaldi, and Tobias Kuhn. 2007. Pro3Gres parser in the CoNLL domain adaptation shared task. In *Proceedings of the CoNLL Shared Task Session of EMNLP-CoNLL 2007*, pages 1161–1165, Prague.

Schneider, Gerold, Fabio Rinaldi, Kaarel Kaljurand, and Michael Hess. 2005. Closing the gap: Cognitively adequate, fast broad-coverage grammatical role parsing. In *ICEIS Workshop on Natural Language Understanding and Cognitive Science (NLUCS 2005)*, Miami, FL, May 2005.

Shatkay, H. and R. Feldman. 2003. Mining the biomedical literature in the genomic era: An overview. *Journal of Computational Biology*, 10 (3):821–855.

Shieber, Stuart. 1983. Direct parsing of ID/LP Grammars. *Linguistics and Philosophy*, 7:2.

Sleator, Daniel and Davy Temperley. 1991. Parsing english with a link grammar. Technical Report CMU-CS-91-196.

Smadja, Frank. 2003. Retrieving collocations from text: Xtract. *Computational Linguistics*, 19:1, Special issue on using large corpora:143–177.

Steedman, Mark. 2000. *Surface Structure and Interpretation*. MIT Press.

Stowell, Tim. 1981. *Origins of Phrase Structure*. Ph.D. thesis, MIT.

Tapanainen, Pasi and Timo Järvinen. 1997. A non-projective dependency parser. In *Proceedings of the 5th Conference on Applied Natural Language Processing*, pages 64–71. Association for Computational Linguistics.

Tarvainen, Kalevi. 1981. *Einführung in die Dependenzgrammatik*. Reihe Germanistische Linguistik 35. Niemeyer, Tübingen.

Telljohann, Heike, Erhard W. Hinrichs, and Sandra Kübler. 2004. The TüBa-D/Z treebank: Annotating German with a context-free backbone. In *Proceedings of the Fourth International Conference on Language Resources and Evaluation*, Lisbon, Portugal.

Tesnière, Lucien. 1959. *Eléments de Syntaxe Structurale*. Librairie Klincksieck, Paris.

Weber, Heinz J. 1997. *Dependenzgrammatik. Ein interaktives Arbeitsbuch. 2. Auflage*. Gunter Narr Verlag, Tübingen.

Weeds, Julie, James Dowdall, Gerold Schneider, Bill Keller, and David Weir. 2005. Using distributional similarity to organise BioMedical terminology. *Terminology*.

Wehrli, Eric. 1997. *L'analyse syntaxique des langues naturelles*. Masson, Paris.

Yamada, Hiroyasu and Yuji Matsumoto. 2003. Statistical dependency analysis with support vector machines. In *Proceedings of IWPT*, pages 195–206.

Younger, D. H. 1967. Recognition and parsing of context-free languages in time n^3. *Information and Control*, 10:189-208.

Zwicky, Arnold. 1985. Heads. *Journal of Linguistics*, 21:1–30.

Appendix A

tgrep Queries for Grammatical Relations

tgrep and tgrep2 are popular query languages for structural searches on annotated Treebank style corpora. In the following, the comprehensive lists of queries for each grammatical relation and sample queries for locality tests are presented to the interested reader.

Active Subject The arbitrary level of nestedness has been spelled out explicitly which accounts for the big number of similar queries. Only pattern instances for which non-zero counts are found in the Penn Treebank are listed. $A < B$ in tgrep stands for A dominates B, or equivalently B dependends on A. $A < -B$ means that A dominates B, and that B is the rightmost dependent. At the terminal NP level, in $NP < -N$ N is usually the head of NP. The $.. operator means succeeding sister. The restriction that the VP head is a verb with no VP sister is expressed by the negation operator !. Due to our treatment of conjunctions, only the first noun of an noun conjunction is extracted. Therefore, only the first (< 1) NP line of a nested NP is descended into.

```
/NP-SBJ$/ <- '(/NN/|PRP|WDT|WP|CD|EX) $.. (VP < ('/VB/ \!$ VP) )
/NP-SBJ$/ <- '(/NN/|PRP|WDT|WP|CD|EX) $.. (VP < (VP < ('/VB/ \!$ VP)) )
/NP-SBJ$/ <- '(/NN/|PRP|WDT|WP|CD|EX) $.. (VP < (VP < (VP < ('/VB/ \!$ VP))) )
/NP-SBJ$/ <- '(/NN/|PRP|WDT|WP|CD|EX) $.. (VP < (VP < (VP < (VP < ('/VB/ \!$ VP)))) )
/NP-SBJ$/ <- '(/NN/|PRP|WDT|WP|CD|EX) $.. (VP < (VP < (VP < (VP < (VP < ('/VB/ \!$ VP))))) )
/NP-SBJ$/ <1 (NP <- '(/NN/|PRP|WDT|WP|CD|EX)) $.. (VP < ('/VB/ \!$ VP) )
/NP-SBJ$/ <1 (NP <- '(/NN/|PRP|WDT|WP|CD|EX)) $.. (VP < (VP< ('/VB/ \!$ VP)) )
/NP-SBJ$/ <1 (NP <- '(/NN/|PRP|WDT|WP|CD|EX)) $.. (VP < (VP< (VP < ('/VB/ \!$ VP))) )
/NP-SBJ$/ <1 (NP <- '(/NN/|PRP|WDT|WP|CD|EX)) $.. (VP < (VP< (VP < (VP < ('/VB/ \!$ VP)))) )
/NP-SBJ$/ <1 (NP<(NP <- '(/NN/|PRP|WDT|WP|CD|EX))) $.. (VP < ('/VB/ \!$ VP) )
/NP-SBJ$/ <1 (NP<(NP <- '(/NN/|PRP|WDT|WP|CD|EX))) $.. (VP < (VP< ('/VB/ \!$ VP)) )
/NP-SBJ$/ <1 (NP<(NP <- '(/NN/|PRP|WDT|WP|CD|EX))) $.. (VP < (VP< (VP < ('/VB/ \!$ VP))) )
```

```
/NP-SBJ$/ <1 (NP<(NP<(NP <- '(/NN/|PRP|WDT|WP|CD|EX)))) $.. (VP < ('/VB/ \!$ VP) )
/NP-SBJ$/ <1 (NP<(NP<(NP <- '(/NN/|PRP|WDT|WP|CD|EX)))) $.. (VP < (VP < ('/VB/ \!$ VP)) )
/NP-SBJ$/ <1 (NP<(NP<(NP <- '(/NN/|PRP|WDT|WP|CD|EX)))) $.. (VP < (VP < (VP < ('/VB/ \!$ VP))) )
/NP-SBJ$/ <1 (NP<(NP<(NP<(NP <- '(/NN/|PRP|WDT|WP|CD|EX))))) $.. (VP < ('/VB/ \!$ VP) )
```

tgrep extraction pattern instances for active subject-verb relations

Object

```
VP << '/VB/ < (/NP$/|NP-PRD <- '(/NN/|PRP|WDT|WP|CD))
VP << '/VB/ < (/NP$/|NP-PRD <1 (NP <- '(/NN/|PRP|WDT|WP|CD))
VP << '/VB/ < (/NP$/|NP-PRD <1 (NP<1(NP <- '(/NN/|PRP|WDT|WP|CD))))
VP << '/VB/ < (/NP$/|NP-PRD <1 (NP<(NP<1(NP <- '(/NN/|PRP|WDT|WP|CD)))))
VP << '/VB/ < (/NP$/|NP-PRD <1 (NP<(NP<(NP<1(NP <- '(/NN/|PRP|WDT|WP|CD))))))
VP << '/VB/ < (/NP$/|NP-PRD <1 (NP<(NP<(NP<(NP<1(NP <- '(/NN/|PRP|WDT|WP|CD)))))))
```

tgrep extraction pattern instances for object-verb relations

Object2 The negated CC sister condition makes sure that the two nouns appearing at the same level are not a conjunction.

```
VP << '/VB/ < (/NP$/ <- (/NN/|PRP|WDT|WP|CD) \!$ /CC/ $.. (/NP$/ <- '(/NN/|PRP|WDT|WP|CD)))
VP << '/VB/ < (/NP$/ <- (/NN/|PRP|WDT|WP|CD) \!$ /CC/ $.. (/NP$/ < (NP <- '(/NN/|PRP|WDT|WP|CD))))
VP << '/VB/ < (/NP$/ <- (/NN/|PRP|WDT|WP|CD) \!$ /CC/ $.. (/NP$/ < (NP<(NP <- '(/NN/|PRP|WDT|WP|CD)))))
VP << '/VB/ < (/NP$/ <- (/NN/|PRP|WDT|WP|CD) \!$ /CC/ $.. (/NP$/ < (NP<(NP<(NP <- '(/NN/|PRP|WDT|WP|CD))))))
VP << '/VB/ < (/NP$/ << (NP <- (/NN/|PRP|WDT|WP|CD)) \!$ /CC/ $.. (/NP$/ << (NP <- '(/NN/|PRP|WDT|WP|CD))))
VP << '/VB/ < (/NP$/ << (NP <- (/NN/|PRP|WDT|WP|CD)) \!$ /CC/ $.. (/NP$/ <- '(/NN/|PRP|WDT|WP|CD)))
```

tgrep extraction pattern instances for object2-verb relations

Passive Subject

```
/NP-SBJ-/ <- '(/NN/|PRP|WDT|WP|CD) $.. \\
   (VP < ('/VBN/ \!$ VP $.. (/NP$/ < (/NONE/)) ) )
/NP-SBJ-/ <- '(/NN/|PRP|WDT|WP|CD) $.. \\
   (VP < (VP < ('/VBN/ \!$ VP $.. (/NP$/ < (/NONE/)) )) )
/NP-SBJ-/ <- '(/NN/|PRP|WDT|WP|CD) $.. \\
   (VP < (VP < (VP < ('/VBN/ \!$ VP $.. (/NP$/ < (/NONE/)) ))) )
/NP-SBJ-/ <- '(/NN/|PRP|WDT|WP|CD) $.. \\
   (VP < (VP < (VP < (VP < ('/VBN/ \!$ VP $.. (/NP$/ < (/NONE/)) )))) )
/NP-SBJ-/ <- '(/NN/|PRP|WDT|WP|CD) $.. \\
   (VP < (VP < (VP < (VP < (VP < ('/VBN/ \!$ VP $.. (/NP$/ < (/NONE/)) ))))) )
/NP-SBJ-/ <1 (NP <- '(/NN/|PRP|WDT|WP|CD)) $.. \\
   (VP < ('/VBN/ \!$ VP $.. (/NP$/ < (/NONE/)) ) )
/NP-SBJ-/ <1 (NP <- '(/NN/|PRP|WDT|WP|CD)) $.. \\
   (VP < (VP< ('/VBN/ \!$ VP $.. (/NP$/ < (/NONE/)) )) )
/NP-SBJ-/ <1 (NP <- '(/NN/|PRP|WDT|WP|CD)) $.. \\
   (VP < (VP< (VP < ('/VBN/ \!$ VP $.. (/NP$/ < (/NONE/)) ))) )
/NP-SBJ-/ <1 (NP <- '(/NN/|PRP|WDT|WP|CD)) $.. \\
   (VP < (VP< (VP < (VP < ('/VBN/ \!$ VP $.. (/NP$/ < (/NONE/)) )))) )
/NP-SBJ-/ <1 (NP <- '(/NN/|PRP|WDT|WP|CD)) $.. \\
   (VP < (VP< (VP < (VP < (VP < ('/VBN/ \!$ VP $.. (/NP$/ < (/NONE/)) ))))) )
/NP-SBJ-/ <1 (NP<(NP <- '(/NN/|PRP|WDT|WP|CD))) $.. \\
   (VP < ('/VBN/ \!$ VP $.. (/NP$/ < (/NONE/)) ) )
/NP-SBJ-/ <1 (NP<(NP <- '(/NN/|PRP|WDT|WP|CD))) $.. \\
   (VP < (VP< ('/VBN/ \!$ VP $.. (/NP$/ < (/NONE/)) )) )
/NP-SBJ-/ <1 (NP<(NP <- '(/NN/|PRP|WDT|WP|CD))) $.. \\
   (VP < (VP< (VP < ('/VBN/ \!$ VP $.. (/NP$/ < (/NONE/)) ))) )
/NP-SBJ-/ <1 (NP<(NP<(NP <- '(/NN/|PRP|WDT|WP|CD)))) $.. \\
   (VP < ('/VBN/ \!$ VP $.. (/NP$/ < (/NONE/)) ) )
/NP-SBJ-/ <1 (NP<(NP<(NP <- '(/NN/|PRP|WDT|WP|CD)))) $.. \\
```

```
         (VP < (VP< ('/VBN/ \!$ VP $.. (/NP$/ < (/NONE/)) )) )
/NP-SBJ-/ <1 (NP<(NP<(NP <- '(/NN/|PRP|WDT|WP|CD)) $.. \\
         (VP < (VP< (VP < ('/VBN/ \!$ VP $.. (/NP$/ < (/NONE/)) )) )
/NP-SBJ-/ <1 (NP<(NP<(NP <- '(/NN/|PRP|WDT|WP|CD))))) $.. \\
         (VP < ('/VBN/ \!$ VP $.. (/NP$/ < (/NONE/)) ) )
```

tgrep extraction pattern instances for subject-passive-verb relations

Control Verbs If we expand this pattern to tgrep queries we get the set shown in fig. A. The last line contains the only object-control query that is needed, as no instance of a complex object-control object has been found.

```
/NP-SBJ-/ <- '(/NN/|PRP|WDT|WP) $.. (VP < ('/VB/ \!$ VP $.. (S < (/NP-SBJ/ < /NONE/))) )
/NP-SBJ-/ <- '(/NN/|PRP|WDT|WP) $.. (VP < (VP <('/VB/ \!$ VP $.. (S < (/NP-SBJ/ < /NONE/)))) )
/NP-SBJ-/ <- '(/NN/|PRP|WDT|WP) $.. (VP < (VP < (VP <('/VB/ \!$ VP $.. (S < (/NP-SBJ/ < /NONE/))))) )
/NP-SBJ-/ <- '(/NN/|PRP|WDT|WP) $.. (VP < (VP < (VP <(VP<('/VB/ \!$ VP $.. (S < (/NP-SBJ/ < /NONE/)))))) )
/NP-SBJ-/ <1 (NP <- '(/NN/|PRP|WDT|WP)) $.. (VP < ('/VB/ \!$ VP $.. (S < (/NP-SBJ/ < /NONE/))) )
/NP-SBJ-/ <1 (NP <- '(/NN/|PRP|WDT|WP)) $.. (VP < (VP <('/VB/ \!$ VP $.. (S < (/NP-SBJ/ < /NONE/)))) )
/NP-SBJ-/ <1 (NP <- '(/NN/|PRP|WDT|WP)) $.. (VP < (VP < (VP <('/VB/ \!$ VP $.. (S < (/NP-SBJ/ < /NONE/))))) )
/NP-SBJ-/ <1 (NP <- '(/NN/|PRP|WDT|WP)) $.. (VP < (VP < (VP <(VP<('/VB/ \!$ VP $.. (S < (/NP-SBJ/ < /NONE/)))))) )
/NP-SBJ-/ <1 (NP< (NP <- '(/NN/|PRP|WDT|WP))) $.. (VP < ('/VB/ \!$ VP $.. (S < (/NP-SBJ/ < /NONE/))) )
/NP-SBJ-/ <1 (NP< (NP <- '(/NN/|PRP|WDT|WP))) $.. (VP < (VP <('/VB/ \!$ VP $.. (S < (/NP-SBJ/ < /NONE/)))) )
/NP-SBJ-/ <1 (NP< (NP <- '(/NN/|PRP|WDT|WP))) $.. (VP < (VP < (VP <('/VB/ \!$ VP $.. (S < (/NP-SBJ/ < /NONE/))))) )
/NP-SBJ-/ <1 (NP<(NP<(NP <- '(/NN/|PRP|WDT|WP)))) $.. (VP < ('/VB/ \!$ VP $.. (S < (/NP-SBJ/ < /NONE/))) )

VP << '/VB/ < (/NP-/|/NP-PRD-/ <- ('/NN/|PRP|WDT|WP|CD)) < (S < (/NP-SBJ/ < (/-NONE-/ < /*-/))) '
```

tgrep extraction pattern instances for control relation

Reduced Relative Clause: the *modpart* relation

```
NP <- '(/NN/|PRP|WDT|WP|CD) $.. (VP < ('/VB/ \!$ VP) )
NP <- '(/NN/|PRP|WDT|WP|CD) $.. (VP < (VP < ('/VB/ \!$ VP)) )
NP <- '(/NN/|PRP|WDT|WP|CD) $.. (VP < (VP <(VP< ('/VB/ \!$ VP))) )
NP < (NP <- '(/NN/|PRP|WDT|WP|CD)) $.. (VP < ('/VB/ \!$ VP) )
NP < (NP <- '(/NN/|PRP|WDT|WP|CD)) $.. (VP < (VP< ('/VB/ \!$ VP)) )
NP < (NP<(NP <- '(/NN/|PRP|WDT|WP|CD))) $.. (VP < ('/VB/ \!$ VP) )

NP << '(/NN/|PRP|WDT|WP|CD) $.. (RRC << (VP <'/VB/))'
```

Locality test sample Queries

Passive subject: How many filler and gap indices coincide in our fixed pattern?
We arbitrarily pick an exemplary pattern instance of medium complexity (line 6) for this and the following passive subject test.

```
/NP-SBJ-/ <1 (NP <- '(/NN/|PRP|WDT|WP|CD)) $.. (VP < ('/VBN/ \!$ VP $.. (/NP$/ < (/NONE/)) ) )
```

The pattern instances A differ from 6.4 as they fail to enforce the identity of the filler and gap index. This gives rise to a first test.

tgrep does not allow the user to do any book-keeping of LDD indices, therefore the most frequent values are tried manually, first without enforcing filler identitiy, then with. The number returned is the number of matches plus 1 (tgrep adds an empty line).

```
tgrep -as " " -n '/NP-SBJ-1$/ <1 ( NP <- (/NN/|PRP|WDT|WP|CD)) $.. \\
        (VP < (VP< (/VBN/ \!$ VP $.. ( /NP$/ < ( /NONE/ < /-/ ) ) ) ) )' | wc -1
            675
tgrep -as " " -n '/NP-SBJ-1$/ <1 ( NP <- (/NN/|PRP|WDT|WP|CD)) $.. \\
        (VP < (VP< (/VBN/ \!$ VP $.. ( /NP$/ < ( /NONE/ < /-1$/ ) ) ) ) )' | wc -1
            675
tgrep -as " " -n '/NP-SBJ-2$/ <1 ( NP <- (/NN/|PRP|WDT|WP|CD)) $.. \\
        (VP < (VP< (/VBN/ \!$ VP $.. ( /NP$/ < ( /NONE/ < /-/ ) ) ) ) )' | wc -1
            73
tgrep -as " " -n '/NP-SBJ-2$/ <1 ( NP <- (/NN/|PRP|WDT|WP|CD)) $.. \\
        (VP < (VP< (/VBN/ \!$ VP $.. ( /NP$/ < ( /NONE/ < /-2$/ ) ) ) ) )' | wc -1
            73
tgrep -as " " -n '/NP-SBJ-3$/ <1 ( NP <- (/NN/|PRP|WDT|WP|CD)) $.. \\
        (VP < (VP< (/VBN/ \!$ VP $.. ( /NP$/ < ( /NONE/ < /-/ ) ) ) ) )' | wc -1
            33
tgrep -as " " -n '/NP-SBJ-3$/ <1 ( NP <- (/NN/|PRP|WDT|WP|CD)) $.. \\
        (VP < (VP< (/VBN/ \!$ VP $.. ( /NP$/ < ( /NONE/ < /-3$/ ) ) ) ) )' | wc -1
            33
tgrep -as " " -n '/NP-SBJ-4$/ <1 ( NP <- (/NN/|PRP|WDT|WP|CD)) $.. \\
        (VP < (VP< (/VBN/ \!$ VP $.. ( /NP$/ < ( /NONE/ < /-/ ) ) ) ) )' | wc -1
            9
tgrep -as " " -n '/NP-SBJ-4$/ <1 ( NP <- (/NN/|PRP|WDT|WP|CD)) $.. \\
        (VP < (VP< (/VBN/ \!$ VP $.. ( /NP$/ < ( /NONE/ < /-4$/ ) ) ) ) )' | wc -1
            9
```

This log shows total identity between the LDD indices.

Passive subject: How many fillers do not find their gap in the passive verb sister? In this experiment, we test in how many cases a filler occurs without a gap position in the position expected by our fixed pattern, i.e. the passive verb object position. In order to exclude some mismatches when using the negation, we restrict ourselves to cases where the gap immediately follows the verb sister.

```
tgrep -as " " -n '/NP-SBJ-/ <1 ( NP <- (/NN/|PRP|WDT|WP|CD)) $.. \\
        (VP < (VP< (/VBN/ \!$ VP $. ( /NP$/ < /NONE/))))' | wc -1
            844
tgrep -as " " -n '/NP-SBJ-/ <1 ( NP <- (/NN/|PRP|WDT|WP|CD)) $.. \\
        (VP < (VP< (/VBN/ \!$ VP $. ( /NP$/ \!< /NONE/))))' | wc -1
            31
```

Of the 30 cases where the NP immediately follows the verb, none involves a verb in the passive voice.

A remark on dub verbs There is a class of verbs, following citelevin93 often called *dub* verbs, that take a noun phrase as object complements. Examples of dub verbs are *name, appoint, consider*, like in *the queen appointed William Cecil her personal secretary*. As dub verbs are in complementary distribution with ditransitive verbs, we give the object complement the secondary object label *obj2*. Dub verbs are very frequently in the passive voice. The (slightly different) extraction patterns for them, involving a small clause, are as follows:

```
/NP-SBJ-/ <- '(/NN/|PRP|WDT|WP|CD) $.. \\
   (VP < ('/VBN/ \!$ VP) < (S< (NP-SBJ < /-NONE-/) ))'
/NP-SBJ-/ <- '(/NN/|PRP|WDT|WP|CD) $.. \\
   (VP < (VP < ('/VBN/ \!$ VP) < (S< (NP-SBJ < /-NONE-/) )))'
/NP-SBJ-/ <- '(/NN/|PRP|WDT|WP|CD) $.. \\
   (VP < (VP < (VP < ('/VBN/ \!$ VP) < (S< (NP-SBJ < /-NONE-/) ))))'
/NP-SBJ-/ <- '(/NN/|PRP|WDT|WP|CD) $.. \\
   (VP < (VP < (VP < (VP < ('/VBN/ \!$ VP) < (S< (NP-SBJ < /-NONE-/) )))))'
/NP-SBJ-/ <1 (NP <- '(/NN/|PRP|WDT|WP|CD)) $.. \\
   (VP < ('/VBN/ \!$ VP) < (S< (NP-SBJ < /-NONE-/) ))'
/NP-SBJ-/ <1 (NP <- '(/NN/|PRP|WDT|WP|CD)) $.. \\
   (VP < (VP< ('/VBN/ \!$ VP) < (S< (NP-SBJ < /-NONE-/) )))'
/NP-SBJ-/ <1 (NP <- '(/NN/|PRP|WDT|WP|CD)) $.. \\
   (VP < (VP< (VP<('/VBN/ \!$ VP) < (S< (NP-SBJ < /-NONE-/) ))))'
```

tgrep extraction pattern instances for subject-passive-verb relations with 'dub' verbs

Control: How many filler and gap indices coincide in our fixed pattern? We take line 3 for our subject control tests, and the single object control pattern for object control tests.

Again, the most frequent values are tried manually, first without enforcing filler identitiy, then with. The number returned is the number of matches plus 1 (tgrep adds an empty line). For subject control, we get:

```
tgrep -as " " -n '/NP-SBJ-1/ <- (/NN/|PRP|WDT|WP) $.. \\
   (VP < (VP <(VP <(/VB/ \!$ VP $.. (S < (/NP-SBJ/ < (/NONE/ < /-/) ))))) ) ' | wc -l
   215
tgrep -as " " -n '/NP-SBJ-1/ <- (/NN/|PRP|WDT|WP) $.. \\
   (VP < (VP <(VP <(/VB/ \!$ VP $.. (S < (/NP-SBJ/ < (/NONE/ < /-1/) ))))) ) ' | wc -l
   210
tgrep -as " " -n '/NP-SBJ-2/ <- (/NN/|PRP|WDT|WP) $.. \\
   (VP < (VP <(VP <(/VB/ \!$ VP $.. (S < (/NP-SBJ/ < (/NONE/ < /-/) ))))) ) ' | wc -l
   74
tgrep -as " " -n '/NP-SBJ-2/ <- (/NN/|PRP|WDT|WP) $.. \\
   (VP < (VP <(VP <(/VB/ \!$ VP $.. (S < (/NP-SBJ/ < (/NONE/ < /-2/) ))))) ) ' | wc -l
   73
tgrep -as " " -n '/NP-SBJ-3/ <- (/NN/|PRP|WDT|WP) $.. \\
   (VP < (VP <(VP <(/VB/ \!$ VP $.. (S < (/NP-SBJ/ < (/NONE/ < /-/) ))))) ) ' | wc -l
   25
tgrep -as " " -n '/NP-SBJ-3/ <- (/NN/|PRP|WDT|WP) $.. \\
   (VP < (VP <(VP <(/VB/ \!$ VP $.. (S < (/NP-SBJ/ < (/NONE/ < /-3/) ))))) ) ' | wc -l
   24
tgrep -as " " -n '/NP-SBJ-4/ <- (/NN/|PRP|WDT|WP) $.. \\
   (VP < (VP <(VP <(/VB/ \!$ VP $.. (S < (/NP-SBJ/ < (/NONE/ < /-/) ))))) ) ' | wc -l
   6
tgrep -as " " -n '/NP-SBJ-4/ <- (/NN/|PRP|WDT|WP) $.. \\
   (VP < (VP <(VP <(/VB/ \!$ VP $.. (S < (/NP-SBJ/ < (/NONE/ < /-4/) ))))) ) ' | wc -l
   6
```

For object control, we get:

```
tgrep -as " " -n '/VP << /VB/ < (/NP-1/|/NP-PRD-1/ <- (/NN/|PRP|WDT|WP|CD)) < \\
   (S < (/NP-SBJ/ < (/-NONE-/ < /*-/))) ' | wc -l
```

```
           149
tgrep -as " " -n 'VP << /VB/ < (/NP-1/|/NP-PRD-1/ <- (/NN/|PRP|WDT|WP|CD)) < \\
    (S < (/NP-SBJ/ < (/-NONE-/ < /*-1/))) ' | wc -1
           149
tgrep -as " " -n 'VP << /VB/ < (/NP-2/|/NP-PRD-2/ <- (/NN/|PRP|WDT|WP|CD)) < \\
    (S < (/NP-SBJ/ < (/-NONE-/ < /*-/))) ' | wc -1
            74
tgrep -as " " -n 'VP << /VB/ < (/NP-2/|/NP-PRD-2/ <- (/NN/|PRP|WDT|WP|CD)) < \\
    (S < (/NP-SBJ/ < (/-NONE-/ < /*-2/))) ' | wc -1
            73
tgrep -as " " -n 'VP << /VB/ < (/NP-3/|/NP-PRD-3/ <- (/NN/|PRP|WDT|WP|CD)) < \\
    (S < (/NP-SBJ/ < (/-NONE-/ < /*-/))) ' | wc -1
            32
tgrep -as " " -n 'VP << /VB/ < (/NP-3/|/NP-PRD-3/ <- (/NN/|PRP|WDT|WP|CD)) < \\
    (S < (/NP-SBJ/ < (/-NONE-/ < /*-3/))) ' | wc -1
            32
tgrep -as " " -n 'VP << /VB/ < (/NP-4/|/NP-PRD-4/ <- (/NN/|PRP|WDT|WP|CD)) < \\
    (S < (/NP-SBJ/ < (/-NONE-/ < /*-/))) ' | wc -1
             9
tgrep -as " " -n 'VP << /VB/ < (/NP-4/|/NP-PRD-4/ <- (/NN/|PRP|WDT|WP|CD)) < \\
    (S < (/NP-SBJ/ < (/-NONE-/ < /*-4/))) ' | wc -1
             9
```

This log shows an almost perfect identity for object-control, and very high identity for subject-control. An example of the few sentences where the subject-control pattern goes astray is:

```
(NP-SBJ-1 (DT Some)
          (NNP Golenbock)
          (NNS lawyers))
(VP (MD wo)
    (RB n't)
    (VP (VB be)
        (VP (VBN invited)
            (NP-2 (-NONE- *-1))
            (S (NP-SBJ (-NONE- *-2))
               (VP (TO to)
                   (VP (VB join)
                       (NP (NNP Whitman)
                           (CC &)
                           (NNP Ransom))))))
        (, ,)
        (PP (VBG according)
            (PP (TO to)
                (NP (NP (NNS partners))
                    (PP-LOC (IN at)
                            (NP (DT both)
                                (NNS firms)))))))))
```

Complex interaction between different types of LDDs, in this case between passive and control, means that the pattern can make errors.

Control: How many fillers do not find their gap in the subordinate subjectless clause? In this experiment, we test in how many cases a filler occurs without a gap position in the position expected by our fixed pattern, i.e. the subordinate clause subject position.

For subject control, we get:

```
tgrep -as " " -n '/NP-SBJ-/ <- (/NN/|PRP|WDT|WP) $.. \\
```

```
(VP < (VP <(VP <(/VB/ \!$ VP $. (S < (/NP-SBJ/ < (/NONE/ < /-/) ))))) ) ' | wc -l
    302
tgrep -as " " -n '/NP-SBJ/- <- (/NN/|PRP|WDT|WP) $.. \\
(VP < (VP <(VP <(/VB/ \!$ VP $. (S < (/NP-SBJ/ \!< (/NONE/ < /-/) ))))) ) ' | wc -l
    9
```

For object control, we get:

```
tgrep -as " " -n 'VP << /VB/ < (/NP-/|/NP-PRD-/ <- (/NN/|PRP|WDT|WP|CD)) < \\
 (S < (/NP-SBJ/ < (/-NONE-/ < /*-/))) ' | wc -l
    334
tgrep -as " " -n 'VP << /VB/ < (/NP-/|/NP-PRD-/ <- (/NN/|PRP|WDT|WP|CD)) < \\
 (S < (/NP-SBJ/ \!< (/-NONE-/ < /*-/))) ' | wc -l
    16
tgrep -as " " -n 'VP << /VB/ < (/NP-TMP/ <- (/NN/|PRP|WDT|WP|CD)) < \\
 (S < (/NP-SBJ/ \!< (/-NONE-/ < /*-/))) ' | wc -l
    14
```

The 8 subject-control cases where no gap is the subordinate clause subject position include a conjunction that triggers a mismatch, an annotation error, a complex interaction between passive and control, and one case where the movement is longer than what the pattern matches, but not a typical case of control:

```
(NP-SBJ-1 (PRP we))
(VP (MD should)
    (VP (VB be)
        (VP (VBG helping)
            (S (NP-SBJ (NNP U.S.)
                      (NNS companies))
               (VP (VB improve)
                   (NP (VBG existing)
                       (NNS products))
                   (PP (RB rather)
                       (IN than)
                       (S-NOM (NP-SBJ (-NONE- *-1))
                              (ADVP-TMP (RB always))
                              (VP (VBG developing)
                                  (NP (JJ new)
                                      (NNS ones)))))))))))
```

The 15 object-control cases where no gap is the subordinate clause subject position include 13 cases where the pattern by mistake matches a temporal expression (TMP) in the object position, made explicit in the last query.

Appendix B

Gradience and Mapping: A Small Selection of Problematic Cases

Inter-annotator-agreement in the Carroll test corpus is "around 95 %" (Carroll, Minnen, and Briscoe, 1999). (Crouch et al., 2002) warn that mapping between differing annotation schemes is a true challenge, and that due to mapping results can only be indicative. Here we briefly discuss some of the cases where different annotators may come to different conclusions, where both the gold standard and Pro3Gres output seem reasonable and correct but are in disagreement. The cases are all from the Carroll test corpus (Carroll, Minnen, and Briscoe, 1999; Carroll, Minnen, and Briscoe, 2003). Our selection of cases cannot be assumed to be complete nor fully representative.

- *What could rescue the bill would be some quick progress on a bill ...*

  In the gold standard, *What could rescue the bill* is analysed as a clausal subject.
  ```
  csubj( 'be' , 'rescue' , _ , 92 ).
  ```
  Pro3Gres gives the analysis in figure B.1, which was intended by the grammar, in which *What could rescue the bill* is analysed as a nominal subject that is modified by a relative clause, analogous to *That which could rescue the bill*.

- *... the measure would provide means of enforcing the law ...*
  ```
  ncsubj( 'enforce' , 'measure' , _ , 21 ).
  ```
  The gold standard assumes a subject control relation between *measure* and *enforce*. It is not clear to us if a control relation across an *of*-genitive, and

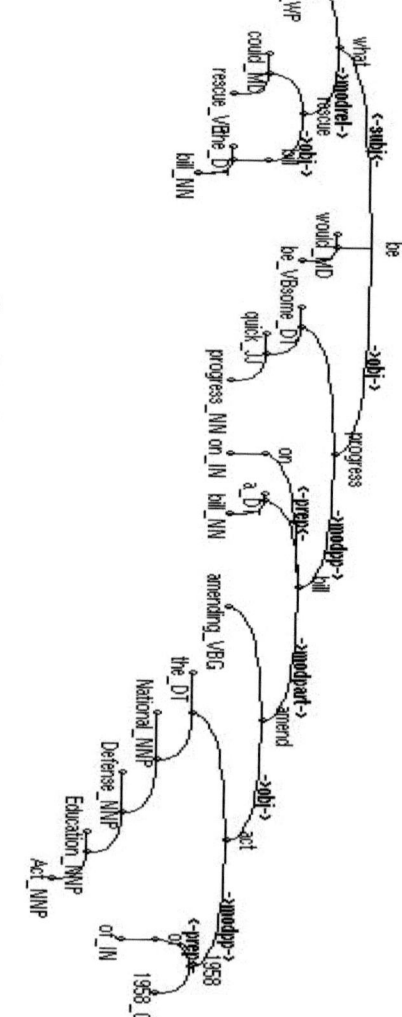

Figure B.1: Aberrant but intentional analysis

to inside the object instead of to inside a subordinate clause, is syntactically possible.

- *... there is nothing left of the conservative party ...*
  ```
  ncsubj( 'nothing' , 'leave' , 'obj' , 71 ). % gold standard: there-movement
  modpart(nothing, leave, _, '→', 71). % parser analysis: reduced relative
  ```
  The gold standard assumes a *there*-movement, while the intentional parser analysis reports a reduced relative clause.

- *... prove [one of the difficult problems] ...*
  ```
  dobj( 'prove' , 'one' , _ , 48 ). % gold standard: syntactical analysis
  obj(prove, problem, _, '→', 48). % parser analysis: based on chunker output
  ```
  The gold standard assumes *one* as the head of the object, which is in turn modified by an *of*-PP. The LTPos chunker analyzes the entire NP *one of the difficult problems* as a base NP. This is syntactically questionable but semantically convincing, and the fact that sequences like *one of, some of, many of, all of* etc. are almost unambiguous cases of nominal PP-attachment can be exploited. But in evaluating Pro3Gres it leads to 3 errors:

  1. an object precision error: `obj(prove, problem, _, '→', 48)`.
  2. an object recall error: `dobj( 'prove' , 'one' , _ , 48 )`.
  3. a nominal PP-attachment recall error: `ncmod('of', 'one', 'problem', _, 48 )`.

- *... (the government) made blunders in Cuba*
  ```
  ncmod( 'in' , 'blunder' , 'cuba' , 51 ). % gold standard: to noun
  pobj(make, cuba, in, '→', 51). % parser: to verb
  ```
  PP-attachment is a classical source of low inter-annotator agreement. Since both the action *make* and the effect *blunders* are in the same location, the PP-attachment disambiguation is semantically vacuous in this case, and hence inherently ambiguous. See also our discussion of PP-attachment in chapter 4.

Die VDM Verlagsservicegesellschaft sucht für wissenschaftliche Verlage abgeschlossene und herausragende

Dissertationen, Habilitationen, Diplomarbeiten, Master Theses, Magisterarbeiten usw.

für die kostenlose Publikation als Fachbuch.

Sie verfügen über eine Arbeit, die hohen inhaltlichen und formalen Ansprüchen genügt, und haben Interesse an einer honorarvergüteten Publikation?

Dann senden Sie bitte erste Informationen über sich und Ihre Arbeit per Email an *info@vdm-vsg.de*.

Sie erhalten kurzfristig unser Feedback!

VDM Verlagsservicegesellschaft mbH
Dudweiler Landstr. 99   Telefon +49 681 3720 174
D - 66123 Saarbrücken   Fax   +49 681 3720 1749
www.vdm-vsg.de

Die VDM Verlagsservicegesellschaft mbH vertritt

Printed by Books on Demand GmbH, Norderstedt / Germany